LANGUAGE!®

The Comprehensive Literacy Curriculum

Jane Fell Greene, Ed.D.

SOPRIS WEST Educational Services
A Cambium Learning Company

BOSTON, MA • NEW YORK, NY • LONGMONT, CO

Editorial Director: Nancy Chapel Eberhardt
Word and Phrase Selection: Judy Fell Woods
English Learners: Jennifer Wells Greene
Lesson Development: Sheryl Ferlito, Donna Lutz,
Isabel Wesley, Straightline Editorial Development, Inc.
Text Selection: Sara Buckerfield, Jim Cloonan
LANGUAGE! eReader is a customized version of the
CAST eReader for Windows® (3.0). CAST eReader
©1995—2003, CAST, Inc. and its licensors. All rights reserved.

SOPRIS
WEST
EDUCATIONAL SERVICES

4093 Specialty Place • Longmont, CO 80504 • (303) 651-2829
www.sopriswest.com

"You must be the change you wish to see in the world."

—Mohandas Gandhi (1869–1948)

Table of Contents

This book contains six units.

Each unit builds knowledge in:

- Sounds and Letters
- Spelling and Words
- Vocabulary and Roots
- Grammar and Usage
- Listening and Reading
- Speaking and Writing

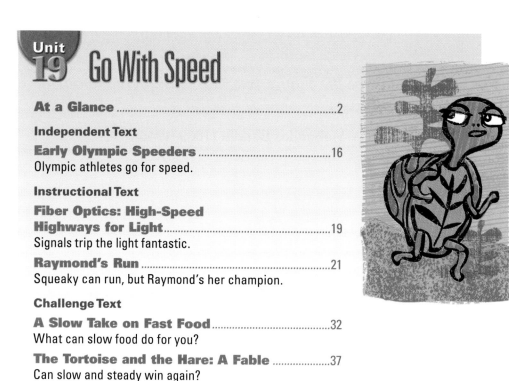

Unit 19 Go With Speed

Unit 20 Play On

Unit 21 Join the Family

22 Solve the Puzzle

Unit 23 Power Up

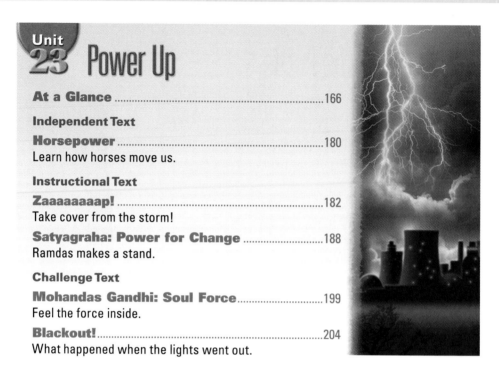

24 Have a Dream

Appendix

Go With
Speed

STEP 1

Phonemic Awareness and Phonics

Unit 19 introduces vowel digraph syllables with the digraphs **ai**, **ee**, and **oa**.

Syllables

Review: Words are made up of **syllables**.

- A syllable is a word, or word part, that has one vowel sound.
- A syllable's type is determined by the syllable's vowel sound.
- A **closed syllable** ends with a consonant and has a short vowel sound.
- An **r-controlled syllable** contains an **r-controlled** vowel sound.
- An **open syllable** ends with a vowel and has a long vowel sound.
- A syllable that ends with vowel + consonant + **e** is a **final silent e syllable**.

Vowel Digraph Syllables

A syllable that contains a vowel digraph is a **vowel digraph syllable**.

- In some syllables, the vowel phoneme is spelled with two vowel letters.
- The vowel sound represented by the vowel digraph is usually long.

Go to the **Vowel Chart** on page A3. Find these long vowel sounds on the chart:

Find / $\bar{a}$ /. Find the cue word **rain**.
Find / $\bar{e}$ /. Find the cue word **see**.
Find / $\bar{o}$ /. Find the cue word **boat**.

More vowel digraphs are introduced in Unit 20.

STEP 2

Word Recognition and Spelling

Prefixes

We can build longer words by adding **prefixes**. These word parts are added to the beginnings of words. Example: **mid** + summer = midsummer

(See Step 3: Vocabulary and Morphology for links to meaning.)

> **Unit 19 Prefixes**
> **fore-, mid-, mis-, over-**

Suffixes

We can build longer words by adding **suffixes**. These word parts are added to the ends of words. Example: agree + **ment** = agreement

(See Step 3: Vocabulary and Morphology for links to meaning and Step 4: Grammar and Usage for function.)

> **Unit 19 Suffixes**
> **-en, -er, -ful, -ist, -less, -ment, -ness**

Essential Words

Unit 19 Essential Words		
abroad	captain	language
against	curtain	nuisance

Spelling Lists

The Unit 19 spelling lists contain three categories:

1. Words with the vowel digraphs **ai**, **ee**, and **oa**

2. Essential Words (in italics)

3. Words with prefixes and suffixes

Spelling Lists

Lessons 1—5

abroad	keeping
against	*language*
captain	*nuisance*
coaching	railroad
curtain	rain check
download	speeding
entertain	training
freestyle	

Lessons 6—10

agreement	explained
aimlessly	foresee
appraiser	midweek
artist	miscalculated
boastful	mistake
colorful	sailor
darkness	waiter
details	

STEP 3

Vocabulary and Morphology

Unit Vocabulary

Sound-spelling correspondences from this unit and previous units make up this unit's vocabulary.

- What do these words mean?
- Do some of them mean more than one thing? Which ones?

UNIT Vocabulary

ai	paint	beef	queen	weed
afraid	praise	between	screen	week
aid	rail	breeze	see	wheel
aim	rain	cheese	seed	
bait	raise	coffee	seek	**oa**
brain	remain	creep	seem	approach
chain	retain	deep	seen	boat
complain	sail	fee	sheep	coal
contain	snail	feed	sheet	coast
daily	tail	feel	sleep	coat
entertain	tailor	feet	speech	float
explain	trail	fifteen	speed	goal
faint	train	free	squeeze	goat
faith	vain	freeze	steel	load
grain	waist	green	steep	loan
jail	wait	greet	street	oak
mail		heel	sweep	road
maintain	**ee**	jeep	sweet	roast
nail	agree	keep	teeth	soap
obtain	asleep	meet	three	throat
pain	bee	need	tree	

Word Relationships

Homophones are words that sound the same but have different spellings and meanings. The context indicates the correct spelling based on the meaning. Example: She **rode** the horse down the dusty **road**. (**Rode** and **road** are homophones.)

Idioms and Expressions Review

Idioms are common phrases that cannot be understood by the meanings of their separate words—only by the entire phrase. The words in an idiom cannot be changed or the idiom loses its meaning. Example: **keep it under your hat** (keep something a secret)

Expressions are common ways of saying something. They occur often in English. An expression is similar to an idiom, but it does not have a specific form. It is simply a common way of saying something. Example: **a rocky road** (a difficult time with a lot of problems)

Meaning Parts

Prefixes

Prefixes can add to or change the meanings of words.

Unit 19 Prefixes	Meanings	Examples
fore-	before, in front of	forehand, foreman, foretell
mid-	middle	midsummer, midterm, midyear
mis-	wrongly, badly, not	misfile, misprint, misunderstand
over-	beyond, above, too much	overdue, overpass, overslept

Suffixes *-er, -ist, -ment, -ness*

Suffixes can add to or change the meanings of words. Some suffixes indicate noun form. When added to a base word, they can change a verb or an adjective to a noun.

Suffixes *-en, -ful, -less*

Other suffixes indicate verb or adjective forms. When added to a base word, they can change an adjective to a verb or a noun to an adjective.

Unit 19 Suffixes (Nouns)	Meanings	Examples
-er	someone who, something that	entertainer, trainer, waiter
-ist	someone who	artist, medalist, motorist
-ment	the state, act, or process of	agreement, ailment, shipment
-ness	the state, quality, condition, or degree of	lateness, sweetness, thickness
(Verbs or Adjectives)	Meanings	Examples
-en	to become, made of, caused to be or have	deepen, stiffen, widen
-ful	full of, characterized by	colorful, painful, skillful
-less	without, lacking	helpless, spotless, useless

Challenge Morphemes

Suffixes	Meanings	Examples
-dom	state or condition of being	freedom, kingdom, stardom
-some	characterized by	loathsome, lonesome, tiresome

STEP
4

Grammar and Usage

Nouns

Review: **Nouns** name people, places, things, or ideas. Which Unit 19 Unit Vocabulary words are nouns?

Suffixes -er, -ist, -ment, and **-ness** added to base words indicate noun function.

Adjectives

Review: Adjectives describe nouns. The suffixes **-en, -ful**, and **-less** added to base words indicate adjective function. The suffix **-er** indicates a comparative adjective.

Tense Timeline

Review: **Verbs** describe an action or a state of being. Verbs also convey time. The **Tense Timeline** shows the relationship between time and verb form.

Yesterday	Today	Tomorrow
Past	Present	Future
-ed	**-s**	**will** + verb
-ing	**-ing**	**-ing**
(with *was/were*)	(with *am/is/are*)	(with *will be*)

Unit 19 Verbs

aid	complain	float	paint
aim	creep	freeze	raise
approach	entertain	greet	roast
coast	faint	obtain	squeeze

Irregular Verbs

Some verbs signal time through irregular verb forms. These Unit 19 verbs have irregular past tense and past participle forms.

Base Verb	Past Tense	Past Participle
bleed	bled	bled
breed	bred	bred
creep	crept	crept
feed	fed	fed
feel	felt	felt
flee	fled	fled
freeze	froze	frozen
keep	kept	kept
meet	met	met
see	saw	seen
seek	sought	sought
sleep	slept	slept
speed	sped	sped
sweep	swept	swept
weep	wept	wept

Unit 19 Irregular Verbs

Linking Verbs

Review: Some verbs can act as main verbs or helping verbs. Forms of **be** belong to this group of verbs. Helping verbs combine with the main verb to form a verb phrase. The helping verb signals the time. Examples: He **is explaining** the project. They **were painting** the fence. She **will be feeding** her cat.

- The verb **be** can also act as a **linking verb**. Linking verbs connect, or link, the subject of the sentence to a word in the predicate.

- A noun that follows a linking verb renames, or tells more about, the subject. This noun is called a **predicate nominative**.

- The subject and the predicate nominative name the same person, place, thing, or idea.

> **Be** as a Linking Verb for a Predicate Nominative
>
> The *girl* **is** a *runner.*
>
> The verb **is** links the subject *girl* to the noun *runner.*

Sentence Pattern

Form: N/LV/N   **noun/linking verb/noun**

Function: S/P/PN   **subject/predicate/predicate nominative**

The **girl** **is** a **runner.**

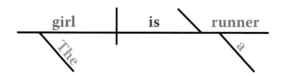

Punctuation

Commas are used to separate items in a series. When three or more words or word groups are listed together in a sentence, a comma separates the items in the series. The last item is usually connected to the others in the series by **and** or **or.**

> **Commas in a Series**
>
> *Skating, swimming,* **and** *running* are speed sports.

Listening and Reading Comprehension

Informational Text

- Some informational text is nonfiction material about a specific topic, event, experience, or circumstance. It is typically found in content area text. Textbooks, biographies, and essays are examples of informational text.

  Some informational text provides **reasons**, which are causes or motives for a topic or event. In this type of text organization, examples or other evidence support the reasons.

  > **Transition Words for Reasons**
  > one reason, the next reason, another reason

Vocabulary in Context

- **Context clues** help us understand new vocabulary. Pronoun referents, meaning signals, and visuals, such as charts and graphs, provide meaning links.

Signal Words

- Different types of sentences can help us think about new information in different ways. Some sentences require us to make judgments based on criteria and standards. These sentences ask us to **Evaluate It**. They are introduced by specific **signal words**.

  > **Signal Words for Evaluate It**
  > assess, justify

Literary Terms and Devices

Genres are types or categories of literature. Unit 19 features two genres:

- **Fiction** is a literary genre that includes stories that are not true. Fiction is sometimes based on real people, places, or events. **"Raymond's Run"** is an example of fiction.

- **Fable** is a literary genre whose main characters are usually animals. A fable teaches a moral lesson. **"The Tortoise and the Hare"** is an example of a fable.

Plot Analysis

- **Plot** refers to a pattern of events in a narrative or drama. The plot guides the author in composing the work. It helps the reader follow the story.

- **Characters** and **setting** are two components of plot analysis. The characters, which can be people, animals, or things, take part in the story. The setting is the story's time and place. Together these two components make up the introduction in the plot's development.

- To understand how a plot develops, we must first be able to identify a story's main **problem** and its **solution**.

- After we become proficient in identifying a story's main problem and solution, we will learn how a plot develops and apply plot development to our writing.

- Plot development usually consists of five elements:

  Introduction (setting and characters);

  Conflict (rising action);

  Climax (turning point);

  Resolution (falling action);

  Conclusion (the situation at the end of the story, with a look to the future).

Speaking and Writing

Signal Words

- Some sentences ask for information. Other sentences require us to make judgments based on criteria and standards. They use specific **signal words**.

> **Signal Words for Evaluate It**
>
> **Assess** your needs for communication.
>
> **Justify** using fiber optics rather than electricity.

Paragraph Organization

- Some paragraphs are organized by **reasons**. The content of these paragraphs includes the reasons, or the causes or motives for a topic or event, with supporting evidence or examples. Specific **transition words** signal this organization. Examples: one reason, the next reason, another reason

Plot Analysis

- Fiction includes characters created by the author. During prewriting, the author thinks about **character traits**. In good writing, each character must become distinct. Some character traits a writer may consider include: the character's personal appearance, personality, relationships with other characters, reactions to various situations, and means of coping with difficulties. Anything that distinguishes a character might be a character trait.

- Good writers usually include information about characters in the plot's introduction. This is because the reader needs to know the characters in order to follow the plot. Good writers can tell the reader about a character by including:

   A description of the character in simple narrative form;

   An incident during which the character interacts with others;

   A dialog in which the character is speaking to others.

More About Words

- **Bonus Words** use the same sound-spelling correspondences that we have studied in this unit and previous units.

- **Idioms** are common phrases that cannot be understood by the meanings of their separate words—only by the entire phrase.

- **Why? Word History** explains the origin of the word **speed**.

UNIT Bonus Words

ai	maize	discreet	referee	cocoa
ail	railroad	eel	screech	croak
attain	raincoat	esteem	seedling	goad
avail	raindrop	feedback	sheepskin	groan
await	remainder	flee	sixteen	inroad
braid	restrain	fleet	sneeze	lifeboat
braille	sailboat	freehand	streetcar	loaf
constrain	sailor	glee	tee	moan
daisy	saint	greed	teen	oat
detail	sprain	indeed	thirteen	oath
domain	stain	keel	upkeep	overcoat
drain	sustain	keen	weekend	reproach
gain		meek	weep	roadside
gait	**ee**	nineteen		roadway
hail	beech	peek	**oa**	soak
ingrain	bleed	peel	boast	toad
laid	cheek	peep	charcoal	toast
lain	creek	peeve	cloak	towboat
mailbox	decree	redeem	coach	
mainland	deed	reed	coastal	
mainstay	degree	reef	coax	

Idioms	
Idiom	**Meaning**
be up to speed	perform at an acceptable level
bite the hand that feeds you	repay generosity or kindness with ingratitude and injury
feed you a line	deceive you
keep it under your hat	keep something a secret
keep your fingers crossed	hope for a successful or advantageous outcome
keep your shirt on	don't get angry; be patient
make a beeline	go straight toward something
miss the boat	arrive too late and miss out on something
rock the boat	make trouble; risk spoiling a plan
take a rain check	ask to do something at a later date

Word History

Speed—We know from **"The Tortoise and the Hare: A Fable"** that speed alone does not make us successful, but yourDictionary.com™ shows us how the words for speed and success are related. The Old English word *spēd*, which our modern word **speed** comes from, originally meant "prosperity, successful outcome, ability, or quickness." A related verb *spēdan*, which our verb **speed** comes from, meant "to succeed, prosper, or achieve a goal." The adjective *spēdig*, the ancestor of our word **speedy**, meant "wealthy, powerful."

Today the words relate only to how fast an action is. The meaning "success" is retained mainly in a Middle English compound word, *Godspeed*. This noun came from a phrase that meant "May you be blessed and prosper."

Early Olympic Speeders

Betty Robinson (center) winning the 100-meter dash in the 1928 Olympics.

Speed matters in some sports. Runners, swimmers, and speed skaters race with amazing speed. Let's look at the speeds of these three sports in the early days.

Early Sprinting: Betty Robinson, Gold Medalist

In 1928, an unknown 16-year-old girl won gold. She was
5 a high school junior. She took first place. The event itself was a first. Women's track and field was new. The sport had just been added to the Olympic Games.

Betty Robinson was that girl. She won the women's 100-meter dash. Robinson had never thought of an Olympic
10 race. One afternoon, she was running to catch a train. A track coach spotted her. Four months later, she won a college championship. Next, she finished second at the Olympic trials. Then, she won the 100-meter run at the Amsterdam games. She set a record at 12.2 seconds.
15 In 1931, Robinson survived a plane crash. They thought she wouldn't walk again. She recovered and trained hard. She ran in the 1936 Olympics. She was on the women's relay team.

Early Swimming: Ethelda Bleibtrey, Gold Medalist

Belgium hosted the 1920 Games. The Games had added
20 women's swimming. There were only three events. Ethelda
Bleibtrey overcame the crippling illness of polio to race. She
raced in all three events. She won three gold medals! She
is the only woman to have won all the women's swimming
events at any Olympics games. Bleibtrey set a new record. It
25 was in the 100-meter freestyle. Her time was 1:13.6.

Over the next two years, Bleibtrey won every race she
entered. She won short races. She won long races. She won
freestyle. She won backstroke. She became a celebrated
athlete.
30 Bleibtrey had spunk in and out of the water. She wanted
to see more swimming pools built for the public. She
swam in a small New York City lake to make her point.
Swimming was not allowed. She was arrested. Many people
were upset. The city responded. It built its first public
35 swimming pool.

Early Ice Speed Skating: Clas Thunberg, Gold Medalist

They called Clas Thunberg the "king of speed skating."
In 1924, he won three gold medals. He also
won a silver and a bronze. Four years later,
he continued his Olympic success. He won
40 two more gold medals. Thunberg set the
1500-meter record. His time was 2:20.8.

Clas Thunberg, the "king of speed skating."

Thunberg was a master bricklayer from
Helsinki, Finland. He won his last Olympic
gold at age 34. He was the oldest Olympic
45 champion in speed skating. He continued
skating until he was 42.

The speeds of Olympic athletes have
always been fast. Over time, however,
these speeds have increased. What are
50 the reasons for increased speeds? Better equipment has
helped. Better training has resulted in faster speeds. The
ways of keeping time during races have also improved.
What else could make athletes speed up?

To see how much times have sped up, look at this
55 chart. It shows the winning times from the 2002 and 2004
Olympic games. Compare these winning times with the
winning times cited in the article.

Recent Olympic Results

Sport	Year	Event	Winner	Nation	Winning Time
Sprinting	2004	100m	Yuliya Nesterenko	BLR	10.93
Swimming	2004	100m freestyle	Jodie Henry	AUS	53.84
Speed Skating	2002	1500m	Derek Parra	USA	1:43.95

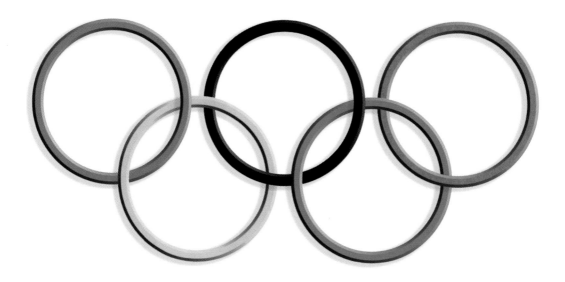

Fiber Optics:

High-Speed Highways for LIGHT

Faster than a bolt of lightning, able to carry billions of light pulses a second, yet thinner than a human hair, it's . . . optical fiber!

What happens when you download research from
5   the Internet? What carries your messages when you chat
online with a friend? You may be using fiber **optics**. Fiber
optic **cables** hide under the streets. They are under many
of our cities and towns. These cables carry all kinds of
information.
10   Fiber optic technology is being used more and more.
It has been around since the 1930s, but, today, as much as
2,000 miles of fiber optic cable are being laid every hour.
Why is the use of fiber optics increasing?
One reason to use fiber optics is the material. It's better.
15   Electric **signals** use wires. The wires carry electric **pulses**.
What is the problem? The electricity moves through the
wires quickly. However, the metal in the wire can slow
down the signal along the way. Fiber optics is different. It
uses long tubes. The tubes are thin. Instead of wires, these
20   tubes are made from glass. The tubes don't carry electricity.
They carry pulses of light. They send out light signals.
A second reason for using fiber optics is speed. Glass
speeds up the light signals. The signals travel at almost the

optics
the science of light; vision; lenses

cables
covered bundles of wire

signals
sounds, images, or messages that are sent or received

pulses
bursts of movement; vibrations

speed of light. Light speeds millions of times faster than
25 racing cars! The glass tubes can even be bent. Light moves at
such quickness that some bending doesn't bother the signal.

A final reason for using fiber optics is space. The
system uses less space. Glass fibers are thin. They are
thinner than wires. More fibers can fit into a cable. This
30 means more signals can be sent.

communications

ways of exchanging
information

The use of fiber optics has improved **communications**.
Light signals send huge amounts of information. Cable TV
is faster because of fiber optics. Thanks to fiber optics, we
have high-speed Internet. Phone lines could never carry
35 this much information this fast.

Fiber optics has changed the way some people do their
work. Doctors can now see into a person's body without
doing major surgery. How? Doctors place special scopes
inside a person's body. Fiber optics is used to send a picture
40 for the doctor to see. Astronomers use fiber optics to
learn more about space. Special optic fibers receive and

interpret

to translate;
figure out

interpret signals. The signals come from telescopes. They
let scientists measure changes in light and temperature for
stars and planets. Fiber optics is also used by engineers.
45 The technology is used for lighting homes and offices. It is
even used to direct solar lighting into buildings.

The fiber optic age has just begun. As it develops, how
will it affect your life?

Adapted from "High-Speed Highways for Light" by Nancy Day

Answer It

1. Justify using fiber optics rather than electricity.

2. Medical costs are rising. Justify a doctor's request for using fiber optics.

3. Imagine you are building a new school. Assess your needs for communication. (television, phone lines, etc.)

4. Summarize ways that fiber optics has changed the way some people work.

5. Do you use fiber optics at school or at home? Predict how fiber optics will affect your life in the future.

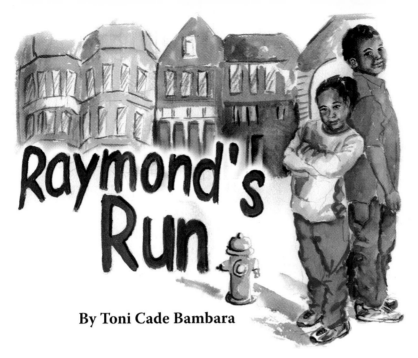

Raymond's Run

By Toni Cade Bambara

I don't have much work to do around the house like some girls. My mother does that. And I don't have to earn my pocket money by hustling; George runs errands for the big boys and sells Christmas cards. And anything else that's got to get done, my father does. All I have to do in life is **mind** my brother Raymond, which is enough.

Sometimes I slip and say my little brother Raymond. But as any fool can see he's much bigger and he's older too. But a lot of people call him my little brother cause he needs looking after cause he's not quite right. And a lot of smart mouths got lots to say about that too, especially when George was minding him. But now, if anybody has anything to say to Raymond, anything to say about his big head, they have to come by me. And I don't play the dozens or believe in standing around with somebody in my face doing a lot of talking. I much rather just knock you down and take my chances even if I am a little girl with skinny arms and a squeaky voice, which is how I got the name Squeaky. And if things get too rough, I run. And as anybody can tell you, I'm the fastest thing on two feet.

There is no track meet that I don't win the first place medal. I use to win the twenty-yard dash when I was a little kid in kindergarten. Nowadays it's the fifty-yard dash.

mind
to take care of; look after

subject

likely to; expected to

subject

prone; having a tendency toward

And tomorrow I'm **subject** to run the quarter-mile relay
25 all by myself and come in first, second, and third. The big
kids call me Mercury cause I'm the swiftest thing in the
neighborhood. Everybody knows that—except two people
who know better, my father and me.

He can beat me to Amsterdam Avenue with me having
30 a two fire-hydrant headstart and him running with his
hands in his pockets and whistling. But that's private
information. Cause can you imagine some thirty-five-year-
old man stuffing himself into PAL shorts to race little kids?
So as far as everyone's concerned, I'm the fastest and that
35 goes for Gretchen, too, who has put out the tale that she
is going to win the first place medal this year. Ridiculous.
In the second place, she's got short legs. In the third place,
she's got freckles. In the first place, no one can beat me and
that's all there is to it.

40 I'm standing on the corner admiring the weather and
about to take a stroll down Broadway so I can practice
my breathing exercises, and I've got Raymond walking on
the inside close to the buildings, cause he's **subject** to
fits of fantasy and starts thinking he's a circus performer
45 and that the curb is a tightrope strung high in the air.
And sometimes after a rain, he likes to step down off his
tightrope right into the gutter and slosh around getting
his shoes and cuffs wet. Then I get hit when I get home.
Or sometimes if you don't watch him, he'll dash across
50 traffic to the island in the middle of Broadway and give the
pigeons a fit. Then I have to go behind him apologizing to
all the old people sitting around trying to get some sun and
getting all upset with the pigeons fluttering around them,
scattering their newspapers and upsetting the waxpaper
55 lunches in their laps. So I keep Raymond on the inside of
me, and he plays like he's driving a stage coach which is
O.K. by me so long as he doesn't run me over or interrupt
my breathing exercises, which I have to do on account of
I'm serious about my running and don't care who knows it.

60 Now some people like to act like things come easy
to them, won't let on that they practice. Not me. I'll high
prance down 34th Street like a rodeo pony to keep my

knees strong even if it does get my mother uptight so that she walks ahead like she's not with me, don't know me, is
65 all by herself on a shopping trip, and I am somebody else's crazy child.

Now you take Cynthia Procter for instance. She's just the opposite. If there's a test tomorrow, she'll say something like, "Oh I guess I'll play handball this afternoon and watch
70 television tonight," just to let you know she ain't thinking about the test. Or like last week when she won the spelling bee for the millionth time, "A good thing you got 'receive,' Squeaky, cause I would have got it wrong. I completely forgot about the spelling bee." And she'll clutch the lace on
75 her blouse like it was a narrow escape. Oh, brother.

But of course when I pass her house on my early morning trots around the block, she is practicing the scales on the piano over and over and over and over. Then in music class, she always lets herself get bumped around so
80 she falls accidentally on purpose onto the piano stool and is so surprised to find herself sitting there, and so decides just for fun to try out the ole keys and what do you know— Chopin's waltzes just spring out of her fingertips and she's the most surprised thing in the world. A regular **prodigy**.
85 I could kill people like that.

I stay up all night studying the words for the spelling bee. And you can see me anytime of day practicing running. I never walk if I can trot and shame on Raymond if he can't keep up. But of course he does, cause if he hangs
90 back someone's liable to walk up to him and get smart, or take his allowance from him, or ask him where he got that great big pumpkin head. People are so stupid sometimes.

So I'm strolling down Broadway breathing out and breathing in on counts of seven, which is my lucky number,
95 and here comes Gretchen and her sidekicks—Mary Louise who used to be a friend of mine when she first moved to Harlem from Baltimore and got beat up by everybody till I took up for her on account of her mother and my mother used to sing in the same choir when they were young girls,
100 but people ain't grateful, so now she hangs out with the new girl Gretchen and talks about me like a dog; and Rosie

prodigy
a genius; someone of great ability

who is as fat as I am skinny and has a big mouth where
Raymond is concerned and is too stupid to know that there
is not a big deal of difference between herself and Raymond
105 and that she can't afford to throw stones. So they are steady
coming up Broadway and I see right away that it's going to
be one of those Dodge City scenes cause the street ain't that
big and they're close to the buildings just as we are. First I
think I'll step into the candy store and look over the new
110 comics and let them pass. But that's chicken and I've got a
reputation to consider. So then I think I'll just walk straight
on through them or over them if necessary. But as they get
to me, they slow down. I'm ready to fight, cause like I said
I don't feature a whole lot of chitchat, I much prefer to just
115 knock you down right from the jump and save everybody a
lotta precious time.

"You signing up for the May Day races?" smiles Mary
Louise, only it's not a smile at all.

A dumb question like that doesn't deserve an answer.
120 Besides, there's just me and Gretchen standing there really,
so no use wasting my breath talking to shadows.

"I don't think you're going to win this time," says Rosie,
trying to **signify** with her hands on her hips all salty,
completely forgetting that I have whupped her behind
125 many times for less salt than that.

> **signify**
> to show; indicate

"I always win cause I'm the best," I say straight at Gretchen who is, as far as I'm concerned, the only one talking in this ventriloquist-dummy routine.

130 Gretchen smiles but it's not a smile and I'm thinking that girls never really smile at each other because they don't know how and don't want to know how and there's probably no one to teach us how cause grown-up girls don't know either. Then they all look at Raymond who has just brought his mule team to a standstill. And they're about to

135 see what trouble they can get into through him.

"What grade you in now, Raymond?"

"You got anything to say to my brother, you say it to me, Mary Louise Williams of Raggedy Town, Baltimore."

"What are you, his mother?" sasses Rosie.

140 "That's right, Fatso. And the next word out of anybody and I'll be their mother too." So they just stand there and Gretchen shifts from one leg to the other and so do they. Then Gretchen puts her hands on her hips and is about to say something with her freckle-face self but doesn't. Then

145 she walks around me looking me up and down but keeps walking up Broadway, and her sidekicks follow her. So me and Raymond smile at each other and he says, "Gidyap" to his team and I continue with my breathing exercises, strolling down Broadway toward the icey man on 145th with

150 not a care in the world cause I am Miss Quicksilver herself.

I take my time getting to the park on May Day because the track meet is the last thing on the program. The biggest thing on the program is the May Pole dancing which I can do without, thank you, even if my mother thinks it's

155 a shame I don't take part and act like a girl for a change. You'd think my mother'd be grateful not to have to make me a white organdy dress with a big satin sash and buy me new white baby-doll shoes that can't be taken out of the box till the big day. You'd think she'd be glad her daughter

160 ain't out there prancing around a May Pole getting the new clothes all dirty and sweaty and trying to act like a fairy or a flower or whatever you're supposed to be when you should be trying to be yourself, whatever that is, which is, as far as I am concerned, a poor Black girl who really can't

165 afford to buy shoes and a new dress you only wear once a
lifetime cause it won't fit next year.

I was once a strawberry in a Hansel and Gretel pageant
when I was in nursery school and didn't have no better
sense than to dance on tiptoe with my arms in a circle over
170 my head doing umbrella steps and being a perfect fool just
so my mother and father could come dressed up and clap.
You'd think they'd know better than to encourage that
kind of nonsense. I am not a strawberry. I do not dance
on my toes. I run. That is what I am all about. So I always
175 come late to the May Day program, just in time to get my
number pinned on and lay in the grass till they announce
the fifty-yard dash.

I put Raymond in the little swings, which is a tight
squeeze this year and will be impossible next year. Then I
180 look around for Mr. Pearson who pins the numbers on. I'm
really looking for Gretchen if you want to know the truth,
but she's not around. The park is jam-packed. Parents in
hats and corsages and breast-pocket handkerchiefs peeking
up. Kids in white dresses and light blue suits. The parkees
185 unfolding chairs and chasing the rowdy kids from Lenox
as if they had no right to be there. The big guys with their
caps on backwards, leaning against the fence swirling
the basketballs on the tips of their fingers waiting for all
these crazy people to clear out the park so they can play.
190 Most of the kids in my class are carrying bass drums and
glockenspiels and flutes. You'd think they'd put in a few
bongos or something for real like that.

Then here comes Mr. Pearson with his clipboard and
his cards and pencils and whistles and safety pins and fifty
195 million other things he's always dropping all over the place
with his clumsy self. He sticks out in a crowd because he's
on stilts. We used to call him Jack and the Beanstalk to get
him mad. But I'm the only one that can outrun him and get
away, and I'm too grown for that silliness now.
200 "Well, Squeaky," he says checking my name off the
list and handing me number seven and two pins. And I'm
thinking he's got no right to call me Squeaky, if I can't call
him Beanstalk.

"Hazel Elizabeth Deborah Parker," I correct
205 him and tell him to write it down on his board.
"Well, Hazel Elizabeth Deborah Parker,
going to give someone else a break this
year?" I squint at him real hard to see
if he is seriously thinking I should
210 lose the race on purpose just to give
someone else a break.
"Only six girls running this time,"
he continues, shaking his head sadly like
it's my fault all of New York didn't turn
215 out in sneakers. "That new girl should give
you a run for your money." He looks around
the park for Gretchen like a periscope in
a submarine movie. "Wouldn't it be a nice
gesture if you were . . . to ahhh . . ."
220　　I give him such a look he couldn't
finish putting that idea into words.
Grownups got a lot of nerve
sometimes. I pin number seven
to myself and stomp away—I'm so

225 burnt. And I go straight for the track
and stretch out on the grass while the
band winds up with "Oh the Monkey
Wrapped His Tail Around the Flag Pole," which my teacher
calls by some other name. The man on the loudspeaker
230 is calling everyone over to the track and I'm on my back
looking at the sky trying to pretend I'm in the country, but
I can't, because even grass in the city feels hard as sidewalk
and there's just no pretending you are anywhere but in a
"concrete jungle" as my grandfather says.
235　　The twenty-yard dash takes all of the two minutes
cause most of the little kids don't know no better than to
run off the track or run the wrong way or run smack into
the fence and fall down and cry. One little kid though has
got the good sense to run straight for the white ribbon
240 up ahead so he wins. Then the second graders line up for
the thirty-yard dash and I don't even bother to turn my
head to watch cause Raphael Perez always wins. He wins

gesture
a thoughtful action

before he even begins by psyching the runners, telling them
they're going to trip on their shoelaces and fall on their
245 faces or lose their shorts or something, which he doesn't
really have to do since he is very fast, almost as fast as I am.
After that is the forty-yard dash which I use to run when
I was in first grade. Raymond is hollering from the swings
cause he knows I'm about to do my thing cause the man
250 on the loudspeaker has just announced the fifty-yard dash,
although he might just as well be giving a recipe for angel
food cake cause you can hardly make out what he's saying
for the static. I get up and slip off my sweat pants and then
I see Gretchen standing at the starting line kicking her
255 legs out like a pro. Then as I get into place I see that ole
Raymond is in line on the other side of the fence, bending
down with his fingers on the ground just like he knew what
he was doing. I was going to yell at him but then I didn't. It
burns up your energy to holler.
260   Every time, just before I take off in a race, I always feel
like I'm in a dream, the kind of dream you have when you're
sick with fever and feel all hot and weightless. I dream I'm
flying over a sandy beach in the early morning sun, kissing
the leaves of the trees as I fly by. And there's always the
265 smell of apples, just like in the country when I was little
and use to think I was a choo-choo train, running through
the fields of corn and chugging up the hill to the orchard.
And all the time I'm dreaming this, I get lighter and lighter
until I'm flying over the beach again, getting blown through
270 the sky like a feather that weighs nothing at all. But once I
spread my fingers in the dirt and crouch over for the Get
on Your Mark, the dream goes and I am solid again and
am telling myself, Squeaky you must win, you must win,
you are the fastest thing in the world, you can even beat
275 your father up Amsterdam if you really try. And then I feel
my weight coming back just behind my knees then down
to my feet then into the earth and the pistol shot explodes
in my blood and I am off and weightless again, flying past
the other runners, my arms pumping up and down and the
280 whole world is quiet except for the crunch as I zoom over
the gravel in the track. I glance to my left and there is no

one. To the right a **blurred** Gretchen who's got her chin jutting out as if it would win the race all by itself. And on the other side of the fence is Raymond with his arms down
285 to his side and the palms tucked up behind him, running in his very own style and it's the first time I ever saw that and I almost stop to watch my brother Raymond on his first run. But the white ribbon is bouncing toward me and I tear past it racing into the distance till my feet with a mind
290 of their own start digging up footfuls of dirt and brake me short. Then all the kids standing on the side pile on me, banging me on the back and slapping my head with their May Day programs, for I have won again and everybody on 151st Street can walk tall for another year.
295   "In first place . . ." the man on the loudspeaker is clear as a bell now. But then he pauses and the loudspeaker starts to whine. Then static. And I lean down to catch my breath and here comes Gretchen walking back for she's overshot the finish line too, huffing and puffing with her hands on
300 her hips taking it slow, breathing in steady time like a real pro and I sort of like her a little for the first time. "In first place . . ." and then three or four voices get all mixed up on the loudspeaker and I dig my sneaker into the grass and

blurred

indistinct; unclear

stare at Gretchen who's staring back, we both wondering
305 just who did win. I can hear old Beanstalk arguing with
the man on the loudspeaker and then a few others running
their mouths about what the stop watches say.

Then I hear Raymond yanking at the fence to call me
and I wave to shush him, but he keeps rattling the fence,
310 but then like a dancer or something he starts climbing up
nice and easy but very fast. And it occurs to me, watching
how smoothly he climbs hand over hand and remembering
how he looked running with his arms down to his side
and with the wind pulling his mouth back and his teeth
315 showing and all, it occurred to me that Raymond would
make a very fine runner. Doesn't he always keep up with
me on my trots? And he surely knows how to breathe in
counts of seven cause he's always doing it at the dinner
table, which drives my brother George up the wall. And
320 I'm smiling to beat the band cause if I've lost this race, or
if me and Gretchen tied, or even if I've won, I can always
retire as a runner and begin a whole new career as a coach
with Raymond as my champion. After all, with a little more
study I can beat Cynthia and her phony self at the spelling
325 bee. And if I bugged my mother, I could get piano lessons
and become a star. And I have a big rep as the baddest
thing around. And I've got a roomful of ribbons and medals
and awards. But what has Raymond got to call his own?

So I stand there with my new plans, laughing out
330 loud by this time as Raymond jumps down from the fence
and runs over with his teeth showing and his arms down
to the side which no one before him has quite mastered
as a running style. And by the time he comes over I'm
jumping up and down so glad to see him—my brother
335 Raymond, a great runner in the family tradition. But of
course everyone thinks I'm jumping up and down because
the men on the loudspeaker have finally gotten themselves
together and compared notes and are announcing "In first
place—Miss Hazel Elizabeth Deborah Parker." (Dig that.)
340 "In second place—Miss Gretchen P. Lewis." And I look over
at Gretchen wondering what the P stands for. And I smile.
Cause she's good, no doubt about it. Maybe she'd like to

help me coach Raymond; she obviously is serious about
running, as any fool can see. And she nods to congratulate
345 me and then she smiles. And I smile. We stand there with
this big smile of respect between us. It's about as real a
smile as girls can do for each other, considering we don't
practice real smiling every day you know, cause maybe we
too busy being flowers or fairies or strawberries instead of
350 something honest and worthy of respect . . . you know . . .
like being people.

Answer It

1. Assess the encounter Squeaky and Raymond had with Gretchen and her
   sidekicks, Mary Louise and Rosie.

2. State reasons the author titled this selection "Raymond's Run."

3. Explain how the relationship between Squeaky and Raymond developed
   from the beginning to the end of the story.

4. Describe the meaning of the smile between Gretchen and Squeaky at the end
   of the story.

5. Discuss lessons that can be learned from the characters in "Raymond's Run."

A SLOW TAKE ON FAST FOOD

Food at Different Speeds

Is it always better to be fast than slow? You would certainly think so if you trained a team of sprinters for the Olympics. But what if you trained a team of doctors for brain surgery? You definitely would *not* want them to rush 5 through an operation, especially if you were the one being operated on!

The point is that faster is not always better. It all depends on the situation. And one situation is the speed at which we eat. That is, not only what we eat, but how fast we eat.

10 For thousands of years, people have eaten in the same basic way all around the world. First, they spend hours, days, weeks, or months just to hunt, gather, fish, or farm for their food. If they are successful in their efforts, they spend hours or days to prepare the food, start a fire, then slowly 15 cook their meal. Given all of the time and effort spent on the whole process, it is easy to imagine that they enjoy every last morsel.

Today, eating for some of us is changing. We can prepare, cook, and eat meals more quickly. However, some 20 people think things have become too fast for our own good. They **promote** *slow food* meals that are carefully planned and slowly prepared, cooked, enjoyed, and shared.

promote

to support or encourage

Early Fast Food

Let's first look at how our eating habits have sped up over time. For thousands of years, people have been drying, salting, and pickling food so that they could eat it later. About two hundred years ago, people figured out how to store products in jars and cans. Preparing food ahead of time made mealtimes quicker.

After the invention of canned food, you could reach for a jar of fruit prepared years ago, open it, and eat right then. It was a revolution in food history, matched only by the later invention of iceboxes, which kept food cold in airtight boxes full of blocks of ice.

Transportation also had a huge impact on our eating habits. It's one thing to store food and another to move it from one place to another. The invention of the steam engine allowed trains and ships to quickly transport food from faraway places. These inventions took place before the twentieth century. So, it's interesting to note that *your* great-grandparents' food already was much faster than that of *their* great-grandparents.

Faster Food

Meanwhile, new events further improved methods for preparing, packaging, and storing food. For example, electric refrigerators were a big improvement on iceboxes. World War II alone saw many advances in food production, storage, and **distribution**. After all, it's hard to win a war on an empty stomach. It's also no easy task to feed millions of soldiers and keep them moving fast across deserts and jungles. Canned meals called C rations fed American soldiers.

After the war, new and faster foods made their way from grocery stores into the home. Refrigerated items, known as "frozen foods," became popular. This included fully prepared meals called "TV dinners," which you could eat while watching TV. There also were frozen concentrates, frozen pizzas, boxes of cereal, and all sorts of foods that were ready to eat after adding water or heating them up.

distribution
the passing out of goods over a wide area

convenient

useful; easy to use

Faster foods were a great help to mothers, who did
60 most of the cooking. More moms than ever were working
full-time jobs, and fast foods saved them precious time. So
did other new, fast, and **convenient** appliances, such as
dishwashers.

Fast Food Goes into Business

The whole world seemed to be speeding up. And the
65 most famous newcomer in fast food never could have
occurred without these developments. It was the fast food
restaurant.

The 1950s saw an explosion in this type of business,
usually in the form of "hamburger joints." Most of these
70 were individual- or family-owned, but all relied on "pre-
processed" foods. This simply refers to items that are ready
to cook or serve with minimum preparation.

Some of these restaurants were extremely popular. It
wasn't long before their owners realized that they could
75 repeat their successes in more than one location. So, they
decided to open one restaurant after another across the
country, like links on a chain. In fact, that's exactly what
they were called—"restaurant chains."

Before long, Americans were eating out at these
80 restaurants on a regular basis. The practice has become
so common that now nearly every community in the
United States includes at least one fast food restaurant,
and often many.

No longer do fast food restaurants offer only
85 hamburgers, and no longer do they operate only in the
United States. Today's fast food restaurants provide many
types of **cuisine** and operate in nearly every country on
the globe. Some of these businesses are now the world's
largest companies.

cuisine

food; French for
"food" and
"kitchen"

The Faults of Fast Food

90 According to supporters of the Slow Food movement,
all of this speed and convenience has come at a great cost.
Carlo Petrini, an Italian food critic, founded the Slow

Food movement in Paris in 1989. Basically, this movement believes that fast food means bad food.

95　　For starters, they believe the taste of fast food is inferior to slow-cooked meals that use fresh ingredients. Just as important, they criticize fast food for using unhealthy ingredients. Of course, everyone may have his or her own tastes, but health experts agree that fast food often includes

100 too much fat and salt and too many calories.

In addition, members of the Slow Food movement believe that fast food encourages us to eat too quickly. Most medical professionals agree that we should not eat too fast, because it is bad for our digestion.

105　　Slow Food promoters also believe that fast food is bad for our mental health. That's because it encourages people to rush through their meals, and, all too often, to eat alone, on the run, in the car, or in unattractive settings.

Slow Is Good

The slow food alternative values healthy whole grains,

110 fruits, and vegetables bought from farmers' markets or local grocers. It prizes planning and cooking meals that are **savored** and shared with good company, like a special occasion dinner. The point isn't to take time or waste time, but to make the most of it with a

115 quality eating experience.

As an added benefit, slow food may reduce **caloric intake**. The reason has to do with how our bodies handle what we eat. As the stomach digests

120 food, it sends chemicals to the brain

savored
enjoyed the taste of

caloric intake
the eating or con-
suming of calories

letting us know when we're full. However, it takes a while for these signals to reach the brain.

Unfortunately, when we quickly gobble down large portions of food, our brain may not get the message that
125 we've eaten too much until the meal is already over! Eating slowly gives the brain time to get the message that the stomach has had enough.

Almost everybody agrees that it is a good thing to slow down our lives once in a while, including our eating. This
130 probably explains why there are now tens of thousands of members of the Slow Food movement throughout roughly fifty countries.

However, is slow food simply too slow and impractical for most people's fast-paced lives? Fast food may give you
135 extra time, but what if one of the best things you can do with your free time is to cook and share a meal? Then again, what if there are other things that you enjoy doing even more with your time, such as visiting friends, reading books, or playing sports? One thing is for sure, whether
140 you think fast food or slow food is better, it's time to think about what's at the end of your fork and what's the best choice for you.

From "Not So Fast" by Diane Voyatzis

Think About It

1. List two inventions that changed the way food was stored or transported.

2. Explain how fast food helps working mothers.

3. Check to see who invented the Slow Food movement. What year was it? Describe the Slow Food movement.

4. Explain how eating alone, on the run, in the car, or in unattractive settings may be bad for your mental health.

5. Justify the need to quickly prepare meals. How does this help you in your life?

6. Assess the author's point of view regarding fast food and the Slow Food movement.

The Tortoise and the Hare: A Fable

One hot and muggy summer afternoon, the Hare was boasting to a huge crowd of animals who had gathered in a **verdant** forest clearing: "I'm the fastest animal in the forest, and no one can beat me, even on my slowest day!"

5　　"Why is it so important to be the fastest?" asked the Tortoise.

"Because faster is superior!" replied the Hare. "My speed is unbeatable, and I can do anything faster than any other animal, so I am the most superior animal in the forest."

10　　"Speed, perhaps, can be a good thing, but it doesn't automatically make one animal more superior or important than any other animal," responded the Tortoise **indignantly**.

"If you really don't think my speed makes me superior, why don't you prove it? Suppose the two of us run a race to

15　see who's right?" exclaimed the Hare. "We can race down the four-mile path along the edge of the forest. You're so slow and sluggish that I'll probably finish the race before you get a third of the way." The Hare began to laugh at the thought of the Tortoise racing, and he fell to the ground in

20　a fit of laughter, snorting and spitting great guffaws.

Although the Tortoise had **disdain** for the Hare's display of insensitive behavior and preferred not to enter into a race with such an **egocentric** fool, he accepted the Hare's challenge because he wanted to confront the

25　Hare's taunting. He stashed a bottle of water in his shell in anticipation of the sweltering race ahead.

verdant
covered with green plants

indignantly
angrily; discontentedly

disdain
contempt; the feeling that someone deserves no respect

egocentric
selfish; self-centered

Without doing anything to prepare for the hot and humid weather, the Hare lined up at the starting line next to the Tortoise. The other animals, hoping for the
30 impossible—that the Hare would get his just rewards— shouted, "Go!" and the Hare took off with unbelievable speed, darted up the first hill, and soon disappeared from sight. The Tortoise set off with a gradual and methodical pace, and steadily climbed up the hill after the Hare. Seeing
35 this, most of the animals calculated that the Tortoise's chances of winning were slim to nil.

After he had finished his repast, he noticed a nearby skateboarding course across the meadow. "I'm so far ahead of that pitiful Tortoise that I still have time for some amusement," considered the Hare. "The Tortoise probably
50 hasn't even reached a mile yet." Chuckling at the Tortoise, and with great confidence in himself, the Hare rented a skateboard, kneepads, and a helmet, and hit the course. He skateboarded at such great speed that he literally "hit" the course and landed on his own tail! The Hare did not

The Hare seemed unstoppable as he passed the three-mile mark on the path. However, because he did not prepare for the hot day, he began languishing in the heat and
40 decided to stop at one of the rest stops along the path for a little refreshment. "I'm so far ahead of that laboriously slow Tortoise that I have lots of time," he concluded. With great confidence in his anticipated victory, he strolled into his favorite fast food restaurant and demanded a jumbo-sized
45 carrot juice and an extra-large salad.

audacity
shameless boldness; overconfidence

55 hurt himself badly, but his great **audacity** left him with a bruised ego. He arose sheepishly and limped off the course.

Following his skateboarding accident, the Hare tried to start sprinting. Because of his bruises and full stomach, he was unable to run as swiftly as before. "Even though I can't
60 run as fast, I'll still beat that tedious Tortoise," proclaimed the Hare. However, the broiling temperature made running difficult, and the Hare soon felt totally exhausted. After running for only a half mile, the Hare decided to take another short rest, and he sat down near a gurgling brook.
65 "I'll just rest here for a few minutes, and then I'll have more

energy for racing." Although he would eventually regret it, the Hare nestled in a bed of leaves, immediately fell asleep, and began snoring very loudly.

70 Meanwhile, the Tortoise continued to trudge along the path at the edge of the forest; he knew that he could not afford to stop, and more importantly, he knew that the overconfident Hare would stop many times. "Even though it's hot, I have plenty of water, so there's no need to stop until I finish the race," the Tortoise told himself. "Plus, it's

75 never a good idea to eat and run."

Soon, the Tortoise was passing the brook where the Hare napped comfortably. The Tortoise heard the Hare's loud snoring, which gave the Tortoise an added degree of confidence. He calculated that if he were able to keep up

80 his steady pace, he had a good chance of finishing first. The Tortoise thanked the Hare for being true to his foolish character, and he continued to plod steadily toward the finish line.

As the Tortoise slowly approached the end of the

85 path, the Hare suddenly awoke and bolted upright from his leaf-nest. Realizing that he could potentially lose the race, the Hare jumped up and raced back onto the path. Unfortunately, his pace was even slower than before because he wasn't yet fully awake and still felt groggy.

90 As the Hare moved along the path as fast as he could, he noticed that the Tortoise was just a few yards away from the finish line. He knew that his only chance of winning was to trick the Tortoise. He called to the Tortoise, "Tortoise, I'm hurt. Can you help me?"

95 The Tortoise stopped and looked back, "How do I know that you're telling the truth?"

"My tail hurts. Please help me," begged the Hare, as he pretended to be in great pain.

Fortunately, the Tortoise had heard the Hare's loud

100 snoring, so he knew that the Hare was trying to deceive him.

"What can I do to help you?" asked the Tortoise.

"Please help me get to the clearing," pleaded the Hare.

"Did you enjoy your sleep?" questioned the Tortoise, immune to the Hare's antics.

105 "Yes . . . err. No, wait!" shouted the harebrained Hare.

"I knew you were sleeping after I heard your loud snoring," declared the Tortoise. "I'll see you on the other side of the finish line."

Despite his **lethargy**, the Hare made a mad dash 110 to catch the Tortoise. But he was too late. The Tortoise crossed the finish line just ahead of the Hare. The Hare crossed the line and collapsed on the ground.

"You boast too much, you're arrogant, and you rarely consider others' feelings, so I'm not surprised that you tried 115 to deceive me," the Tortoise said calmly.

All the animals cheered gleefully. It was clear that speed alone was not enough to make the Hare finish first.

The Moral: Slow and steady wins the race.

Adapted from "The Hare and the Tortoise," *Aesop's Fables*

lethargy

a lack of energy; sluggishness

Think About It

1. Explain why the Tortoise accepted the Hare's challenge. Do you think that the Tortoise believed that he had a chance of winning?

2. Tell what the Tortoise did to prepare for the race in hot weather.

3. Find the idioms "slim to nil" in line 36 and "made a mad dash" in line 109. Use the context to figure out the meanings. Write an explanation of one of the idioms.

4. Explain the meaning of the Tortoise's statement to the Hare, "I'm not surprised that you tried to deceive me." What does this statement reveal about the Hare's character?

5. Justify the challenge made by the Hare. Explain what you would have done.

6. Assess the moral of the fable. What is another way to express "slow and steady wins the race"?

Unit 20

Play On

STEP
1

Phonemic Awareness and Phonics

Unit 20 expands vowel digraph syllables to include the digraphs **ay**, **ea**, **ie**, **ey**, **ow**, and **oe**.

Syllables

Review: Words are made up of **syllables**.

- A syllable is a word, or word part, that has one vowel sound.

- A syllable's type is determined by the syllable's vowel sound.

- A **closed syllable** ends with a consonant and has a short vowel sound.

- An **r-controlled syllable** contains an **r-controlled** vowel sound.

- An **open syllable** ends with a vowel and has a long vowel sound.

- A syllable that ends with vowel + consonant + **e** is a **final silent e syllable**.

Vowel Digraph Syllables

A syllable that contains a vowel digraph is a **vowel digraph syllable**.

- In some syllables, the vowel phoneme is spelled with two vowel letters.

- The vowel sound represented by the vowel digraph is usually long.

- In this unit the vowel digraphs are: **ay**, **ea** (for / $\bar{a}$ / and / $\bar{e}$ /), **ey**, **ie** (for / $\bar{e}$ / and / $\bar{\imath}$ /), **ow**, and **oe**.

Go to the **Vowel Chart** on page A3. Find these long vowel sounds on the chart and the vowel digraphs that represent them:

Find / $\bar{a}$ /. Find the cue words **play** and **great**.

Find / $\bar{e}$ /. Find the cue words **eat**, **chief**, and **key**.

Find / $\bar{\imath}$ /. Find the cue word **pie**.

Find / $\bar{o}$ /. Find the cue words **show** and **toe**.

Word Recognition and Spelling

Prefixes

Review: We can expand words and change meaning by adding **prefixes**. These word parts are added to the beginnings of words. Examples: **pre** + date = predate; **re** + name = rename; **un** + clean = unclean

(See Step 3: Vocabulary and Morphology for links to meaning.)

> **Unit 20 Prefixes**
>
> **de-, ex-**

Suffixes

Review: We can expand words and change meaning by adding **suffixes**. These word parts are added to the ends of words. Examples: decay + **ed** = decayed; chose + **en** = chosen; neat + **er** = neater; brave + **est** = bravest; heal + **ing** = healing

(See Step 3: Vocabulary and Morphology for links to meaning and Step 4: Grammar and Usage for function.)

> **Unit 20 Suffix**
>
> **-y**

Roots

We can build words using roots. We usually attach a prefix or suffix to make it a word. Example: ex + **tract** = extract

> **Unit 20 Roots**
>
> **form, port, tract**

Essential Words

Unit 20 Essential Words

course	guarantee	guess
friend	guard	guest

Spelling Lists

The Unit 20 spelling lists contain three categories:

1. Words with the vowel digraphs **ay**, **ea** (for / $\bar{a}$ / and / $\bar{e}$ /), **ey**, **ie** (for / $\bar{e}$ /), and **ow**

2. Essential Words (in italics)

3. Words with prefixes, roots, and suffixes

Spelling Lists

Lessons 1–5		Lessons 6–10	
chimney	*guard*	contract	squeaky
course	*guess*	decay	subtracted
decrease	*guest*	exporter	supported
delay	hollow	extracted	tractor
feast	meanwhile	formula	tricky
friend	relieve	informal	unblocked
great	shallow	payment	uninformed
guarantee		pretest	

STEP 3

Vocabulary and Morphology

Unit Vocabulary

Sound-spelling correspondences from this unit and previous units make up this unit's vocabulary.

- What do these words mean?

- Do some of them mean more than one thing? Which ones?

UNIT Vocabulary

ay for / ā /	**ea** for / ā /	easy	monkey	grow
away	break	eat	valley	hollow
bay	great	feast		low
clay		grease	**ie** for / ē /	own
day	**ea** for / ē /	increase	believe	shadow
decay	beam	lead	chief	shallow
delay	beast	leaf	factories	show
hay	beat	lean	field	slow
lay	beneath	least	priest	snow
may	cheap	leave	shield	sow
maybe	clean	meal		window
pay	cream	mean	**ie** for / ī /	yellow
play	deal	meanwhile	lie	
pray	decrease		tie	**oe** for / ō /
ray	disease	**ey** for / ē /		toe
say	each	chimney	**ow** for / ō /	hoe
stay	eager	donkey	blow	
tray	ease	key	borrow	
way	east	money	bowl	

Word Relationships

Homophones are words that sound the same but have different spellings and meanings. The context indicates the correct spelling based on the meaning. Example: He has felt **weak** from the flu for about a **week**. (**Weak** and **week** are homophones.)

Meaning Parts

Prefixes

Review: Prefixes can add to or change the meanings of words. Examples: predate (**pre** = before); rename (**re** = again); recall (**re** = back); unclean (**un** = not); uncap (**un** = opposite of)

Unit 20 Prefixes	Meanings	Examples
de-	from	decode, deduct, defrost
ex-	out, from	excavate, expand, expel

Suffixes

Review: Adding the suffix **-er** to an adjective compares two people, places, or things. Example: neat**er**. Adding the suffix **-est** to an adjective compares one person, place, or thing to two or more others. Example: brav**est**

Review: Other suffixes, when added to a base word, permit a verb form to function as an adjective. Examples: decay**ed**, chos**en**, heal**ing**

Suffixes can add to or change the meanings of words. Some suffixes indicate adjective form. When added to a base word, they can change the base word to an adjective. The Unit 20 suffix is -**y**.

Unit 20 Suffix	Meanings	Examples
-y	characterized by, consisting of, the quality or condition of	funny, stormy, tricky

Roots

- A **root** is the basic meaning part of a word. It carries the most important part of the word's meaning.
- The root usually needs a prefix or suffix to make it into a word.
- Roots of English words often come from other languages, especially Latin.

> **Root**
>
> ex + **tract** = extract
>
> ex = out   **tract** = pull
>
> extract = to pull out

Unit 20 Roots	Meanings	Examples
form	to shape	inform, reform, transform
port	to carry	deport, export, report
tract	to pull	detract, extract, retract

Challenge Morphemes

Root	Meanings	Examples
pend/ pens	to hang, pay, or weigh	compensate, pendulum, pensive, spender, stipend

Grammar and Usage

Adjectives

Review: **Adjectives** describe nouns. They answer: **Which one? How many?** and **What kind?**

Adjectives

> **Fifty unbeaten marble** players **from each state** competed.

Which ones?	**from each state** (prepositional phrase that acts as an adjective)
How many?	**fifty** (single word that acts as an adjective)
What kind?	**unbeaten, marble** (past participle that acts as an adjective; single word)

Irregular Verbs

Review: Some verbs signal past time through irregular verb forms.

Unit 20 Irregular Verbs

Base Verb	Past Tense	Past Participle
beat	beat	beaten
blow	blew	blown
break	broke	broken
deal	dealt	dealt
eat	ate	eaten
grow	grew	grown
lay (= put)	laid	laid
lead	led	led
leave	left	left
lie (= recline)	lay	lain
pay	paid	paid
read	read	read
say	said	said
show	showed	shown
speak	spoke	spoken

Tense Timeline

Review: **Verbs** describe an action or a state of being. Verbs also convey time. The **Tense Timeline** shows the relationship between time and verb form.

Yesterday	Today	Tomorrow
Past	Present	Future
was/were	*am/is/are*	*will be*

Linking Verbs

Review: Some verbs can act as main verbs or helping verbs. Forms of **be** belong to this group of verbs. Helping verbs combine with the main verb to form a verb phrase. The helping verb signals the time. Examples: He **is playing** the cello. It **was snowing** during the night. She **will be increasing** their pay.

- The verb **be** can also act as a **linking verb**. Linking verbs connect, or link, the subject of the sentence to a word in the predicate.

- A noun that follows a linking verb renames, or tells more about, the subject. This noun is called a **predicate nominative**.

- The subject and the predicate nominative name the same person, place, thing, or idea. Example: *Kokopelli* **is** a *flute player.* The verb **is** links the subject *Kokopelli* to the noun *flute player.*

Predicate Adjectives

An adjective that follows a linking verb describes the subject. This adjective is called a **predicate adjective**. It describes the subject.

> *Be* **as a Linking Verb for a Predicate Adjective**
>
> Kokopelli's *music* **is** *beautiful.*
>
> The verb **is** links the adjective *beautiful* to the subject *music.*

Sentence Pattern

Form: N/LV/ADJ   noun/linking verb/adjective

Function: S/P/PA   subject/predicate/predicate adjective

Kokopelli's **music is** beautiful.

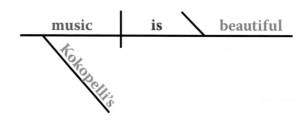

Punctuation

Review: We use **commas** to separate items **in a series**. When three or more words or word groups are listed together in a sentence, a comma separates the items in the series. The last item is usually connected to the others in the series by **and** or **or**.

Example: Nash's poems played with words, provided humor, and increased interest in poetry.

Commas in Addresses

A comma separates the building number and street name from the city. Another comma separates the city from the state. If the address is in a sentence, a comma follows the state.

> **Commas in Addresses**
>
> We are moving to 300 New Street, Old Town, Massachusetts, in August.

Commas in Dates

A comma separates the month and day from the year. If the date is in a sentence, a comma follows the year.

> **Commas in Dates**
>
> On April 11, 2010, I will turn sixteen.

Listening and Reading Comprehension

Informational Text

■ Some informational text is nonfiction material about a specific topic, event, experience, or circumstance. It is typically found in content area text. Textbooks, biographies, and essays are examples of informational text.

Some informational text provides **reasons**, which are causes or motives for a topic or event. In this type of text organization, examples or other evidence support the reasons.

> **Transition Words for Reasons**
> one reason, the next reason, another reason

Vocabulary in Context

■ **Context clues** help us understand new vocabulary. Pronoun referents, meaning signals, and visuals, such as charts and graphs, provide meaning links.

Signal Words

■ Different types of sentences can help us think about new information in different ways.

Some sentences require us to make judgments based on criteria and standards. These sentences ask us to **Evaluate It**. They are introduced by specific **signal words**.

> **Signal Words for Evaluate It**
> critique, judge

Literary Terms and Devices

Genres are types or categories of literature. Unit 20 features the genre **fiction**. Fiction is based on a plot.

- **Fiction** is a literary genre that includes stories that are not true. Fiction is sometimes based on real people, places, or events. **"The Marble Champ"** and **"A Game of Catch"** are examples of fiction.

- **Plot** is a literary term referring to the pattern of events in a narrative or drama. Both stories in Unit 20 illustrate plot.

Plot Analysis

- **Plot** refers to a pattern of events in a narrative or drama. The plot guides the author in composing the work. It helps the reader follow the story.

- **Characters** and **setting** are two components of plot analysis. The characters, which can be people, animals, or things, take part in the story. The setting is the story's time and place. Together these two components make up the introduction in the plot's development.

- To understand how a plot develops, we must first identify a story's main **problem** and its **solution**.

- After we become proficient in identifying a story's main problem and solution, we will learn how a plot develops and apply plot development to our writing.

- Plot development usually consists of five elements:

  Introduction (setting and characters);

  Conflict (rising action);

  Climax (turning point);

  Resolution (falling action);

  Conclusion (the situation at the end of the story, with a look to the future).

Speaking and Writing

Signal Words

- Some sentences ask for information. Other sentences require us to make judgments based on criteria and standards. They use specific **signal words**.

> **Signal Words for Evaluate It**
>
> **Critique** "The Marble Champ" as a book reviewer.
>
> **Judge** Lupe's decision to compete in the sport of marbles.

Paragraph Organization

- Some paragraphs are organized by **reasons**. The content of these paragraphs includes the reasons, or the causes or motives for a topic or event, with supporting evidence or examples. Specific **transition words** signal this organization. Examples: one reason, the next reason, another reason

Plot Analysis

- Fiction includes characters created by the author. During prewriting, the author thinks about **character traits**. In good writing, each character must become distinct. Some character traits a writer may consider include: the character's personal appearance, personality, relationships with other characters, reactions to various situations, and means of coping with difficulties. Anything that distinguishes a character might be a character trait.

- Good writers usually include information about characters in the plot's introduction. This is because the reader needs to know the characters in order to follow the plot. Good writers can tell the reader about a character by including:

  A description of the character in simple narrative form;

  An incident during which the character interacts with others;

  A dialog in which the character is speaking to others.

More About Words

- **Bonus Words** use the same sound-spelling correspondences that we have studied in this unit and previous units.

- **Idioms** are common phrases that cannot be understood by the meanings of their separate words—only by the entire phrase.

- **Why? Word History** shows how knowledge of a Latin root, **tract**, expands vocabulary.

UNIT Bonus Words

ay for / ā /	bean	reveal	**ie** for / ē /	follow
birthday	beaver	scream	achieve	glow
crayon	breathe	sea	belief	minnow
daytime	cheat	seal	brief	owe
display	defeat	season	diesel	pillow
driveway	heal	squeak	handkerchief	row
gray	heap	squeal	relief	rowboat
jay	heat	steal	relieve	sorrow
layer	jeans	tea	thief	throw
okay	leak	teach		widow
relay	leap	underneath	**ie** for / ī /	
spray	pea	weave	die	**oe** for / ō /
subway	peach		pie	doe
	peacock	**ey** for / ē /		foe
ea for / ā /	peanut	alley	**ow** for / ō /	oboe
steak	preach	barley	below	
	reach	hockey	bow	
ea for / ē /	real	honey	crow	
appeal	really	turkey	elbow	
beach	release		fellow	
beak	retreat		flow	

Idioms	
Idiom	**Meaning**
blow a gasket	explode with anger
break a leg	used to wish someone success in a performance
eat your words	retract something you have said
get this show on the road	get started with an act or project
let sleeping dogs lie	don't make someone angry by stirring up trouble or talking about something that has caused problems in the past
play into the hands of	act or behave so as to give an advantage to (an opponent)
play possum	pretend to be sleeping or dead
play the game	behave according to the accepted customs
play with fire	take part in a dangerous or risky activity
step on your toes	offend or hurt someone's feelings

 **Word History**

Tractor—Did you know that the word **tractor** comes from Latin? As many as 60 percent of English words contain Latin roots. If we know the meaning of the Latin root, we can often work out the meaning of the English word. The root **tract** means "to pull" and the prefix **ex-** means "out." So what is the meaning of **extract**? "To pull out."

More than 130 English words have **tract** as their root. What does **detract** mean? Use your knowledge of **tract** and **de-** to figure it out.

Nash's Bashes

Word Play

Some folks use words to get attention.
Most folks use words to get things done.
Bad folks say words we shouldn't mention.
But Ogden Nash used words for fun.

Ogden Nash became famous. He was known for playing. But his kind of play was unique. He was a 20th century poet. He became famous for playing with words.

The times were bleak. His career was young. Life
5 offered few opportunities for play. *The New Yorker* magazine was a prominent publication. It was first to publish his poetry. The year was 1930. The Great Depression had begun. The stock market had crashed in 1929. Banks and businesses closed. Investors lost vast sums
10 of money. Unemployment was common. By 1930, it hit one person in five. People suffered.

Nash knew he could help people. He understood words. He knew they were a great source of laughter. He knew something else. Humor could relieve despair. Humor
15 could decrease hopelessness. He knew, too, that words held power. And he knew that words were *free*.

It's his word play that stops us. It makes us pay attention. It is funny. It makes us think. It's humor for people who like having fun with words.

20 Often, Nash plays with sounds in words. This helps create his word play. He knew what word repetition could do. He knew what rhythm could do. He knew what rhyme could do. They all triggered memory. They all helped him celebrate language. A celebration is a *bash*. Nash had a bash
25 with words. We can have fun with him. Let's enjoy his word play. A few of Nash's bashes follow.

The Eel

I don't mind eels,
except as meals.

The Rhinoceros

The rhino is a homely beast,
For human eyes he's not a feast.
Farewell, farewell, you old rhinoceros,
I'll stare at something less prepoceros.

The Cow

The cow is of the bovine ilk;
One end is moo, the other, milk.

The Termite

Some primal termite knocked on wood
And tasted it, and found it good,
And that is why your Cousin May
Fell through the parlor floor today.

The Wasp

The wasp and all his numerous family
I look upon as a major calamily.
He throws open his nest with prodigality,
But I distrust his waspitality.

The Lama

The one-l lama,
He's a priest.
The two-l llama,
He's a beast.

And I will bet
A silk pajama
There isn't any
Three-l lllama.

The Ostrich

The ostrich roams the great Sahara.
Its mouth is wide, its neck is narra.
It has such long and lofty legs.
I'm glad it sits to lay its eggs.

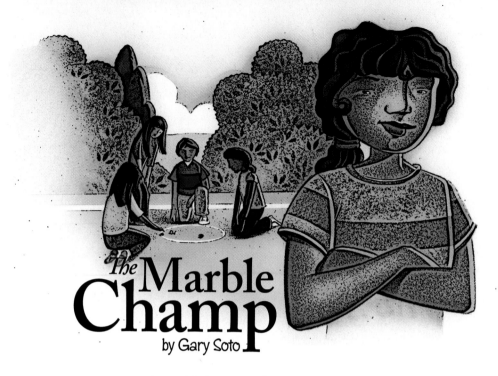

The Marble Champ
by Gary Soto

Lupe Medrano, a shy girl who spoke in whispers, was the school's spelling bee champion, winner of the reading contest at the public library three summers in a row, blue ribbon awardee in the science fair, the top student at her
5 piano recital, and the playground grand champion in chess. She was a straight-A student and—not counting kindergarten, when she had been stung by a wasp—never missed one day of elementary school. She had received a small trophy for this honor and had been congratulated by
10 the mayor.

But though Lupe had a razor-sharp mind, she could not make her body, no matter how much she tried, run as fast as the other girls'. She begged her body to move faster, but could never best anyone in the fifty-yard dash.
15 The truth was that Lupe was no good in sports. She could not catch a pop-up or figure out in which direction to kick the soccer ball. One time she kicked the ball at her own goal and scored a point for the other team. She was no good at baseball or basketball either, and even had a hard
20 time making a hula-hoop stay on her hips.

It wasn't until last year, when she was eleven years old, that she learned how to ride a bike. And even then she had

to use training wheels. She could walk in the swimming pool but couldn't swim, and chanced roller-skating only
25 when her father held her hand.

"I'll never be good at sports," she fumed one rainy day as she lay on her bed gazing at the shelf her father had made to hold her awards. "I wish I could win something, anything, even marbles."

30 At the word "marbles," she sat up. "That's it. Maybe I could be good at playing marbles." She hopped out of bed and **rummaged** through the closet until she found a can full of her brother's marbles. She poured the rich glass treasure on her bed and picked five of the most beautiful
35 marbles.

She smoothed her bedspread and practiced shooting, softly at first so that her aim would be **accurate** . The marble rolled from her thumb and clicked against the targeted marble. But the target wouldn't budge. She tried
40 again and again. Her aim became accurate, but the power from her thumb made the marble move only an inch or two. Then she realized that the bedspread was slowing the marbles. She also had to admit that her thumb was weaker than the neck of a newborn chick.

45 She looked out the window. The rain was letting up, but the ground was too muddy to play. She sat cross-legged on the bed, rolling her five marbles between her palms. Yes, she thought, I could play marbles, and marbles is a sport. At that moment she realized that she had only two weeks
50 to practice. The playground championship, the same one her brother had entered the previous year, was coming up. She had a lot to do.

To strengthen her wrists, she decided to do twenty push-ups on her fingertips, five at a time. "One, two,
55 three . . ." she groaned. By the end of the first set she was breathing hard, and her muscles burned from exhaustion. She did one more set and decided that was enough push-ups for the first day.

She squeezed a rubber eraser one hundred times,
60 hoping it would strengthen her thumb. This seemed to work because the next day her thumb was sore. She could

rummaged
searched

accurate
precise; without error

hardly hold a marble in her hand, let alone send it flying
with power. So Lupe rested that day and listened to her
brother, who gave her tips on how to shoot: get low, aim
65 with one eye, and place one knuckle on the ground.

"Think 'eye and thumb'—and let it rip!" he said.

After school the next day she left her homework in her
backpack and practiced three hours straight, taking time
only to eat a candy bar for energy. With a popsicle stick,
70 she drew an odd-shaped circle and tossed in four marbles.
She used her shooter, a milky agate with hypnotic swirls, to
blast them. Her thumb had become stronger.

After practice, she squeezed the eraser for an hour.
She ate dinner with her left hand to spare her shooting
75 hand and said nothing to her parents about her dreams of
athletic glory.

Practice, practice, practice. Squeeze, squeeze, squeeze.
Lupe got better and beat her brother and Alfonso, a
neighbor kid who was supposed to be a champ.
80 "Man, she's bad!" Alfonso said. "She can beat the other
girls for sure, I think."

The weeks passed quickly. Lupe worked so hard that
one day, while she was drying dishes, her mother asked why
her thumb was swollen.
85 "It's muscle," Lupe explained. "I've been practicing for
the marbles championship."

"You, honey?" Her mother knew Lupe was no good at sports.

"Yeah. I beat Alfonso, and he's pretty good."

90 That night, over dinner, Mrs. Medrano said, "Honey, you should see Lupe's thumb."

"Huh?" Mr. Medrano said, wiping his mouth and looking at his daughter.

"Show your father."

95 "Do I have to?" an embarrassed Lupe asked.

"Go on, show your father."

Reluctantly, Lupe raised her hand and flexed her thumb. You could see the muscle.

The father put down his fork and asked, "What
100 happened?"

"Dad, I've been working out. I've been squeezing an eraser."

"Why?"

"I'm going to enter the marbles championship."

105 Her father looked at her mother and then back at his daughter. "When is it, honey?"

"This Saturday. Can you come?"

The father had been planning to play racquetball with a friend Saturday, but he said he would be there. He knew
110 his daughter thought she was no good at sports and he wanted to encourage her. He even rigged some lights in the backyard so she could practice after dark. He squatted with one knee on the ground, **entranced** by the sight of his daughter easily beating her brother.

115 The day of the championship began with a cold blustery sky. The sun was a silvery light behind slate clouds.

"I hope it clears up," her father said, rubbing his hands together as he returned from getting the newspaper. They ate breakfast, paced nervously around the house waiting
120 for 10:00 to arrive, and walked the two blocks to the playground (though Mr. Medrano wanted to drive so Lupe wouldn't get tired). She signed up and was assigned her first match on baseball diamond number three.

Reluctantly
hesitantly; unwillingly

entranced
enchanted; fascinated

Lupe, walking between her brother and her father, shook from the cold, not nerves. She took off her mittens, and everyone stared at her thumb. Someone asked, "How can you play with a broken thumb?" Lupe smiled and said nothing.

She beat her first **opponent** easily, and felt sorry for the girl because she didn't have anyone to cheer for her. Except for her sack of marbles, she was all alone. Lupe invited the girl, whose name was Rachel, to stay with them. She smiled and said, "OK." The four of them walked to a card table in the middle of the outfield, where Lupe was assigned another opponent.

She also beat this girl, a fifth-grader named Yolanda, and asked her to join their group. They proceeded to more matches and more wins, and soon there was a crowd of people following Lupe to the finals to play a girl in a baseball cap. This girl seemed dead serious. She never even looked at Lupe.

"I don't know, Dad, she looks tough."

Rachel hugged Lupe and said, "Go get her."

"You can do it," her father encouraged. "Just think of the marbles, not the girl, and let your thumb do the work."

The other girl broke first and earned one marble. She missed her next shot, and Lupe, one eye closed, her thumb quivering with energy, blasted two marbles out of the circle but missed her next shot. Her opponent earned two more before missing. She stamped her foot and said, "Shoot!" The score was three to two in favor of Miss Baseball Cap.

The referee stopped the game. "Back up, please, give them room," he shouted. Onlookers had gathered too tightly around the players.

Lupe then earned three marbles and was set to get her fourth when a gust of wind blew dust in her eyes and she missed badly. Her opponent quickly scored two marbles, tying the game, and moved ahead six to five on a lucky shot. Then she missed, and Lupe, whose eyes felt scratchy when she blinked, relied on instinct and thumb muscle to score the tying point. It was now six to six, with only three marbles left. Lupe blew her nose and studied the angles.

opponent

a person who takes the opposite side in a game or contest

She dropped to one knee, steadied her hand, and shot so hard she cracked two marbles from the circle. She was the
165 winner!

"I did it!" Lupe said under her breath. She rose from her knees, which hurt from bending all day, and hugged her father. He hugged her back and smiled.

Everyone clapped, except Miss Baseball Cap, who
170 made a face and stared at the ground. Lupe told her she was a great player, and they shook hands. A newspaper photographer took pictures of the two girls standing shoulder-to-shoulder, with Lupe holding the bigger trophy.

Lupe then played the winner of the boys' division, and
175 after a poor start beat him eleven to four. She blasted the marbles, shattering one into sparkling slivers of glass. Her opponent looked on **glumly** as Lupe did what she did best—win!

The head referee and the President of the Fresno
180 Marble Association stood with Lupe as she displayed her trophies for the newspaper photographer. Lupe shook hands with everyone, including a dog who had come over to see what the commotion was all about.

glumly
sadly; unhappily

That night, the family went out for pizza and set the
185 two trophies on the table for everyone in the restaurant
to see. People came up to congratulate Lupe, and she
felt a little embarrassed, but her father said the trophies
belonged there.

Back home, in the privacy of her bedroom, she
190 placed the trophies on her shelf and was happy. She had
always earned honors because of her brains, but winning
in sports was a new experience. She thanked her tired
thumb. "You did it, thumb. You made me champion."
As its reward, Lupe went to the bathroom, filled the
195 bathroom sink with warm water, and let her thumb swim
and splash as it pleased. Then she climbed into bed and
drifted into a hard-won sleep.

Answer It

1. Wanting to win at something, Lupe made a decision
   to participate in the sport of marbles. Judge Lupe's
   decision to compete in the sport of marbles.

2. Explain why Lupe was reluctant to show her thumb
   to her father.

3. Identify evidence that Lupe's father supported her
   decision to compete in marbles.

4. Compare the personality traits of Lupe, in "The
   Marble Champ," and Squeaky, in "Raymond's Run."
   Include examples from each story.

5. Pretend you review books and movies for the local
   newspaper. Critique "The Marble Champ." Be sure
   to include your opinion about whether this story
   should appear on the newspaper's recommended
   reading list.

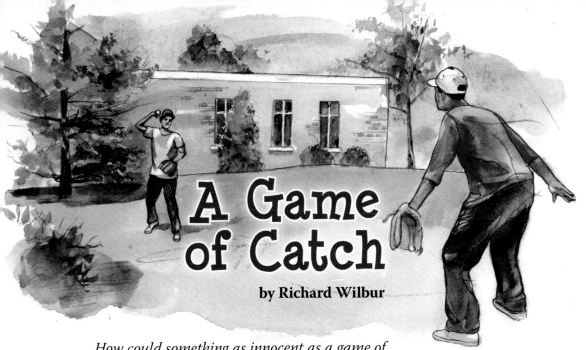

A Game of Catch

by Richard Wilbur

How could something as innocent as a game of catch result in such painful consequences?

Monk and Glennie were playing catch on the side lawn of the firehouse when Scho caught sight of them. They were
5 good at it, for seventh-graders, as anyone could see right away. Monk, wearing a catcher's mitt, would lean easily sidewise and back, with one leg lifted and his throwing hand almost down to the grass, and then lob the white ball straight up into the sunlight. Glennie would shield his eyes
10 with his left hand and, just as the ball fell past him, snag it with a little dart of his glove. Then he would burn the ball straight toward Monk, and it would spank into the round mitt and sit, like a still-life apple on a plate, until Monk flipped it over into his right hand and, with a negligent flick
15 of his hanging arm, gave Glennie a fast grounder.

They were going on and on like that, in a kind of slow, mannered, **luxurious** dance in the sun, their faces perfectly blank and entranced, when Glennie noticed Scho dawdling along the other side of the street and called hello
20 to him. Scho crossed over and stood at the front edge of the lawn, near an apple tree, watching.

"Got your glove?" asked Glennie after a time. Scho obviously hadn't.

luxurious
extremely enjoy-able, self-indulgent

"You could give me some easy grounders," said Scho. 25 "But don't burn 'em."

"All right," Glennie said. He moved off a little, so the three of them formed a triangle, and they passed the ball around for about five minutes, Monk tossing easy grounders to Scho, Scho throwing to Glennie, and Glennie 30 burning them in to Monk. After a while, Monk began to throw them back to Glennie once or twice before he let Scho have his grounder, and finally Monk gave Scho a fast, bumpy grounder that hopped over his shoulder and went into the brake on the other side of the street.

35 "Not so hard," called Scho as he ran across to get it.

"You should've had it," Monk shouted.

It took Scho a little while to find the ball among the ferns and dead leaves, and when he saw it, he grabbed it up and threw it toward Glennie. It struck the trunk 40 of the apple tree, bounced back at an angle, and rolled steadily and stupidly onto the cement apron in front of the firehouse, where one of the trucks was parked. Scho ran hard and stopped it just before it rolled under the truck, and this time he carried it back to his former position on 45 the lawn and threw it carefully to Glennie.

"I got an idea," said Glennie. "Why don't Monk and I catch for five minutes more, and then you can borrow one of our gloves?"

"That's all right with me," said Monk. He socked his fist 50 into his mitt, and Glennie burned one in.

"All right," Scho said, and went over and sat under the tree. There in the shade he watched them resume their skillful play. They threw lazily fast or lazily slow—high, low, or wide—and always handsomely, their expressions 55 **serene**, changeless, and forgetful. When Monk missed a low backhand catch, he walked **indolently** after the ball and, hardly even looking, flung it sidearm for an imaginary put-out. After a good while of this, Scho said, "Isn't it five minutes yet?"

60 "One minute to go," said Monk, with a fraction of a grin.

serene
very calm; peaceful

indolently
lazily

Scho stood up and watched the ball slap back and forth for several minutes more, and then he turned and pulled himself up into the crotch of the tree.

65 "Where you going?" Monk asked.

"Just up the tree," Scho said.

"I guess he doesn't want to catch," said Monk.

Scho went up and up through the fat light-
70 gray branches until they grew slender and bright and gave under him. He found a place where several supple branches were knit to make a dangerous chair, and sat there with his head coming out of the
75 leaves into the sunlight. He could see the two other boys down below, the ball going back and forth between them as if they were bowling on the grass, and Glennie's crew-cut head looking like a sea urchin.

80 "I found a wonderful seat up here," Scho said loudly. "If I don't fall out." Monk and Glennie didn't look up or comment, and so he began **jouncing** gently in his chair of branches and singing "Yo-ho, heave ho" in an exaggerated way.

85 "Do you know what, Monk?" he announced in a few moments. "I can make you two guys do anything I want. Catch that ball, Monk! Now you catch it, Glennie!"

"I was going to catch it anyway," Monk suddenly said. "You're not making anybody do anything when they're
90 already going to do it anyway."

"I made you say what you just said," Scho replied joyfully.

"No, you didn't," said Monk, still throwing and catching but now less serenely absorbed in the game.

95 "That's what I wanted you to say," Scho said.

The ball bounded off the rim of Monk's mitt and plowed into a gladiolus bed beside the firehouse, and Monk ran to get it while Scho jounced in his treetop and sang, "I wanted you to miss that. Anything you do is what I wanted
100 you to do."

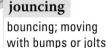

jouncing
bouncing; moving with bumps or jolts

"Let's quit for a minute," Glennie suggested.

"We might as well, until the peanut gallery shuts up," Monk said.

They went over and sat cross-legged in the shade of
105 the tree. Scho looked down between his legs and saw them
on the dim, spotty ground, saying nothing to one another.
Glennie soon began abstractedly spinning his glove
between his palms; Monk pulled his nose and stared out
across the lawn.

110 "I want you to mess around with your nose, Monk," said
Scho, giggling. Monk withdrew his hand from his face.

"Do that with your glove, Glennie," Scho persisted.
"Monk, I want you to pull up hunks of grass and chew on
it."

115 Glennie looked up and saw a self-delighted, intense face
staring down at him through the leaves. "Stop being a dope
and come down and we'll catch for a few minutes," he said.

Scho hesitated, and then said, in a **tentatively** mocking
voice, "That's what I wanted you to say."

120 "All right, then, nuts to you," said Glennie.

"Why don't you keep quiet and stop bothering people?"
Monk asked.

"I made you say that," Scho replied, softly.

"Shut up," Monk said.

125 "I made you say that, and I want you to be standing
there looking sore. And I want you to climb up the tree. I'm
making you do it!"

Monk was scrambling up through the branches,
awkward in his haste, and getting snagged on twigs. His
130 face was furious and foolish, and he kept telling Scho to
shut up, shut up, shut up, while the other's **exuberant** and
panicky voice poured down upon his head.

"Now you shut up or you'll be sorry," Monk said,
breathing hard as he reached up and threatened to shake
135 the cradle of slight branches in which Scho was sitting.

"I want—" Scho screamed as he fell. Two lower
branches broke his rustling, crackling fall, but he landed
on his back with a deep thud and lay still, with a strangled
look on his face and his eyes clenched. Glennie knelt down

---

tentatively

shyly; hesitantly

---

exuberant

high-spirited;
enthusiastic

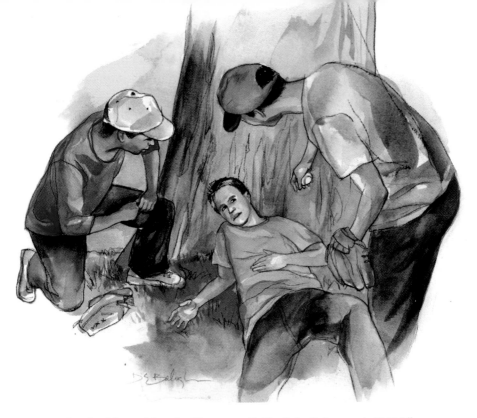

140 and asked breathlessly, "Are you O.K., Scho? Are you O.K.?"
while Monk swung down through the leaves crying that
honestly he hadn't even touched him, the crazy guy just let
go. Scho doubled up and turned over on his right side, and
now both the other boys knelt beside him, pawing at his
145 shoulder and begging to know how he was.

Then Scho rolled away from them and sat partly up,
still struggling to get his wind but forcing a species of smile
onto his face.

"I'm sorry, Scho," Monk said. "I didn't mean to make
150 you fall."

Scho's voice came out weak and gravelly, in gasps.
"I meant—you to do it. You—had to. You can't do—
anything—unless I want—you to."

Glennie and Monk looked helplessly at him as he sat
155 there, breathing a bit more easily and smiling fixedly, with
tears in his eyes. Then they picked up their gloves and the
ball, walked over to the street, and went slowly away down
the sidewalk, Monk punching his fist into the mitt, Glennie
juggling the ball between glove and hand.

160   From under the apple tree, Scho, still bent over a little for lack of breath, croaked after them in triumph and misery, "I want you to do whatever you're going to do for the whole rest of your life!"

Answer It

1. Monk threw a fast, bumpy grounder to Scho. Explain why Monk might have behaved in this manner.

2. Glennie and Monk continued to play catch longer than the agreed upon five minutes, when Scho was supposed to be able to play with them again. Explain how Scho responded as the other boys continued to play on and on without him.

3. Pretend you are a judge. Decide which boy is responsible for Scho being left alone at the end of the story: Glennie, Monk, or Scho. Explain your answer.

4. List ways to help a person feel included, rather than excluded.

5. Select one of the characters in the story: Glennie, Monk, or Scho. Describe how that character could have handled the situation differently.

Yo-Yo Ma Plays the World

"It is so easy to be cynical. It's an accurate reflection of reality. It's much harder; it takes a philosophical point of view, to be optimistic. You have to work at it every day. One of the joys of working with children is that they are still unspoiled by cynicism." — Yo-Yo Ma

Yo-Yo Ma, famous cellist.

Who Is He?

Who is Yo-Yo Ma? Is he a great philosopher? Is he a great humanist? Is he a great counselor? Is he a great philanthropist? Is he a cultural ambassador to the world? Yo-Yo Ma is all of these, and more.

5　　Yo-Yo Ma has created a global music community. One of the finest **cellists** of all time, he is one of the world's best-selling solo artists. He has recorded more than 60 albums and has won 16 Grammy awards. Fans pack concert halls regularly to witness the rapturous way he bows his
10　beloved instrument, in tribute to the great composers. Ma says he's striving to create music that helps to interpret what it means to be human.

　　Ma's colossal **stamina** has led to comparisons with great athletes. Conductor David Zinman, a frequent
15　collaborator, says, "I see Tiger Woods as the Yo-Yo Ma of golf." (Others have called Michael Jordan the Yo-Yo Ma of

cellists
musicians who play the cello

stamina
ability to do something for a long time; endurance

basketball, Yo-Yo Ma the Wayne Gretzky of music, and so forth.) "On our last tour," says Zinman, "Ma said, 'You have to expend energy in order to produce energy. If you empty 20 yourself, you're going to fill yourself even more.' Sometimes he sleeps; sometimes he doesn't. He's one of those people who can sleep on a dime. If he has 10 minutes before a concert, he can just *zzzzzz* out, then throw some water on his face and be radiant."

An Extraordinary Life

25   Yo-Yo Ma was born in Paris in 1955 to a talented Chinese family. At four, he began cello lessons; at five, he gave his first **recital**. But his life hasn't followed a typical classical music path. Yes, he plays million-dollar instruments, including a 1733 Montagnana cello from 30 Venice and a 1712 Davidoff Stradivarius cello, but Yo-Yo Ma doesn't play classical music exclusively. He also plays a wide variety of contemporary music, folk music, and lesser-known works—sometimes by unknown composers.

    Ma has jammed with Argentine tango bands, traded 35 tunes with bushmen in the Kalahari, and even performed with the Muppets on Sesame Street. "I'm proud to say," he boasts a little, "that I knew Elmo before he became Tickle-Me Elmo, the star. When he was starting the violin, I helped him learn a very difficult note." Ma's appearances 40 on *Sesame Street*, with Mister Rogers, and as a giant bespectacled gray bunny on *Arthur*, he says, are "the things I am most proud of; I love being invited into the world of children."

Early Beginnings

    Ma's father, Hiao-Tsiun Ma, a violinist and a professor 45 at Nanjing University, left China for Paris in 1936. His mother, Marina, a singer from Hong Kong and former student of Hiao-Tsiun's, immigrated to Paris in 1949, where she and Hiao-Tsiun were married. In 1955, Yo-Yo was born. Some years ago, he told interviewer David Blum that "Yo," 50 which in Chinese means "friendship," was the generational

> **recital**
>
> a formal performance in front of an audience

character chosen for him and his sister, Yeou-Cheng, M.D., now a violinist and pediatrician, who is four years older than he. "With me," he laughs, "they seem to have got lazy and been unable to think of anything else, so they added
55 another Yo."

At his first public concert at the University of Paris when he was five, he played both the piano and cello. His father "was the **pedagogue** of the family, very strict. I was born when he was 49, so he was an older parent, very old-
60 world. He loved painting, and himself studied musicology, composition, and violin in Paris." Hiao-Tsiun tutored Yeou-Cheng and Yo-Yo in French and Chinese history, calligraphy, and, of course, music. Each day, Ma had to memorize two measures of Bach; by the time he was four
65 he was already playing a Bach suite.

pedagogue
demanding teacher

At about this time, an important friend and advocate, violinist Isaac Stern, entered Ma's life. "When Yo-Yo was about six," recalled Stern, "a good friend of mine in Paris said to me, 'You know, there's this young Chinese boy that
70 you must hear.' I went to listen to him, six years old, and the cello was larger than he was. It was extraordinary." Stern was to be invaluable in helping the family get established when they immigrated to the United States.

Growing Up

When he was seven, Ma, his sister, and his parents
75 moved to New York City, where the children would grow up. In New York, Ma continued his cello studies. Soon, the ever-watchful Isaac Stern buttonholed his friend, the great cellist Leonard Rose. He said, "Lenny, you have to teach this boy," so Ma played for Leonard Rose, and Rose
80 instantly took him as a student. He studied with Lenny for many years in the Juilliard precollege program. Isaac Stern recalled that everybody noticed Ma's extraordinary talent, including his natural feel for being on stage, the way most people feel in their old clothes in their own living rooms.
85 As children, Ma and his sister played at a fundraiser in Washington D.C. The event, attended by President and

Mrs. Kennedy, was hosted and conducted by Leonard Bernstein. It was one of television's first specials. The film clips show a boy who is already displaying what Isaac
90 Stern later called " **charisma** in spades." Yo-Yo Ma was introduced to the international music community. They loved him.

charisma

personal charm and appeal

Working with Young People

Yo-Yo Ma recalls the difficulties of being young, and helping young people has become an important part of his
95 life. He sees education as the key to young people's success. He brings young audiences into contact with music and allows them to participate in its creation. While touring, he conducts master classes as well as informal programs for students—musicians and non-musicians alike.
100 "Often," he has said, "I meet young people getting really involved in music early. You know, the child-prodigy syndrome. Based on my own experience, I tell these kids and their parents: 'Remember that what you do between the ages of, say, 12 and 21 is creating your emotional bank
105 account. You'll be withdrawing from that account the rest of your life, so make sure you put in stuff that really counts. If you do nothing but tour during those years, if you are center stage from concert hall to hotel to limo rides to the airport, that is what you will be withdrawing from because
110 that is all you'll know.'" And competitions? He laughs. "Are you kidding? I lost every competition, except once when I was five. Today, I won't even be a judge. I'm against them."

Ma's Silk Road and Other Cultural Pursuits

His life has been about stretching boundaries; in 1998, he founded the Silk Road Project, his most ambitious
115 stretch of all, a fusion of all his roads into one. Its goal is to study the ebb and flow of ideas among different cultures along the ancient Silk Road that connected Europe to Asia, finding and performing traditional music and commissioning new works. "This is the most exciting

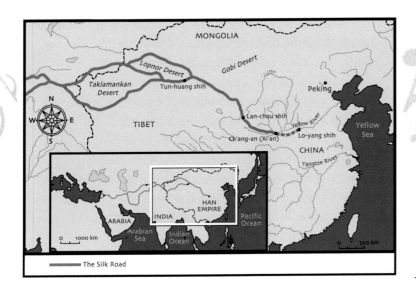

The Silk Road served as a trade route between China and the Mediterranean region for thousands of years.

120 thing I've ever done," he says. "The Silk Road is a metaphor for a number of things: as the Internet of **antiquity**, the trade routes were used for commerce, by religious people, adventurers, scientists, storytellers. Everything from algebra to Islam moved along the Silk Road. It's the local-global

125 thing. In the cultural world, you want to make sure that voices don't get lost, that fabulously rich traditions continue to live, without becoming generic." Ma's Silk Road Project has been called his "senior thesis, his grand unification, his Sistine Chapel."

130   Yo-Yo Ma founded the Silk Road Project to explore the musical currents of countries along the ancient Central Asian trade routes. His objective was to promote study of the cultural, artistic, and intellectual traditions along the ancient Silk Road trade route, from the Mediterranean Sea

135 to the Pacific Ocean.

    One of Ma's life goals has been the exploration of music as communication and as a vehicle for the migrations of ideas across cultures throughout the world. Ma says, "We live in a world of increasing awareness and

140 interdependence, and I believe that music can act as a magnet to draw people together. . . . I'm seeking to join, to connect things that were not previously joined together:

> **antiquity**
> very old, ancient times

from Bach to the Kalahari to music along the Silk Road, to country fiddling and the tango. . ." His large and diverse
145 body of work is a testament to this idea.

Today, Yo-Yo Ma is household name. He and his wife, Jill, have two children, Nicholas and Emily. Jill and both children are musicians as well. Ma's life is full, with projects and goals beyond the imaginations of most people. Yo-
150 Yo Ma's story includes a unique combination of prodigy, celebrity, musicianship, and humanity. Recently, he has set dozens of new goals, exploring the worlds of folk, crossover music, and multimedia experimentation. This isn't the end of Yo-Yo Ma's life story. It's just getting good.

Excerpted from "Yo-Yo Ma's Journeys" by Janet Tassel

Think About It

1. List reasons why Yo-Yo Ma's life is extraordinary.

2. Describe Yo-Yo Ma's father, Hiao-Tsiun.

3. Isaac Stern said that everybody noticed Ma's extraordinary talent, including his natural feel for being on stage, the way most people feel in their old clothes in their own living rooms. Analyze the meaning of Stern's statement. Why do you think some people are so comfortable, and others so ill at ease, on a stage?

4. What does Yo-Yo Ma say is the key to success for young people? Evaluate his statement. Is the key to success more complicated than he describes? Explain.

5. What is the Silk Road?

6. Cite any three of Yo-Yo Ma's life goals.

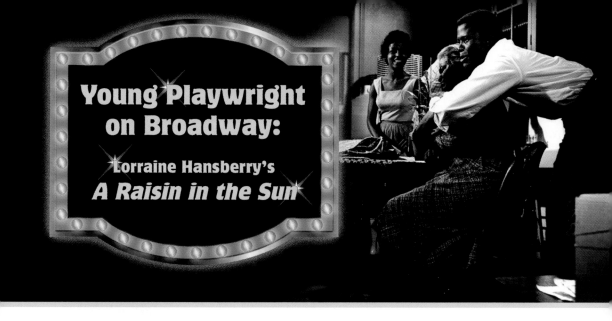

Young Playwright on Broadway:
Lorraine Hansberry's
A Raisin in the Sun

A Rave Review

New York City is world famous for the quality of its theater productions. When a play opens on Broadway, a playwright's dream comes true. That's what happened to Lorraine Hansberry. Her play, *A Raisin in the Sun*, opened
5 on Broadway on March 11, 1959. But there was something very different about this play. There was something very different about its author. Hansberry was young, and she was female. She was also African American. *A Raisin in the Sun* was the first play by a black woman ever to be
10 produced on Broadway. *A Raisin in the Sun* became one of the most highly regarded plays of all time.

Lorraine Hansberry.

New York Times theater reviews are famous for making or breaking a play. The famous theater critic, Brooks Atkinson, wrote the play's first *New York Times* review.
15 He wrote:

"In *A Raisin in the Sun*, which opened at the Ethel Barrymore last evening, Lorraine Hansberry touches on some serious problems. No doubt, her feelings about them are as strong as anyone's.
20 But she has not tipped her play to prove one thing or another. The play is honest. She has told the inner as well as the outer truth about a Negro family in the South Side of Chicago at the present time. Since the performance is also honest and since Sidney Poitier is a candid actor, *A*

25 *Raisin in the Sun* has vigor as well as veracity and is likely to destroy the **complacency** of anyone who sees it.

The family consists of a firm-minded widow, her daughter, her restless son, and his wife and son. The mother has brought up her family in a **tenement** that is
30 small, battered but personable. All the mother wants is that her children adhere to the code of honor and self-respect that she inherited from her parents.

The son is dreaming of success in a business deal. And the daughter, who is race-conscious, wants to become
35 a physician and heal the wounds of her people. After a long delay the widow receives $10,000 as the premium on her husband's life insurance. The money projects the family into a series of situations that test their individual characters.

40 What the situations are does not matter at the moment. For *A Raisin in the Sun* is a play about human beings who want, on the one hand, to preserve their family pride and, on the other hand, to break out of the poverty that seems to be their fate. Not having any axe to grind, Miss Hansberry
45 has a wide range of topics to write about—some of them hilarious, some of them painful in the extreme.

You might, in fact, regard *A Raisin in the Sun* as a Negro *The Cherry Orchard*.[1] Although the social scale of the characters is different, the knowledge of how character
50 is controlled by environment is much the same, and the alternation of humor and **pathos** is similar.

If there are occasional crudities in the craftsmanship, they are redeemed by the honesty of the writing. And also by the rousing honesty of the stage work. For Lloyd
55 Richards has selected an admirable cast and directed a bold and stirring performance.

Mr. Poitier is a remarkable actor with enormous power that is always under control. Cast as the restless son, he

---

[1] In the play *The Cherry Orchard*, Anton Chekhov tells the story of the Ranevskaya family, and, in doing so portrays the major political, social, and economic shifts taking place in Russia at the beginning of the 20th century.

vividly communicates the tumult of a high-strung young
60 man. He is as **eloquent** when he has nothing to say
as when he has a pungent line to speak. He can convey
devious processes of thought as graphically as he can clown
and dance.

As the **matriarch**, Claudia McNeil gives a heroic
65 performance. Although the character is simple, Miss
McNeil gives it nobility of spirit. Diana Sands' amusing
portrait of the over-intellectualized daughter; Ivan Dixon's
quiet, sagacious student from Nigeria; Ruby Dee's young
wife burdened with problems; Louis Gossett's supercilious
70 suitor; John Fiedler's
timid white man, who
speaks sanctimonious
platitudes—bring variety
and excitement to a first-
75 rate performance.

All the crises and
comic sequences take
place inside Ralph
Alswang's set, which
80 depicts both the poverty
and the taste of the family.
Like the play, it is honest.
That is Miss Hansberry's
personal contribution
85 to an explosive situation in which simple honesty is the
most difficult thing in the world. And also the most
illuminating."

> **eloquent**
> persuasive, power-
> ful expression

> **matriarch**
> the female head of
> a family

*A Raisin in the Sun
opened on Broadway in
1959 to rave reviews.*

Raisin Plays On

More "firsts" awaited the young playwright. In 1959,
Lorraine Hansberry became the youngest playwright and
90 the first African American playwright to win the New York
Drama Critics Circle Award. She was the fifth woman and
the youngest American to ever have done so. (This award
was an even greater honor, knowing that two of America's
most celebrated playwrights, Eugene O'Neill and Tennessee

95 Williams, also had plays at that time on Broadway.) It was
ranked the best American play of the year.

Two years later, the play was turned into a film.
Hansberry wrote the screenplay for the film. For her
screenplay, she was nominated for the Screen Writers Guild
100 award. Then, in 1973, it became a musical, titled *Raisin*.
It won the Tony Award for the best musical of 1974. *A
Raisin in the Sun* has been translated into over 30 different
languages and is still produced on stages around the
country each year. Lorraine Hansberry has earned a place
105 in theater history. She is one of the greatest playwrights in
the history of the American stage.

Playing with the Title

Many theatergoers wondered about the play's title.
Where did Hansberry get the phrase "raisin in the sun"?
Half a century ago, many people were unfamiliar with great
110 literature composed by African Americans. Few outside
the black community knew the works of the brilliant poet,
Langston Hughes.
Interestingly, when
Hansberry began
115 to write this play,
she had titled it
"The Crystal Stair,"
which is a line
from a different
120 Langston Hughes
poem—"Mother
to Son." Langston
Hughes' poetry sings
of the struggles
125 of his people. The
phrase "a raisin in
the sun" comes from
his poem, "Harlem,"
from his poetry
130 collection *Montage
of a Dream Deferred.*

> **Harlem**
> by Langston Hughes
>
> What happens to a dream
> deferred?
>
> Does it dry up
> like a raisin in the sun?
> Or fester like a sore—
> And then run?
> Does it stink like
> rotten meat?
> Or crust and sugar over—
> like a syrupy sweet?
>
> Maybe it just sags
> like a heavy load.
>
> *Or does it explode?*

Today, things have changed. Langston Hughes' poems and
Lorraine Hansberry's *A Raisin in the Sun* are recognized as
great literature. Both are taught in schools and universities
135 around the world.

The Playwright

On the night that *A Raisin in the Sun* opened on
Broadway, Lorraine Hansberry must have thought about
her journey. She was only 28 years old, and *this* was her
first published play. Born in 1930 to a middle-class, African
140 American family in Chicago, she was the youngest of four
siblings. Her father, Carl Hansberry, was a successful real
estate broker. Her uncle was an African American scholar
at Howard University. Many in her family were involved in
civil rights. As a young girl, Lorraine had the opportunity
145 to meet numerous famous African Americans of the time,
right in her parents' living room. Guests included the
classical actor Paul Robeson, great jazz musician Duke
Ellington, and Olympic gold medalist Jesse Owens.

When Hansberry was eight years old, her father bought
150 a house in a previously all-white neighborhood. When the
Hansberry family moved in, it upset the neighborhood,
since Chicago was still legally **segregated**; however, as a
result of a lawsuit brought by Hansberry's father, the Illinois
Supreme Court declared Chicago's housing segregation
155 laws unconstitutional. The experience of living through
this time influenced Hansberry.

segregated
separated or
isolated

Hansberry attended the University of Wisconsin and
studied art education. Later, she studied painting at the Art
Institute of Chicago. In 1950, she moved to New York and
160 worked at several different jobs—including reporting and
editing—while she continued to write plays and fiction.
Before she finished her masterpiece, *A Raisin in the Sun,*
she had written three plays and a novel.

After she had finished writing *A Raisin in the Sun,*
165 Hansberry recalled that she could not quite believe what
she had accomplished. Later, in her autobiographical work,
To Be Young, Gifted and Black, she described her feeling:

. . . I had turned the last page out of the typewriter
and pressed all the sheets neatly together in a pile, and
170 *gone and stretched out face down on the living room floor.*
I had finished a play; a play I had no reason to think or
not think would ever be done; a play that I was sure no one
would quite understand . . .

Hansberry began another play, *The Sign in Sidney*
175 *Brustein's Window*. Although it was less successful, it ran
on Broadway for over 100 performances. It closed on the
day of Hansberry's death, January 12, 1965. She died of
cancer at the age of 35, after a brief illness. These lines,
taken from her last play, adorn her tombstone:

180 *I care. I care about it all. It takes too much energy not*
to care . . . the why of why we are here is an intrigue for
adolescents; the how is what must command the living.

Adapted from "Raisin in the Sun" by Vicki Hambleton

Think About It

1. Explain what the author means by ". . . reviews are famous for making or breaking a play."

2. What was unusual about Lorraine Hansberry writing this play?

3. Summarize Brooks Atkinson's review of *A Raisin in the Sun*.

4. Explain why Lorraine Hansberry rewrote her play.

5. Explain how the play got its title. What was the source of the title?

6. List some reasons why Lorraine Hansberry was able to write a play that dealt with such difficult issues during that time period.

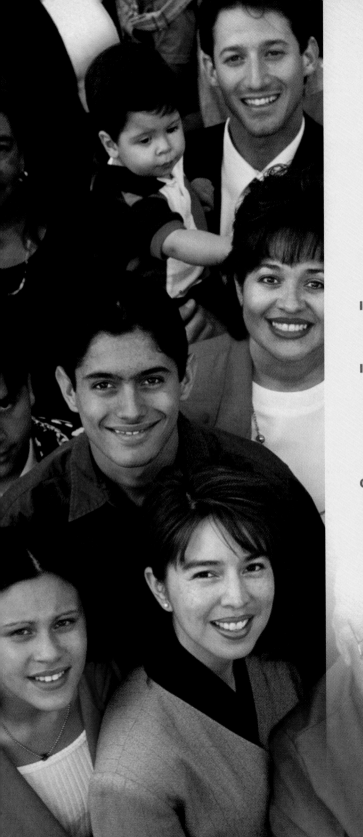

Join the Family

STEP 1

Phonemic Awareness and Phonics

Unit 21 explains the role of stress and schwa in multisyllable words.

Syllables

Review: Words are made up of **syllables**.

- A syllable is a word, or a word part, that has one vowel sound.
- A syllable's type is determined by the syllable's vowel sound. The types of syllables include: closed, **r**-controlled, open, final silent **e**, and vowel digraph.

Syllable Stress

Stress in words and the **schwa** go together. Stress is the emphasis that syllables have in words.

- If a syllable is stressed, the vowel is usually long or short.
- If the syllable is not stressed, the vowel is usually reduced to schwa. Schwa sounds like / ŭ /, but is more reduced.

An **a** that begins or ends a word is often reduced to schwa.

> **Schwa for the Letter a**
>
> a like'   / ə-līk' /
>
> The **a** in **alike** is reduced to schwa. The **a** sounds like / ŭ /.

In a multisyllable word, the second syllable is often reduced to schwa.

> **Schwa in Multisyllable Words**
>
> mul' ti ply'   / mŭl' tə-plī' /
>
> The second syllable **ti** is reduced to schwa. The **i** sounds like / ŭ /.

Go to the Vowel Chart on page A3. Find ə for the reduced sound for **a** in **alike**. Find the cue word **about**.

Word Recognition and Spelling

Prefixes

We can expand words and change meaning by adding **prefixes**.
These word parts are added to the beginnings of words.
Example: **con** + form = conform

(See Step 3: Vocabulary and Morphology for links to meaning.)

> **Unit 21 Prefixes**
>
> **con-, in-**

Suffixes

We can expand words and change meaning by adding **suffixes**.
These word parts are added to the ends of words.
Example: conduct + **or** = conductor

(See Step 3: Vocabulary and Morphology for links to meaning and
Step 4: Grammar and Usage for function.)

> **Unit 21 Suffix**
>
> **-or**

Roots

We can build words using roots. We usually attach a prefix or suffix to
make a root into a word. Example: in + **scribe** = inscribe

> **Unit 21 Roots**
>
> **duc/duct, scrib/script**

Essential Words

Unit 21 Essential Words

beautiful	business	leopard
beauty	busy	women

Spelling Lists

The Unit 21 spelling lists contain three categories:

1. Words with the schwa sound
2. **Essential Words** (in italics)
3. Words with prefixes, roots, and suffixes

Spelling Lists

Lessons 1–5		Lessons 6–10	
accuse	history	compressor	merchants
among	industry	confident	products
beautiful	*leopard*	correct	recommend
beauty	level	director	salary
business	melody	dollars	senator
busy	opposite	inability	several
extra	*women*	income	transcripts
formal		incomplete	

Vocabulary and Morphology

Unit Vocabulary

Sound-spelling correspondences from this unit and previous units make up this unit's vocabulary.

- What do these words mean?

- Do some of them mean more than one thing? Which ones?

UNIT Vocabulary

Begin or end with a
alike
among
amuse
apart
ashamed
aside
astonish
camera
extra

Unaccented syllable in two-syllable words
accuse
admire
afford
arrest
attend
attract
canal
combine
compete
confuse
cruel
custom

dollars
formal
frequent
grammar
instant
kitchen
lessen
lesson
level
merchant
model
modest
moral
neglect
offend
prefer
refresh
regret
retire
rival
sacred
seldom
travel
trial
wicked
witness

Unaccented syllable in multisyllable words
accustom
animal
consider
consonant
cultivate
delicate
determine
diamond
different
difficult
family
favorite
finally
funeral
hesitate
history
holiday
horizon
hospital
imitate
immediate
important
industry

melody
multiply
mystery
numeral
opposite
particular
permanent
practical
president
probably
recommend
regular
remedy
restaurant
salary
separate
several
similar
sympathy
theater
umbrella
universe
violent

Word Relationships

Antonyms are words that have opposite meanings. Example: **Alike** and **different** are antonyms.

Meaning Parts

Prefixes

Prefixes can add to or change the meanings of words. The Unit 21 prefixes have the following meanings.

Unit 21 Prefixes	Meanings	Examples
con-	with, together	confident, conformist, contribute
in-	not; into, toward	inactive, incomplete, independent; income, ingrained, insider

A prefix often assimilates to the base word or root to which it is attached. In **assimilation**, the last letter of the prefix changes or sounds similar to the first letter of the base or root. This change makes pronunciation easier. The meaning of the prefix does not change when it is assimilated.

> **Assimilation**
>
> **in** + **legal** = **illegal**
>
> **con** + **bine** = **combine**

Suffixes

Review: **Suffixes** can add to or change the meanings of words. Some suffixes indicate noun form. When added to a base word or root, they can change the base word or root to a noun to mean "someone who." Examples: sing**er**, botan**ist**

Another suffix also changes the base word or root to a noun to mean "someone who." The Unit 21 suffix is **-or**.

Unit 21 Noun Suffix	Meanings	Examples
-or	someone who, something that	director, donor, protector

Roots

Roots are the basic meaning part of a word. A root usually needs a prefix or suffix to make it into a word. Roots of English words often come from another language, especially Latin.

Example: con + **duct** = conduct

Unit 21 Roots	Meaning	Examples
duc/duct	to lead	conduct, educate, product
scrib/script	to write	describe, inscribe, transcript

Challenge Morphemes

Root	Meanings	Examples
rect/reg	right, straight	correct, direct, regal

STEP 4

Grammar and Usage

Nouns

Review: **Nouns** name people, places, things, and ideas. Nouns usually function as a subject, a direct object, an indirect object, or the object of a preposition. Example: The **family** was in hiding. (subject)

■ Sometimes a noun functions as an adjective.

> **Noun as Adjective**
> Anne Frank enjoyed a good **family** life.

Adjectives

Review: **Adjectives** describe nouns. They answer: **Which one? How many?** and **What kind?**

> **Adjectives**
> **All** members **of the species** watch over the **growing** babies.
>
> Which ones? **of the species** (prepositional phrase that acts as an adjective)
> How many? **all** (single word that acts as an adjective)
> What kind? **growing** (present participle that acts as an adjective)

Tense Timeline

Review: **Verbs** describe an action or a state of being. Verbs also convey time. The **Tense Timeline** shows the relationship between time and verb form.

Yesterday	Today	Tomorrow
Past	Present	Future
was/were	*am/is/are*	*will be*
had	*have*	*will have*

Helping Verbs and Linking Verbs

Review: Some verbs can act as main verbs or helping verbs. Forms of **have** and **be** belong to this group of verbs. Helping verbs combine with the main verb to form a verb phrase. The helping verb signals the time. Examples: She **is writing** a diary. They **were growing** into adults. It **will be leaving** its parents.

- Verb phrases with forms of **have** signal time in special ways:
  Ann *had* received a diary a few weeks before she went into hiding. (past perfect tense)
  Millions *have* read her diary. (present perfect tense)
  By Friday I *will have* finished it. (future perfect tense)

- The verb **be** can also act as a **linking verb.** Linking verbs connect, or link, the subject of the sentence to a word in the predicate.

Predicate Nominative

- A noun that follows a linking verb renames, or tells more about, the subject. This noun is called a **predicate nominative**.

- The subject and the predicate nominative name the same person, place, thing, or idea. Example: *Anne Frank* **was** a young *girl*. The verb **was** links the subject *Anne Frank* to the noun *girl*.

Predicate Adjective

- An adjective that follows a linking verb describes the subject. This adjective is called a **predicate adjective**. It describes the subject. Example: *Anne Frank* **was** *observant*. The verb **was** links the adjective *observant* to the subject *Anne Frank*.

Sentence Patterns

Form:	N/LV/N	noun/linking verb/noun
Function:	S/P/PN	subject/predicate/predicate nominative

Anne Frank **was** a young girl.

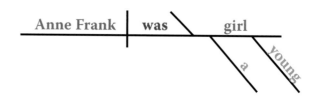

Form:	N/LV/ADJ	noun/linking verb/adjective
Function:	S/P/PA	subject/predicate/predicate adjective

Anne Frank **was** observant.

Anne Frank | was \ observant

Punctuation

Quotation Marks

We use **quotation marks** in text to record the exact words a person has spoken. They are placed before the first word and after the last word spoken. Usually there are words before or after the quotation that indicate who is speaking.

> **Quotation Marks**
> "Try to get the tape off," Jack said.

Commas

Review: We use **commas** to separate the items **in a series**. When three or more words or word groups are listed together in a sentence, commas separate the items in the series. The last item is usually connnected to the others in the series by **and** or **or**. Example: Anne Frank was in hiding with her *mother, father, sister,* **and** *brother.*

Commas are also used at the end of spoken words **inside quotation marks**.

> **Commas in Quotation Marks**
> "Let me try," he said.

Listening and Reading Comprehension

Informational Text

■ Some **informational text** is nonfiction material about a specific topic, event, experience, or circumstance. It is typically found in content area text. Textbooks, biographies, and essays are examples of informational text.

Vocabulary in Context

■ **Context clues** help us understand new vocabulary. Pronoun referents, meaning signals, and visuals, such as charts and graphs, provide meaning links.

Signal Words

■ Different types of sentences can help us think about new information in different ways.

Some sentences require us to make judgments based on criteria and standards. These sentences ask us to **Evaluate It**. They are introduced by specific **signal words**.

> Signal Words for Evaluate It
> assess, critique, judge, justify

Literary Terms and Devices

📖 **Genres** are types or categories of literature. Unit 21 features the genre **fiction**. Fiction is based on a plot.

■ **Fiction** is a literary genre that includes stories that are not true. Fiction is sometimes based on real people, places, or events. **"My Side of the Story"** is an example of fiction.

■ **Plot** is a literary term referring to the pattern of events in a narrative or drama. Both stories in Unit 21 illustrate plot.

Plot Analysis

■ **Plot** refers to a pattern of events in a narrative or drama. The plot guides the author in composing the work. It helps the reader follow the story.

■ **Characters and setting** are two components of plot analysis. The characters, which can be people, animals, or things, take part in the story. The setting is the story's time and place. Together these two components make up the introduction in the plot's development.

■ To understand how a plot develops, we must first identify a story's main **problem** and its **solution**.

■ After we become proficient in identifying a story's main problem and solution, we will learn how a plot develops and apply plot development to our writing.

■ Plot development usually consists of five elements:

Introduction (setting and characters);

Conflict (rising action), climax (turning point);

Resolution (falling action);

Conclusion (the situation at the end of the story, with a look to the future).

STEP 6

Speaking and Writing

Signal Words

- Some sentences ask for information. Other sentences require us to make judgments based on criteria and standards. They use specific **signal words**.

> **Signal Words for Evaluate It**
>
> **Assess** the challenges that Anne Frank faced in her life.
>
> **Critique** Adam's actions.
>
> Make a **judgment** about which character caused the problem in this story.
>
> Explain how Anne **justified** her desire *not* to be treated like a child.

Paragraph Organization

- Some paragraphs are summaries. A **summary** paragraph is a condensed form of the main points of what we read. The organization helps us identify the most important information to use in a summary. A character trait summary identifies the main traits displayed in a character.

Plot Analysis

- Fiction includes characters created by the author. During prewriting, the author thinks about **character traits**. In good writing, each character must become distinct. Some character traits a writer may consider include: the character's personal appearance, personality, relationships with other characters, reactions to various situations, and means of coping with difficulties. Anything that distinguishes a character might be a character trait.

- Good writers usually include information about characters in the plot's introduction. This is because the reader needs to know the characters in order to follow the plot. Good writers can tell the reader about a character by including:

    A description of the character in simple narrative form;

    An incident during which the character interacts with others;

    A dialog in which the character is speaking to others.

More About Words

- **Bonus Words** use the same sound-spelling correspondences that we have studied in this unit and previous units.

- **Idioms** are common phrases that cannot be understood by the meanings of their separate words—only by the entire phrase.

- **Why? Word History** tells about the word **family**—then and now.

UNIT Bonus Words

Begin or end with <u>a</u>
abandon
address
adjust
alarm
atomic
banana
panda

Unaccented syllable in two-syllable words
bacon
bias
camel
carbon
collapse
comfort
confer
confine
conform
converse
dial
effort
label
lizard
mustard
oven

Unaccented syllable in multisyllable words
accurate
advocate
allocate
analyze
annual
benefit
buffalo
calendar
carpenter
colony
compensate
component
concurrent
contradict
critical
definite
delivery
democrat
demonstrate
deposit
domestic
dominant
dominate
eleven

enemy
estimate
evident
external
factory
federal
festival
forthcoming
illustrate
innovate
internal
interval
isolate
justify
liberal
lullaby
manual
maximize
medical
memory
mercury
microscope
minimize
minimum
modify
molecule
museum
occupy

octopus
organize
potato
protocol
radical
realize
recognize
regulate
relevant
republican
senator
statistic
stimulate
telegram
terminate
thermometer
typical
ultimate
uniform
valentine
vertical
vitamin

Idioms	
Idiom	**Meaning**
be a horse of a different color	be another matter entirely; something else
be your own worst enemy	believe things that prevent you from becoming successful
bring home the bacon	support a family by working; earn a living
come apart at the seams	become so upset that you lose all self-control
cut the mustard	perform up to expectations or to a standard
drop you like a hot potato	get rid of someone or something as quickly as possible
go bananas	go crazy
have a domino effect	have a cumulative effect produced when one event sets off a chain of related events
have a skeleton in your closet	have a source of shame or disgrace that is kept secret
run in the family	be characterized by something common to many members of the same family

Why? Word History

Family—It may surprise you that in the 15th century, one definition of **family** was "the servants of a household." In fact, the word **family** originally comes from the Latin word for servant, *famulus.* Certainly people today would not describe their family as servants. The meanings of **family** clearly have changed over the centuries.

Today, in informal speech some people refer to their family as *the fam.* This shortened form of **family** came into use quite recently; however, shortened forms of English words for family members have been in use for much longer. For example, *ma* and *pa*, shortened versions of *mama* and *papa*, have been in use for more than a century. So have *grandma* and *grandpa*.

Words such as *fam* are known as *clipped words*. Many clipped words are used in English. Some examples are: *limo* from *limousine, ref* from *referee, ad* from *advertisement*, and *sub* from *submarine*.

PlantFamilies

You know what cousins are. Imagine a tomato. Now, imagine a potato. Did you know that tomatoes and potatoes are cousins? Does that sound weird? It's true. Plants have families, too. They're placed in families according to a
5 "taxonomy." Taxonomy is a method. It organizes things. It classifies. It categorizes. It helps scientists in their work.

Scientists called botanists study plants. They consider all parts. They examine the stem. They study the seeds and the flowers. They inspect the roots. They decide which
10 plants belong in the same families. They study plant parts that can be seen. They also study plants' genes. They search for similar features. Then, they group similar plants. Plants fit into families.

A plant's flower is important. It often gives the best clue
15 to its family. Flowers that are shaped like crosses indicate

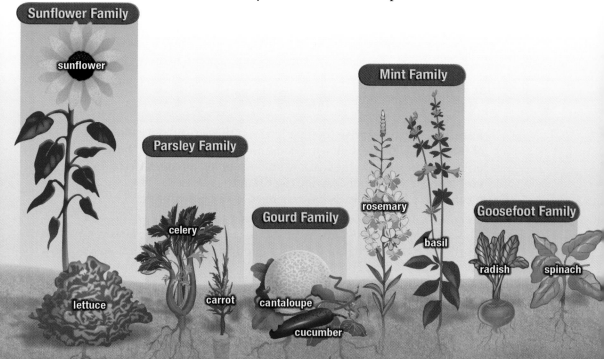

Sunflower Family
sunflower
lettuce

Parsley Family
celery
carrot

Gourd Family
cantaloupe
cucumber

Mint Family
rosemary
basil

Goosefoot Family
radish
spinach

the *Cruciferae* or Cabbage family. The scientific name comes from a word that means "cross."

Can you tell what plants are related? It isn't always easy to spot relatives. As in human families, they don't
20 always look alike. Think of a rose and an apple. They don't look alike. But roses and apple trees are in the same family. Now, picture that potato again. Next, picture a chili pepper. The potato grows below ground. Its taste is mild. The pepper grows above ground. It tastes spicy. But,
25 you guessed it. Both belong to the same family.

Most vegetables belong to one of nine families. They include the lily, mint, and pea families. They include the gourd and goosefoot families. The parsley, sunflower, and cabbage families are vegetable families, too. And
30 what family do the chili pepper and potato belong to? Both belong to the ninth family. Their family name is nightshade.

Go outside. Look around. Find a garden. Take a close look. Look for plants with similar features. You might see
35 some family resemblances!

Wild roses and apples belong to the same family—can you see the resemblance?

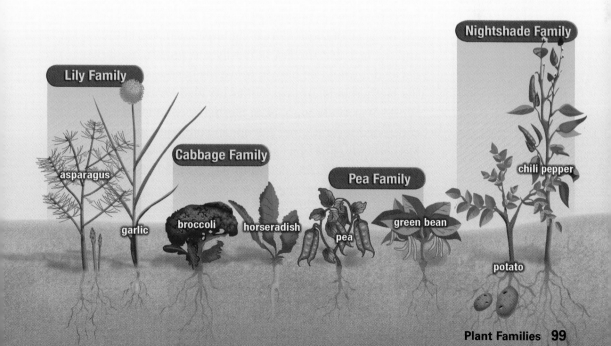

Lily Family

asparagus

garlic

Cabbage Family

broccoli

horseradish

Pea Family

pea

green bean

Nightshade Family

chili pepper

potato

A Family in Hiding:

Anne Frank's Diary

Anne Frank with her family.

Anne Frank started writing her diary when she was 13 years old.

Anne Frank was born on June 12, 1929, in Frankfurt, Germany. Anne's father, Otto Frank, was a respected businessman. For Anne and her older sister, Margot, the world of early childhood was a secure place inhabited by
5 loving parents and relatives. But beyond their family's comfortable environment, the world around them was not so pleasant. By 1933, the Nazi movement had gained control of the German government, and Adolf Hitler was made the chancellor of Germany. Freedom of speech and assembly
10 were suspended, and the Nazi government decreed a boycott of Jewish businesses.

Because of these increasing tensions in Germany and the fact that the Frank family was Jewish, her father decided it would be best to move his business and family to
15 the Netherlands. In 1939, Hitler invaded Poland and started World War II. By 1940, Nazi Germany conquered and controlled several other European countries, including the Netherlands. The Nazi government made Jewish citizens wear yellow stars on their clothing. As the Holocaust
20 gained momentum, the Nazis began deporting Jewish citizens and others from these countries to German concentration camps.[1] The Frank family was no longer safe. In 1942, Anne celebrated her thirteenth birthday

---

[1] The word "Holocaust" comes from the Greek word, *holokauston,* meaning "a sacrifice burned by fire." It refers to the destruction of the Jews in Europe during the Nazi regime. Over 6 million Jewish people along with many others were killed during World War II.

in Amsterdam with her family and received a diary as a
25 birthday present. A few weeks later, Anne, her parents,
and her older sister were forced to go into hiding with four
other people in a Secret Annex of a warehouse that was
part of her father's factory.

While in hiding, Anne Frank wrote in her diary about
30 everything that happened to her and her family. She was
a teenager who was experiencing all the emotions and
conflicts that a typical teenager would, but she was doing
so under extraordinarily difficult circumstances. Her
family and the four others with them lived for 25 months in
35 cramped quarters, worrying every day about the progress
of the war and about what would happen to them if they
were discovered. These excerpts from her diary reveal some
of Anne Frank's feelings about her family and about the
events going on around her.

Saturday, June 20, 1942

40 Writing in a diary is a really strange experience for
someone like me. Not only because I've never written
anything before, but also because it seems to me that
later on neither I nor anyone else will be interested in the
musings of a thirteen-year-old schoolgirl. Oh well, it
45 doesn't matter. I feel like writing and I have an even greater
need to get all kinds of things off my chest. . . .

My father, the most adorable father I've ever seen,
didn't marry my mother until he was thirty-six and she was
twenty-five. My sister Margot was born in Frankfurt-am-
50 Main in Germany in 1926. I was born on June 12, 1929. I
lived in Frankfurt until I was four. Because we're Jewish, my
father immigrated to Holland in 1933, when he became the
Managing Director of the Dutch Opteka Company. . . .

Our lives were not without anxiety since our relatives
55 in Germany were suffering under Hitler's anti-Jewish laws.
. . . In 1938 my two uncles (my mother's brothers) fled
Germany, finding safe refuge in North America. My elderly
grandmother came to live with us. She was seventy-three

musings
deep thoughts

years old at the time. . . . Grandma died in January 1942.
60 No one knows how often I think of her and still love her. . . .

**On July 9, the Frank family went into hiding in the
Secret Annex after Anne's sister, Margot, received a
call-up to be sent to a labor camp. They were helped
by friends, who brought them food and news from the
65 outside. On July 13, they were joined in hiding by another
Jewish family, Mr. and Mrs. van Daan and their fifteen-
year-old son, Peter. The seven of them, living so closely
together, became an extended family.**

Friday, August 21, 1942

Now our Secret Annex has truly become secret. . . . Mr.
70 Kugler thought it would be better to have a bookcase built
in front of the entrance to our hiding place. It swings out
on its hinges and opens like a door. . . .

There's little change in our lives here. Peter's hair was
washed today, but that's nothing special. Mr. van Daan
75 and I are always at loggerheads with each other. Mama
always treats me like a baby, which I can't stand. For the
rest, things are going better. I don't think Peter's gotten any
nicer. He's an obnoxious boy who lies around on his bed
all day, only rousing himself to do a little carpentry work
80 before returning to his nap. . . .

Mama gave me another one of her dreadful sermons
this morning. We take the opposite view of everything.
Daddy's a sweetheart. He may get mad at me, but it never
lasts longer than five minutes.

Friday, October 9, 1942

85 Today I have nothing but dismal and depressing news
to report. Our many Jewish friends and acquaintances
are being taken away in droves. The Gestapo is treating
them very roughly and transporting them in cattle cars
to Westerbork. . . . It must be terrible in Westerbork. The
90 people get almost nothing to eat, much less to drink, as water

is available only one hour a day, and there's only one toilet and sink for several thousand people. Men and women sleep in the same room, and women and children often have their heads shaved. Escape is almost impossible. Many people look
95 Jewish, and they're branded by their shorn heads.

If it's that bad in Holland, what must it be like in those faraway and **uncivilized** places where the Germans are sending them? We assume that most of them are being murdered. . . .

uncivilized
primitive; barbarous, without basic services or humanity

100   **On November 17, Mr. Albert Dussel joined the others in hiding in the Secret Annex and became a part of this secret family.**

Thursday, November 19, 1942

Just as we thought, Mr. Dussel is a very nice man. . . . The first day Mr. Dussel was here he asked me all
105 sorts of questions—for example, what time the cleaning lady comes to the office, how we've arranged to use the washroom, and when we're allowed to go to the toilet. You may laugh, but these things aren't so easy in a hiding place. During the daytime we can't make any
110 noise that might be heard downstairs. And when someone else is there, like the cleaning lady, we have to be extra careful. . . .

Saturday, November 28, 1942

Mr. Dussel, the man who was said to get along so well with children and absolutely adore them, has turned
115 out to be an old-fashioned disciplinarian and preacher of unbearably long sermons on manners. . . . Since I am generally considered to be the worst behaved of the three young people, it's all I can do to avoid having the same old scoldings and admonitions repeatedly flung at my
120 head and pretend not to hear. This wouldn't be so bad if Mr. Dussel weren't such a tattletale and hadn't singled out Mother to be the **recipient** of his reports. If Mr.

recipient
one who receives

Dussel's just read me the riot act, Mother lectures me all over again, this time throwing the whole book at me. And
125 if I'm really lucky, Mrs. van D. calls me to account five minutes later and lays down the law as well!

Really, it is not easy being the badly brought-up center of attention in a family of nit-pickers. . . .

Friday, February 5, 1943

. . . Margot and Peter aren't exactly what you'd call
130 "young"; they're both so quiet and boring. Next to them, I stick out like a sore thumb and I am always being told, "Margot and Peter don't act that way. Why don't you follow your sister's example!" I hate that.

I confess that I have absolutely no desire to be like
135 Margot. She is too weak-willed and **passive** to suit me; she lets herself be swayed by others and always backs down under pressure. I want to have more spunk! But I keep ideas like these to myself. They'd only laugh at me if I offered this in my defense.

passive

accepting without resistance or struggle

Monday Evening, November 8, 1943

140   I see the eight of us in the Annex as if we were a patch of blue sky surrounded by menacing clouds. The perfectly round spot on which we're standing is still safe, but the clouds are moving in on us, and the ring between us and the approaching danger is being pulled tighter and tighter.
145 We're surrounded by darkness and danger, and in our desperate search for a way out, we keep bumping into each other. We look at the fighting down below and the peace and beauty up above. In the meantime, we've been cut off by the dark mass of clouds, so that we can go neither up
150 nor down. It looms before us like an impenetrable wall, trying to crush us, but not yet able to. I can only cry out and implore, "Oh ring, ring, open wide and let us out!"

Friday, December 24, 1943

. . . Believe me, if you've been shut up for a year and a half, it can get to be too much for you sometimes.

155 But feelings can't be ignored, no matter how unjust or
ungrateful they seem. I long to ride a bike, dance, whistle,
look at the world, feel young and know that I'm free, and
yet I can't let it show. Just imagine what would happen if all
eight of us were to feel sorry for ourselves or walk around
160 with the discontent clearly visible on our faces. Where
would that get us? . . .

Sunday, January 2, 1944

This morning, when I had nothing to do, I leafed
through the pages of my diary and came across so many
letters dealing with the subject "Mother" in such strong
165 terms that I was shocked. I said to myself: "Anne, is that
really you talking about hate? Oh, Anne, how could you?". . .

Wednesday Evening, January 19, 1944

. . . You know that I always used to be jealous of
Margot's relationship with Father. There's not a trace of
my jealousy left now. I still feel hurt when Father's nerves
170 cause him to be unreasonable toward me, but then I think,
"I can't blame you for being the way you are. You talk so
much about the minds of children and adolescents but you
don't know the first thing about them!". . .

Saturday, March 11, 1944

I haven't been able to sit still lately. I wander upstairs
175 and down and then back again. I like talking to Peter, but
I'm always afraid of being a nuisance. He's told me a bit
about the past, about his parents and about himself, but
it's not enough, and every five minutes I wonder why I find
myself longing for more. He used to think I was a real pain
180 in the neck, and the feeling was mutual. I've changed my
mind, but how do I know he's changed his? I think he has,
but that doesn't necessarily mean we have to become the
best of friends, although, as far as I am concerned, it would
make the time here more bearable. But I won't let this drive
185 me crazy. . . .

Friday, March 17, 1944

. . . For both of us [Anne and Margot], it's been quite a blow to suddenly realize that very little remains of the close and **harmonious** family we used to be at home! This is mostly because everything's out of kilter here. By that I mean
190 that we're treated like children when it comes to external matters, while, inwardly, we're much older than other girls our age. Even though I'm only fourteen, I know what I want. I know who's right and who's wrong. I have my own opinions, ideas, and principles. And though it may sound
195 odd coming from a teenager, I feel I'm more of a person than a child—I feel I'm completely independent of others. . . .

Friday, March 24, 1944

I often go up to Peter's room after dinner nowadays to breathe in the fresh evening air. You can get around to meaningful conversations more quickly in the dark than
200 with the sun tickling your face. It's cozy and snug sitting beside him on a chair and looking outside. The van Daans and Dussel make the silliest remarks when I disappear into his room. . . . "Is it proper for a gentleman to receive young girls in his room at night. . .?" Peter has amazing presence
205 of mind in the face of these so-called witticisms. My Mother, incidentally, is also bursting with curiosity and simply dying to ask what we talk about, only she's secretly afraid I'd refuse to answer. Peter says that grown-ups are just jealous because we're young and that we shouldn't take their obnoxious
210 comments to heart. . . .

Tuesday, April 11, 1944

. . . None of us have ever been in such danger as we were that night. . . . Just think—the police were right at the bookcase, the light was on, and still no one had discovered our hiding place! "Now, we're done for!" I'd whispered at
215 that moment, but once again we were spared. . . .

I'm becoming more and more independent of my parents. Young as I am, I face life with more courage and have a better and truer sense of justice than Mother. I know what I want. I have a goal. I have opinions. . . . If only I

harmonious
in agreement; working well together

220 can be myself, I'll be satisfied. I know that I'm a woman, a
woman with inner strength and a great deal of courage.

Saturday, July 15, 1944

. . . So if you're wondering whether it's harder for
the adults here than for the children, the answer is no.
It's certainly not. Older people have an opinion about
225 everything and are sure of themselves and their actions. It's
twice as hard for us young people to hold on to our opinions
at a time when ideals are being shattered and destroyed,
when the worst side of human nature **predominates** . . . .

predominates
overshadows or
overpowers others

It's utterly impossible for me to build my life on a
230 foundation of chaos, suffering, and death. I see the world
being slowly transformed into a wilderness, I hear the
approaching thunder that, one day, will destroy us too. I feel
the suffering of millions. And yet, when I look up at the sky,
I somehow feel that everything will change for the better,
235 that this cruelty too will end, that peace and tranquility
will return once more. In the meantime, I must hold on to
my ideals. Perhaps the day will come when I'll be able to
realize them.

Tuesday, August 1, 1944, is the date of the last entry
240 in Anne Frank's diary. On August 4, 1944, Gestapo officers
and Dutch members of the Security Police arrested the
eight people hiding in the
Secret Annex and brought them
to a prison in Amsterdam.
245 They were then transferred to
Westerbork, the transport camp
for Jews in north Holland. They
were deported on September
3, 1944, on the last transport
250 to leave Westerbork, and
arrived three days later in the
Auschwitz concentration camp
in Poland. The men and women
were separated there. Margot

Auschwitz concentration camp in Poland.

255 and Anne were transferred to Bergen-Belsen, another
concentration camp in Germany. A typhus epidemic broke
out there in the winter of 1944–45, and both Margot and
Anne became ill and died. The camp was liberated by
British troops on April 12, 1945.

260   All the others who had hidden in the Secret Annex died
in concentration camps as well, except for Anne's father,
Otto Frank. One of the family's friends had saved Anne's
diary and gave it to him. He published the first edition in
1947. Anne Frank's *The Diary of a Young Girl* has since
265 been translated into 47 languages and is one of the most
widely read books in the world.

Excerpted from *The Diary of a Young Girl: Anne Frank,*
The Definitive Edition edited by Otto H. Frank and Mirjam Pressler

Answer It

1. Explain why Anne and her family were forced to hide in the Annex.

2. Assess the challenges that Anne faced in her life. Were they the same challenges that a typical teen faces? Why or why not?

3. In her diary, Anne repeatedly voiced her desire not to be treated like a child. Explain how she justified this desire.

4. Make a generalization about the type of person whom Anne admired.

5. Reread lines 222–228. Describe why Anne thought that it was particularly difficult for children to live in the conditions brought on by World War II and the Holocaust.

MY SIDE OF THE STORY

BY ADAM BAGDASARIAN

I was sitting at my desk in my bedroom practicing my signature when my brother came in and asked me if I wanted to throw the ball around or shoot baskets.

"No," I said. So he looked over my shoulder at the
5   signatures, went into the bathroom for a few seconds, came out, went to his own desk, unraveled an entire roll of Scotch tape and stuck it on my head.

Naturally, I was outraged. "What did you do that for?" I asked. It was a stupid question because I knew very well
10 why he had done it. He had done it for the same reason he had stuffed me in the laundry hamper and tied me to a chair with my best ties. He had done it because he was fourteen and had the great good fortune to be blessed with a little brother he could **bedevil** at will.

bedevil

to annoy or harass; torment

15 "Try to get it off," he said.

This I attempted to do, but he had rubbed the Scotch tape so hard into my scalp that it had become a part of my head.

"Let me try," he said.

justice
fairness

righteous
right; justified

enormity
great evil; outrage

integrity
strong morals;
honesty

20 So he tried, and I yowled, and he stopped. Then he
gently pulled a piece of the Scotch tape off the side of my
head, along with six or seven of my temple hairs.

Even at the age of nine I knew that I had been mightily
wronged; even at nine I knew that this violated every code
25 of **justice** and fair play that I had ever been taught. And so,
my heart full of **righteous** rage and indignation, I leaped
out of my chair, past my brother, in search of justice.

In those days justice looked a good deal like my mother.
It had lovely brown hair, a warm enchanting smile, and
30 a soft, understanding voice. It was comforting to know
that in a matter of seconds my mother would hear the
evidence, weigh the evidence, and punish my brother.
Generally, things were murkier. Generally, I did something
by accident, then my brother did something back, and I
35 did something back, and on and on until it was impossible
to tell who was at fault. But this—this was the case of a
lifetime. And the best part of all was that the evidence was
stuck to my head.

When I reached my mother's room, I saw that the door
40 was closed. For a moment I hesitated, wondering if she was
sleeping, but I was so sure of my case, so convinced of the
general rightness of my mission that I threw open the door
and burst into the room screaming, "Mom! Mom! Skip
put—"

45 And then I realized that I was talking to my father, not
my mother.

In order to understand the **enormity** of the mistake
I had made, you have to understand my father. My father
was five feet seven and a half inches tall, stocky, powerfully
50 built, and larger than life in laughter, strength, character,
integrity, humor, appetite, wit, intelligence, warmth,
curiosity, generosity, magnetism, insight, and rage.
Consequently, he was not concerned with the little things
in life, such as sibling shenanigans, rivalries, or disputes.
55 His job, as he saw it, was to make us the best human beings
we could possibly be—to guide us, love us, and teach us
the large laws of honor, courage, honesty, and self-reliance.
He was the only man to turn to if you had a severed artery,

broken ribs, or any serious disease or financial problems, but he was not the kind of man one would knowingly burst

60 in upon screaming anything less than "The house is on fire!" or "Somebody stole your car!"

    I knew this, of course, which is why I had run to my mother's room in the first place, and why, when I saw my father, most of the color drained from my face. My first

65 impulse was to walk backward out of the room, closing the door gently before me as I did so, but I had shifted so suddenly from offensive indignation to defensive fear and astonishment that I felt a little **disoriented**. For a moment I considered telling him that I smelled smoke or saw

disoriented
confused

70 someone stealing his car, but I couldn't lie. I couldn't tell the truth, either. In fact, for a moment, I couldn't speak.

    "What on earth are you doing?" my father said.

    I started to say, "I was sitting at my desk minding my own business, when—" and I stopped. I stopped

75 because I knew instinctively that Scotch tape on my head was not enough, not nearly enough to warrant my wild, unannounced entrance into this room.

    "When what?"

    "Nothing."

80   "You ran in here screaming about something. What happened?"

    "I didn't . . ."

    "You didn't what?"

    "I didn't know you were here."

85   "So what! You knew someone was here! What did Skip do?"

    "Skip . . . uh. I was sitting at my desk, and Skip . . ."

    "Skip what? Tell me!"

    "Put Scotch tape on my head."

90   This apparently was all my father needed to set the wheels of his anger in motion.

    "You came running in here without knocking because Skip put Scotch tape on your head?"

    "No, I—"

95   "You didn't care that the door was closed? You didn't care that your mother might have been sleeping?"

I wanted to explain to him that this had been going on for years, that Mom and Skip and I had an understanding, but I knew that we weren't having a discussion. I also knew that he was working himself into a rage and that anything I said would only make it worse.

"Is that what you do? You run into rooms screaming?" He was on his feet now and advancing toward me. "You don't knock?"

"No. Yes."

At this point my brother entered the room, saw what was happening, and stood transfixed.

"Here!" my father said. "Here's what we do with Scotch tape!" And with that he pulled the whole wad off my head, along with fifty or sixty of my hairs.

I knew that he was only a few seconds away from his closing arguments now, and my calculations were just about right.

"You don't *ever* come in here without knocking! Do you hear me?" my father bellowed. Silence. "Do you hear . . ."

At this point I heard a wheeze of escaping laughter where my brother was standing, and saw him run out of the room.

"Do you?"

"Yes, Pop, yes. I hear you."

"Are you ever going to come in here without knocking again?"

"No, no."

"Ever!"

125 "No."

"Now get out of here!"

And I got out and heard the door slam behind me.

There was not much to do after that but sit at my desk and wonder what had happened. I had been signing my
130 name, Skip put Scotch tape on my head, I ran to tell Mom, found Pop, and the lights went out. Where, I wondered, was the justice in that? Obviously, when I burst into my mother's room, I had entered a larger world of justice, a world where screaming, whining, mother dependence, not
135 knocking on closed doors, and startling one's father were serious crimes. That part I understood. The part I didn't understand was the part about why my brother, who had started the whole thing by putting Scotch tape on my head, hadn't been punished. So, in the interest of a smaller
140 justice, I went over to his trophy shelf, picked up one of his baseball trophies, and gradually wrested the little gold-plated athlete off its mount.

With a little luck, my brother would want to tell Pop about it.

Answer It

1. Explain what the author meant when he wrote, "In those days, justice looked a good deal like my mother."

2. Explain why Adam thought he had "a case of a lifetime."

3. Describe some of the characteristics of Adam's father.

4. Assess how the story would have been different if the mother had been in the room instead of the father.

5. Make a judgment about which character caused the problem in this story.

Bringing Up BABY

Family Life in the Animal World

At some point in your life, an adult has probably forbidden you from doing something or going somewhere, explaining, "You just aren't old enough, yet!" That phrase, which is **reiterated** by parents everywhere, can certainly
5 be annoying. But there's a valid reason for parents evaluating your maturity before they give you permission to do something. Among all animals, human beings take the longest time to reach maturity—to achieve adulthood and independence. That's because human babies and
10 children have a tremendous amount to learn before they can function on their own in the world. In contrast, some members of the animal world are ready for independence the moment they are born. Read on to find out what "childhood" means to different kinds of creatures and what
15 family life is like for them.

reiterated

repeated

You're On Your Own, Baby!

An eight-inch alligator hatches from an egg in a Florida swamp. With the exception of its yellow markings, the baby looks exactly like its parents—a miniature adult alligator. Born hungry, it immediately begins looking for food.
20 From that moment on, the alligator is almost completely on its own. Its mother's job is to protect the eggs from

predators, and she may defend the babies after they are born. However, the baby alligator is born with all of the instincts and skills it needs to survive in its environment.

25 Many animal babies are like the alligators. They do not necessarily need the protection and nurturing of a parent, because they are born with an **innate** understanding of how to survive in their world.

Like alligators, most insects are born ready to survive
30 independently. Even some insects that evolve through several stages of **metamorphosis** on the way to adulthood don't need a parent to help them through the process. A female fly will simply deposit her eggs in a safe spot and abandon them there; she usually deposits her eggs near a
35 food supply so the babies can eat immediately after they hatch.

Most snakes, too, are ready to wriggle into the world as soon as they are born. That's why a group of scientists were mystified when they observed female black-tailed
40 rattlesnakes in Arizona staying protectively near their young for nine days. Scientists speculate that the mothers were waiting for the young snakes to shed their skin. Until these babies shed the opaque skin that covers their eyes, they cannot see with accuracy. Once the young snakes
45 can see, the mothers consider them old enough to fend for themselves, and they unceremoniously slide away from the area.

Not So Fast

Some animals are born with a lot to learn. In many species, parents must teach their young the skills they
50 need to survive. Bears, lions, gorillas, and humans all go through a long period of **maturation** . In order to live independently, they must learn how to obtain food, protect themselves, and relate to other members of their own species. These animals would die if left entirely to their
55 own devices as youngsters. They need time to grow and nurturing by their parents in order to survive and mature into adults.

innate
born with; possessed at birth

metamorphosis
a change; transformation

maturation
becoming fully grown

frigid

extremely cold; freezing

Polar bear cubs are born small with very fine coats in a snow den during the Arctic winter—a seemingly harsh

60 entrance into a **frigid** world. The cubs, however, never come into contact with the sub-zero conditions outside the den. Their mother's belly provides a place to sleep, eat, and stay toasty warm. When they do venture into the world outside, the mother bear keeps her cubs away from male

65 polar bears, who sometimes attack and kill cubs, and, in the spring, she teaches her cubs how to hunt for seals and other animals. Most polar bear cubs stay with their mothers until they are 2 years old, skilled at hunting, and large enough to protect themselves from the aggression of older bears.

70 Lion cubs are born blind and completely helpless. When a lion mother goes to hunt, she skillfully hides her young in tall grass. After three months, the lion cubs can accompany their mother wherever she goes. At this point, a mother and her cubs usually rejoin the mother's

75 pride, or family of lions. Lion cubs begin to participate in hunting by 11 months of age. However, they cannot survive independently until their second year of life. Male cubs are usually forced to leave the pride when they are about 3 years old, and do not join a group again until they are

80 adults, at about age 5.

Gorilla babies are also born totally helpless. Mothers carry their newborns in their arms for the first two or three months of life. A young gorilla sleeps in its mother's nest and rides around on her back. Until the age of 4, baby

A baby gorilla rides on its mother's back.

85 gorillas depend on their mothers and other adults in the
group for all their needs.

A human being takes longer than any other animal
to reach maturity. Childhood for humans lasts for 12 to
14 years. Scientists estimate that a human child could
90 learn how to survive in the wilderness by about 9 years
of age, but more time is needed for the child to learn the
skills required for living in a complex social group. In
fact, although most human children are mature by the
age of 18 to 20 or so, many do not leave the nest until they
95 are older. For human adults, survival means much more
than just knowing where to find food. Young people must
also learn how to interact with other members of their
communities. Learning to walk and talk, going to school,
and acquiring life skills and job skills are just some of the
100 many tasks human youngsters must accomplish. Like polar
bears, lions, and gorillas, humans are not born with the
instincts, strength, or abilities to survive without assistance
from their parents, and humans often need the advice
and support of many others of their kind to achieve full
105 maturity.

Which Parent Does the Work?

In most animal families, females are the main
caregivers for the young. In some animal species, however,
the father enthusiastically takes on this role. After a
female Emperor Penguin lays an egg in Antarctica, the
110 male penguin begins to incubate it and continues to keep
it warm for 60 days. He rests the egg on his feet, covers it
with a flap of skin, and does not move from the egg—not
even to eat! When the chick hatches, the father finally
excuses himself to eat a large fishy meal. But then he
115 quickly returns to care for the chick, helping the mother
feed it for the next six months.

The male unarmored threespine stickleback, a type
of fish, also has fabulous fatherly instincts. In the spring,
this male stickleback labors to create the perfect "nursery."
120 After finding a shallow, sandy location for the "nursery," he
digs an **elaborate** nest in the sand. He lines the nest with

*An Emperor Penguin
father helps the mother
take care of the baby
for six months.*

elaborate

complex; detailed

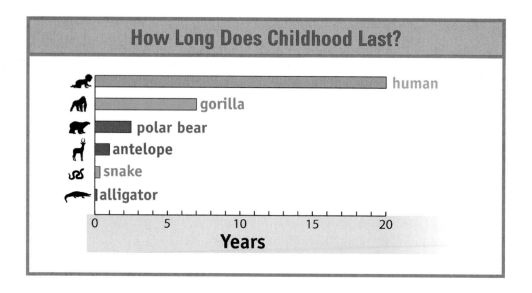

How Long Does Childhood Last?

human
gorilla
polar bear
antelope
snake
alligator

0 5 10 15 20

Years

water plants and algae and then cements the walls with a sticky material produced by his kidneys. After he carves out a tunnel for entering and exiting the nest, he is finally
125 ready to breed. He undergoes a color change from dull gray to brilliant dark green and orange-red. He uses this spectacular coloration to attract a female fish to his nest, where she lays eggs. He then chases her away and fertilizes the eggs.
130   For the next seven days, the male guards the nest full of eggs. He cleans the eggs with his mouth and circulates water over them by fanning them with his tail. Once the eggs hatch, he continues to guard the babies for several weeks. He dutifully herds the baby fish to keep them
135 together. If another male fish, or anything bearing the color red, appears, he may suck the babies protectively into his mouth to guard them from danger.
      For some creatures, "family" doesn't just mean mom or dad; it means the entire community. Wolves, gorillas, and
140 elephants are all animals that raise their young collectively, as a group. Baby elephants are raised in groups led by a female called the matriarch. All of the adult females in the group look out for the elephant babies. As the youngsters grow, they become big sisters or big brothers who help raise
145 the young.

Many insects have no family life, but there are a few exceptions. Ants, termites, and many kinds of bees are social insects. They live together in a community in which each insect has a job, and all of the community members
150 depend on each other for survival. Young honeybees spend 16 to 24 days in a special bee nursery. There, older bees feed the worm-shaped larvae a mixture of honey and pollen. The young bees chew their way out of the wax cells once they have grown into adults. They spend the rest of their
155 lives doing their assigned jobs for the hive.

Clearly, the length of time it takes living creatures to grow up and gain independence varies greatly. Family life also differs from one animal species to the next. However, one thing is true for all creatures: most parents do their
160 best to give their offspring what they need for survival, no matter how little or how much that may be.

Think About It

1. Why do some animals need to be raised by their parents?

2. Compare the responsibilities of a mother alligator to the responsibilities of a mother fly.

3. Explain why scientists think female black-tailed rattlesnakes stay near their young for nine days.

4. Describe the sacrifice that the male Emperor Penguin makes for his young.

5. How are elephants and bees similar?

6. Reread the last paragraph of the selection. Assess the generalization the author makes about animal and human parents.

Who Cares About Great-Uncle Edgar?

We come across an old family photograph. The photo is in black and white. It's faded and cracked. The person in the picture stands stiffly against a background of drapes, plants, and fancy furniture.

5   This old-fashioned studio portrait was taken in the early 1900s. Who is this person in the picture? Is it your great-grandfather's brother? He was the first member of the family to become a famous brain surgeon. He was fondly and respectfully known as Great-Uncle Edgar. Or is

10 it your great-grandfather himself, the most studious boy in his class? He had to drop out of school to work and never fulfilled his dream of becoming a brilliant lawyer.

   Possibly you are wondering why you should even care about your ancestors. Your great-grandparents may

15 have died before you were born. Or, if they are alive, they may live in a distant place. The same may be true of your grandparents.

   These days, it's easy to lose touch even with our own parents. They may have separated. They may be divorced.

20 One or both of them may have remarried. We may find ourselves part of a stepfamily, with a whole new set of

relatives. Or possibly we are being raised by just one parent. Many young Americans today can't even *name* all four of their parents' parents.

25 Yet, whether we know our ancestors or not, we are each a link in a human chain. We share our genes—the tiny units in our body cells that are responsible for **inherited** traits—with our ancestors. And we'll pass on new combinations of these traits to our children and our
30 children's children.

inherited
passed from parent to child

The word *genealogy* means the study of family lines of descent. It is related to the word *gene*. Our genes are what determine certain traits. Genes determine the color of our eyes and hair. Genes determine the shape of our bodies.
35 They also determine the special workings of our brains. Genes are what give us our inborn talent for music, science, or sports. Even certain diseases, how long we will live, and what we will eventually die of may be traceable to our genes.

40 Scientists believe that there may be as many as 3,500 inherited, or genetic, diseases. Some are as mild as a mere tendency toward hay fever. Others are as serious as hemophilia. This disease is caused by the blood's failure to clot and can lead to uncontrollable bleeding from even
45 a tiny cut or scrape. In many cases, healthy parents are the carriers of the disease-causing genes. Death in infancy or early childhood can result from genetic abnormalities passed on by healthy parents.

On a happier note, we can also inherit a trait such
50 as great musical talent from our ancestors. An amazing example is found in the family of the famous composer Johann Sebastian Bach. Bach's earliest-known musical ancestor was born in the late 1500s. Forty out of sixty of this ancestor's descendants, many of whom lived during the
55 1700s, became accomplished musicians!

Heredity—the Bach "bloodline"—was an important factor in producing so much musical talent. But was it the only reason? The Bach family's children all grew up in strongly disciplined households. Music was at the center of

heredity
the passing of genes from parent to child

60 family life. These surroundings helped their inborn abilities
to blossom. Similar abilities in children who were not
exposed to music may have withered because their talents
were never encouraged.

   In other words, our home, our schooling, and the time
65 and place in which we live are all important influences
on how we develop. They form part of what we call our
environment. It isn't only sharing certain genes that leads
to similarities among family members. We often are alike
because of our shared experiences.

70   Adopted children, for example, may be closer in
mannerisms, attitudes, and even appearance to their
adoptive family than to their natural, or biological, family.
They "take after" their adoptive parents to whom they
have no "blood" ties. This may be due to their close family
75 environment.

   Does heredity or environment link us more closely to
our ancestors? The answer is probably a combination of the
two. You may grow up to have the tall, broad-shouldered
build of your great-great-grandfather. That's heredity.

80   On the other hand, if your great-great-grandparents
hadn't bravely crossed the Atlantic as a young couple nearly
one hundred years ago, would you be living in America
today? In moving to America, your ancestors changed not
only their own environment. They changed yours as well.

85   Who were the very first people to keep records of
their family lines? Why did they keep track? People have
been searching for their "roots" and constructing their
"family trees" since earliest times. They have done so out
of curiosity. They have done so out of a sense of family
90 pride. And, often, they wish to establish inheritance claims.
According to many traditions, rights to rulership, land
holdings, and other possessions have been handed down
from parent to child.

   Even before they kept written records, many peoples
95 relied on oral history to recall their ancestors. This was
true among the ancient Scandinavians, Irish, Scots, and
Welsh. Storytellers and poet-singers known as bards passed
on the names and heroic deeds of earlier generations to

---

mannerisms

behaviors or
expressions

---

younger members of the clan or tribe. They wanted these
100 stories to be memorized for safekeeping. We think of a
generation as the time span between *our* being born and
the birth of our children—usually twenty-five to thirty
years. But there have been—and still are—peoples among
whom a new generation is produced as often as every
105 fifteen to twenty years.

Among certain Africans, Indonesians, and Pacific
Islanders, oral history is still very much alive. In recent
times, a chieftain of the Maori, the Polynesian people native
to New Zealand, recited a thirty-four-generation history
110 of his people. He did so as a claim to the **inheritance** of a
certain piece of land in that country. His recital was said to
have taken three days!

Oral history endures, of course, only as long as it is
both remembered and retold. In 1966, a group of high
115 school English students in Rabun Gap, Georgia, interviewed
the neighboring Appalachian mountain people. Many, in
fact, were older members of the students' own families.
Under the guidance of their teacher, Eliot Wigginton, the
students published a magazine called *Foxfire*. It contained
120 the spoken rememberings of the mountain dwellers.

As the wealth of material grew, the magazine developed
into a numbered series of best-selling *Foxfire*
books. These books covered traditional crafts and
skills—from banjo making to bear hunting. They
125 contained stories, songs, and other mountain lore.
Foxfire not only preserved the rich **heritage** of
a fast-disappearing segment of American life. It
also enriched the young people who collected the
folkways of the southern Appalachians.
130 Probably the most famous personal experience
with oral history in our time is the one that Alex
Haley wrote about in his book *Roots: The Saga of
an American Family.* Published in 1976, Haley's
story described what he learned as a result of his
135 successful search for his African ancestry.

Haley's first slave ancestor, as revealed in
Roots, was a man named Kunta Kinte. He had

inheritance
the property received when someone dies

heritage
beliefs, traditions, and history passed from one generation to the next

Author Alex Haley published Roots *in 1976.*

been brought to America in the 1760s. During Haley's childhood years, his grandmother had told him stories she had heard as a child about a man called "Kintay." He had been kidnapped by slavers near the "Kamby Bolongo" in Africa and taken by ship to a place called "Naplis" in the United States. There he was sold to a plantation owner who brought him to work in Virginia, under the slave name of Toby.

The spoken memories of Haley's grandmother made a deep impression on him. As a grown man, he began a twelve-year search for his roots. "Naplis," he discovered, was Annapolis, a port city in Maryland. The "Kamby Bolongo" was the Gambia River in the West African country of Gambia. Haley learned that there were tribal historians in Gambia known as *griots*. He traveled to that country. There, a *griot* recited for Haley the history of his family, the Kinte clan. The *griot* traced the line all the way back to the time of Kunta Kinte's grandfather in the early 1700s.

The people who kept the first written records of their ancestry were probably the ancient Egyptians and Chinese. Such records were especially important to the wealthier classes in these civilizations because they had the most to gain through inheritance. At the very top of the heap were the royal families, known as dynasties. Dynasties ruled in both Egypt and China for thousands of years. Enormous power and untold wealth were passed on to the members of those noble family lines.

Among the Chinese, the common people, too, kept detailed family records. This was because the devotion of sons to fathers and the worship of ancestors were important parts of the teachings of Confucius. Confucius was a Chinese philosopher who lived twenty-five hundred years ago. Confucianism spread through all levels of Chinese society. Even the poorest homes had altars inscribed with the names of ancestors. It was the duty of the eldest son in the family to burn incense and make offerings at the altar.

The Chinese philosopher, Confucius, worshiped his ancestors.

As European society developed, from the Middle Ages onward, members of the upper classes often referred to their family history as their "pedigree." Today this word makes us think of some prize-winning animal, like a carefully bred racehorse or a fancy show poodle. Actually, the word *pedigree* comes from the Middle French *pie de grue*, meaning "foot of a crane." This is because, on old genealogy charts, the lines showing who was descended from whom formed a pattern. The pattern resembled the shape of a crane's foot.

In America, searching for a well-known ancestor didn't become fashionable until the 1800s. Once the Revolutionary War was over, some Americans who had begun to enjoy increased wealth looked for a way to add to their family's **dignity**. One mark of distinction was to be able to say that they were descended from a passenger who had arrived on the *Mayflower*. The *Mayflower* was the ship that carried the first Pilgrims to America in 1620. Another was to trace their roots to one of the "first families of Virginia." The first families formed a colony of the English king in 1624.

dignity
respect;
worthiness

Being related to a signer of the Declaration of Independence or to someone who fought in the American Revolution was also a great honor for a family to claim. Some Americans seeking a glorious past made some real mistakes, though. Imagine those who claimed that they were direct descendants of George Washington. History tells us that the famous "father of his country" never had any children of his own!

Today many of us go ancestor hunting because we both appreciate and are proud of the struggles and achievements of the earlier generations of our family. At the same time, getting to know our roots gives us a sense of stability in an uncertain and rapidly changing world. Finding out where we came from can help explain and clarify the present and may make it easier for us to look forward to the future.

Excerpted from "Who Cares About Great-Uncle Edgar?"
from *The Great Ancestor Hunt* by Lila Perl

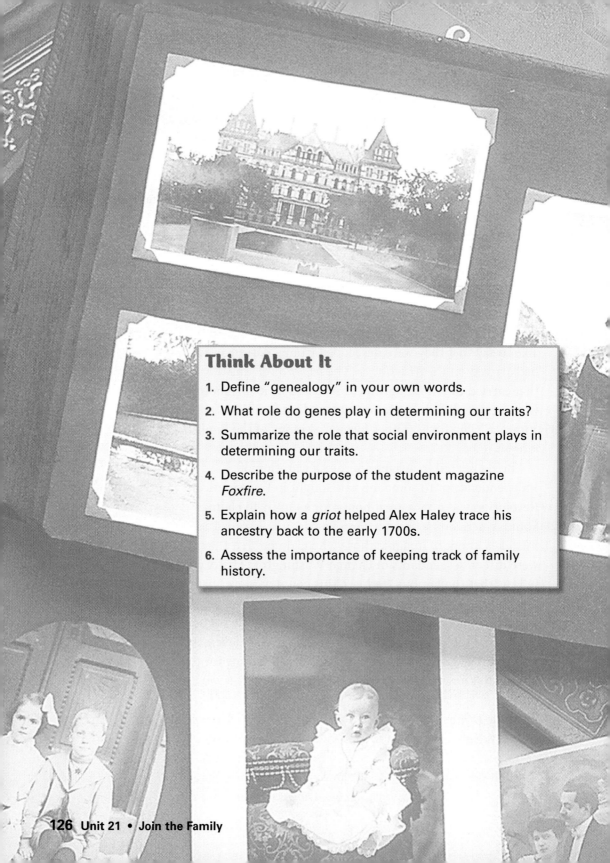

Think About It

1. Define "genealogy" in your own words.

2. What role do genes play in determining our traits?

3. Summarize the role that social environment plays in determining our traits.

4. Describe the purpose of the student magazine *Foxfire*.

5. Explain how a *griot* helped Alex Haley trace his ancestry back to the early 1700s.

6. Assess the importance of keeping track of family history.

Solve the Puzzle

STEP
1

Phonemic Awareness and Phonics

Unit 22 introduces the vowel digraphs **ea**, **ou**, and **ui** for short vowel sounds. It also introduces the final consonant + **le** syllable type.

Syllables

Review: Words are made up of **syllables**.

■ A syllable is a word, or word part, that has one vowel sound.

■ A syllable's type is determined by the syllable's vowel sound. The types of syllables include: closed, **r**-controlled, open, final silent **e**, and vowel digraph.

Vowel Digraph Syllables

A syllable that contains a vowel digraph is a **vowel digraph syllable**.

■ In some syllables, the vowel phoneme is spelled with two vowel letters.

■ The vowel sound represented by the vowel digraph is usually long.

■ Some vowel digraphs represent a short vowel sound. They are: **ea** (for / ĕ /), **ou** (for / ŭ /), and **ui** (for / ĭ /).

Go to the **Vowel Chart** on page A3. Find these short vowel sounds on the chart and the vowel digraphs that represent them.
Find / ĕ /. Find the cue word **head**.
Find / ŭ /. Find the cue word **tough**.
Find / ĭ /. Find the cue word **build**.

Final Consonant + le Syllables

A syllable type and spelling pattern that:

■ Exists only at the ends of words;

■ Exists only in words that have more than one syllable;

■ Is pronounced / əl /, rather than / le /.

Examples: able, eagle, purple, puzzle

Word Recognition and Spelling

Prefixes

We can expand words and add meaning by adding **prefixes**. These word parts are added to the beginnings of words.
Example: **pro** + spect = prospect

(See Step 3: Vocabulary and Morphology for links to meaning.)

> **Unit 22 Prefixes**
> **dis-, pro-**

Suffixes

Review: We can expand words and add meaning by adding **suffixes**. These word parts are added to the ends of words.
Examples: touch + **ed** = touched; threat + **en** = threaten; young + **er** = younger; young + **est** = youngest; build + **ing** = building

(See Step 3: Vocabulary and Morphology for links to meaning.)

> **Unit 22 Suffixes**
> **-able, -ous**

Roots

We can build words using roots. Roots carry the most important part of the word's meaning. We usually attach a prefix or suffix to make a root into a word.
Example: re + **spect** = respect

> **Unit 22 Roots**
> **dic/dict, spect**

Spelling: The Drop e Rule

The **Drop e Rule** is used with words ending with a final consonant + **le** syllable.

1. If the suffix begins with a vowel, drop the **e** from the base word. Example: puzzle + ing = puzzling

2. If the suffix begins with a consonant, do not drop the **e** from the base word. Example: puzzle + ment = puzzlement

Essential Words

Unit 22 Essential Words

colleague	iron	journey
extraordinary	journal	peculiar

Spelling Lists

The Unit 22 spelling lists contain four categories:

1. Words with final consonant + **le** syllables

2. Words with the vowel digraphs **ea** (/ ĕ /), **ou** (/ ŭ /), and **ui** (/ ĭ /)

3. **Essential Words** (in italics)

4. Words with prefixes, roots, and suffixes

Spelling Lists

Lessons 1–5		Lessons 6–10	
apple	*journey*	distracted	saddled
build	*peculiar*	inspector	spectator
colleague	puzzle	nervous	suspect
cousin	ready	predictable	trouble
extraordinary	table	predicted	unanimous
guilty	touch	professor	vehicle
iron	weather	regrettable	verdict
journal		ridiculous	

STEP

3

Vocabulary and Morphology

Unit Vocabulary

Sound-spelling correspondences from this unit and previous units make up this unit's vocabulary.

- What do these words mean?

- Do some of them mean more than one thing? Which ones?

UNIT Vocabulary

final consonant	idle	title	steady
+ le	jungle	tremble	sweat
able	kettle	triangle	thread
angle	little	uncle	threaten
ankle	marble	vehicle	wealth
apple	middle	whistle	weapon
article	needle		weather
assemble	nibble	**ea** for / ĕ /	widespread
battle	pimple	ahead	
bottle	puddle	bread	**ou** for / ŭ /
bubble	purple	breakfast	country
buckle	puzzle	breath	couple
bundle	rattle	breath	cousin
candle	riddle	dead	double
cattle	saddle	deaf	southern
cripple	sample	death	touch
eagle	settle	feather	trouble
enable	simple	head	young
example	single	health	
fiddle	stable	heaven	**ui** for / ĭ /
freckles	steeple	heavy	build
gargle	syllable	instead	built
giggle	table	lead	guild
handle	tangle	leather	guilty
hobble	tattle	pleasant	
humble	tickle	ready	
		spread	

Word Relationships

Attributes are words that tell more about other words such as size, parts, shape, color, and function. Examples: needle/tiny (size); apple/peel (part); marble/spherical (shape); grapes/purple (color); candle/burn (function)

Meaning Parts

Prefixes

Prefixes can add to or change the meanings of words. The Unit 22 prefixes have the following meanings.

Unit 22 Prefixes	Meanings	Examples
dis-	not, absence of, apart	disgust, disinterest, discuss
pro-	forward, in front of	progress, protect

Review: A prefix often assimilates to the base word or root to which it is attached. In **assimilation**, the last letter of the prefix changes or sounds more similar to the first letter of the base or root. This change makes pronunciation easier. The meaning of the prefix does not change when it is assimilated.
Example: **dis + fuse = diffuse**

Suffixes

Review: Suffixes can add to or change the meanings of words. Some suffixes indicate adjective form. When added to a base word or root, they can change the base word or root to an adjective. Adding **-y** to a base word changes the base word to an adjective.
Examples: **bubbly, feathery**

Review: Adding **-ed**, **-en**, or **-ing** to a base word that is a verb permits the verb form to function as an adjective.
Examples: angl**ed**, threat**en**, puzzl**ing**

The Unit 22 adjective suffixes have the following meanings.

Unit 22 Suffixes	Meanings	Examples
-able	capable of, can do	available, dependable, lovable
-ous	full of, having, characterized by	humorous, rigorous, nervous

Roots

Roots are the basic meaning part of a word. Roots of English words often come from another language, especially Latin. A root usually needs a prefix or suffix to make it into a word.

Example: pro + **spect** = prospect (pro = forward; spect = look at, see, watch; prospect = to look forward)

Unit 22 Roots	Meanings	Examples
dic/dict	to say, tell	dedicate, indicate, predict
spect	to look at, see, watch	inspect, spectator, expect

Challenge Morphemes

Root	Meanings	Examples
pel/puls	to drive, push	compel, expel, pulsate, pulse, repel, repulse

Grammar and Usage

Adjectives

Review: **Adjectives** describe nouns. They answer: **Which one? How many?** and **What kind?**

Adjectives

Many puzzling tales involve riddles **with a tricky twist**.

Which ones?	**with a tricky twist** (prepositional phrase that acts as an adjective)
How many?	**many** (single word that acts as an adjective)
What kind?	**puzzling** (present participle that acts as an adjective)

Prepositions and Prepositional Phrases

Review: **Prepositions** show the **positions** or **relationships** of nouns or pronouns. Prepositions often show a position in space or in time; this is indicated by the base word of preposition, **position**. Some prepositions show both time and space.

Prepositional phrases begin with a preposition and usually end with a noun or pronoun. A prepositional phrase can appear at the beginning, middle, or end of a sentence. A prepositional phrase can act as an adjective or as an adverb.
Examples: **with many pieces**, **within a complex maze**

Prepositions in Unit 22

amid	behind	onto	toward	within
among	except	outside	upon	without

Phrasal Verbs

A **phrasal verb** consists of a verb and a word whose form looks like a preposition. But the second word does not function as a preposition. Instead, it is part of the meaning of the phrasal verb. The meaning of the phrasal verb is usually different from the meanings of its individual words.

> **Phrasal Verbs**
>
> Curious students **catch on** quickly to new puzzles.
>
> In this sentence, **on** is connected to **catch**. **Catch on** is a phrasal verb meaning "learn or understand."

Phrasal Verbs in Unit 22

catch on	give back	pass down	run into
dream up	go on	pick out	show up
eat out	hand in	put off	take after
fill out	leave out	put out	take down
fill up	look into	puzzle out	try on
find out	look up	puzzle over	turn down
get by	make up	run across	wake up

Linking Verbs

Review: Some verbs can act as main verbs or helping verbs. Forms of **be** belong to this group of verbs. Helping verbs combine with the main verb to form a verb phrase. The helping verb signals the time. Examples: He **is solving** the puzzle. She **was investigating** the crime. They **will be predicting** the results of the puzzle contest.

- When the verb **be** is the main verb, it acts as a linking verb. Linking verbs connect, or link, the subject of the sentence to a word in the predicate.

- A noun that follows a linking verb renames, or tells more about, the subject. This noun is called a **predicate nominative**. The subject and the predicate nominative name the same person, place, thing, or idea. Example: The *exit* **was** the *fire escape*. The verb **was** links the subject *exit* to the noun *fire escape*.

■ An adjective that follows a linking verb describes the subject. This adjective is called a **predicate adjective**. It describes the subject. Example: The detective's *work* was *dangerous*. The verb **was** links the adjective *dangerous* to the subject *work*.

Sentence Patterns

Review: **Conjunctions** join words, phrases, or clauses in a sentence. Any sentence part can be joined by a conjunction to create a compound component.

Predicate nominatives and **predicate adjectives** can be compounded with the conjunctions **and**, **or**, and **but**.

> **Compound Predicate Nominative**
> The exits were the *fire escape* **and** the *stairs*.

> **Compound Predicate Adjective**
> The detective's work was *dangerous* **and** *hazardous*.

Punctuation

Comma Use	Explanation	Unit 22 Examples
Series	Commas are used to separate items in a series. When three or more words or word groups are listed together in a sentence, a comma separates the items in the series. The last item is usually connected to the others in the series by **and** or **or**.	Puzzles can be *riddles*, *crosswords*, **or** *mysteries*. *Some people like to read mysteries, others like to solve puzzles*, **and** *others like to go fishing*.
Dates	A comma is used to separate the month and day from the year. If the date is written in a sentence, a comma is used after the year.	The crossword puzzle contest begins on *May 1, 2006*. On *July 4, 2006*, they will identify the contest winner.
Addresses	Commas separate the building number and street name from the city, and the city from the state. When an address appears in a sentence, a comma follows the state.	The crossword puzzle contest will be held at *10 West Putnam Avenue, Los Angeles, California*, in July.

Listening and Reading Comprehension

Informational Text

■ Some **informational text** is nonfiction material about a specific topic, event, experience, or circumstance. It is typically found in content area text. Textbooks, biographies, and essays are examples of informational text.

Some informational text outlines a **procedure**, which provides a series of steps to follow.

> **Transition Words for Procedures**
> first, then, next, finally

Vocabulary in Context

■ **Context clues** help us understand new vocabulary. Pronoun referents, meaning signals, and visuals, such as charts and graphs, provide meaning links.

Signal Words

■ Different types of sentences can help us think about new information in different ways.

Some sentences require us to assemble or reorganize elements into a new pattern or structure. These sentences ask us to **Create It**. They are introduced by specific **signal words**.

> **Signal Words for Create It**
> compose, design, plan

Literary Terms and Devices

Genres are types or categories of literature. Unit 22 features two genres:

- A **mystery** is a literary genre in which the author creates suspense around an unknown and provides clues for the reader, who tries to predict the unknown. "Whodunits" are popular forms of mystery. **"The Disappearing Man"** is an example of a mystery.

- A **folktale** is a literary genre consisting of an old story, told over many generations, about a hero or nature. Early folktales were told orally and often changed as they were retold. **"A Collection of Puzzling Tales"** is an example of folktales.

Plot Analysis

- **Plot** refers to a pattern of events in a narrative or drama. The plot guides the author in composing the work. It helps the reader follow the story.

- **Characters** and **setting** are two components of plot analysis. The characters, which can be people, animals, or things, take part in the story. The setting is the story's time and place. Together, these two components make up the introduction in the plot's development.

- To understand how a plot develops, we must first identify a story's main **problem** and its **solution**.

- After we become proficient in identifying a story's main problem and solution, we will learn how a plot develops and apply plot development to our writing.

- Plot development usually consists of five elements:

  Introduction (setting and characters);

  Conflict (rising action);

  Climax (turning point);

  Resolution (falling action);

  Conclusion (the situation at the end of the story, with a look to the future).

Speaking and Writing

Signal Words

- Some sentences ask for information. Other sentences require us to assemble or reorganize elements into a new pattern or structure. They use specific **signal words**.

> **Signal Words for Create It**
>
> **Compose** a puzzling tale.
>
> **Design** a crossword puzzle.
>
> **Plan** a modern-day solution to the problem presented in **"The Cleverest Son."**

Paragraph Organization

- Some paragraphs describe. A **descriptive** paragraph creates a mental image. It paints a picture with words. Through the use of sensory information, examples, and comparisons, a descriptive paragraph helps readers form a picture in their minds.

Plot Analysis

- Fiction includes characters created by the author. During prewriting, the author thinks about **character traits**. In good writing, each character must become distinct. Some character traits a writer may consider include: the character's personal appearance, personality, relationships with other characters, reactions to various situations, and means of coping with difficulties. Anything that distinguishes a character might be a character trait.

- Good writers usually include information about characters in the plot's introduction. This is because the reader needs to know the characters in order to follow the plot. Good writers can tell the reader about a character by including:

    A description of the character in simple narrative form;

    An incident during which the character interacts with others;

    A dialog in which the character is speaking to others.

More About Words

- **Bonus Words** use the same sound-spelling correspondences that we have studied in this unit and previous units.

- **Idioms** are common phrases that cannot be understood by the meanings of their separate words—only by the entire phrase.

- **Why? Word History** tells how **prospectors** and **spectators** are alike.

UNIT Bonus Words

final consonant + le	gaggle	ruffle	**ea** for / ĕ /
ample	gamble	sable	breastbone
axle	gobble	scribble	dealt
babble	grapple	scuffle	dread
barnacle	grumble	shingle	endeavor
battlefield	hassle	shuffle	headquarters
beetle	huddle	shuttle	heather
boggle	jumble	spectacle	homestead
bridle	ladle	sprinkle	peasant
bristle	maple	staple	realm
brittle	mingle	startle	sweater
bugle	multiple	stifle	tread
cable	muzzle	struggle	
chuckle	noble	stumble	**ou** for / ŭ /
coddle	nobleman	supple	countryside
crackle	nozzle	tackle	couplet
cradle	paddle	temple	troublemaker
dangle	pebble	throttle	troublesome
dazzle	pickle	timetable	
dimple	pineapple	topple	**ui** for / ĭ /
disgruntle	ramshackle	trample	buildup
dribble	rattlesnake	trifle	guilt
fable	rectangle	tumble	rebuild
frizzle	rifle	ventricle	
gable	ripple	wiggle	
	rubble	wobble	

Idioms	
Idiom	**Meaning**
be fit as a fiddle	be in good health
be in a pickle	be in trouble or out of luck; be in a difficult situation with little hope of getting out of it
be on pins and needles	be in a state of tense anticipation
blow the whistle on someone or something	expose a wrongdoing in the hope of bringing it to a halt
burn the candle at both ends	work from early in the morning until late at night and so get very little rest
cry uncle	show a willingness to give up a fight
have an iron in the fire	have an undertaking or project in progress
lay your cards on the table	discuss the issue honestly
weave a tangled web	be involved in a complicated situation
whistle in the dark	attempt to keep up your courage

 **Word History**

The root *spect*—Did you know that gold diggers and football fans at games have something in common? Gold diggers are called **prospectors**. Fans at games are called **spectators**. Both of these words have the same root, **spect**. What does that root mean? "To look at, see, or watch."

Prospectors are people who look for natural deposits of valuable minerals such as gold, silver, or oil. Prospectors are inclined to be adventuresome characters who take risks in the hope they will become rich. Spectators watch or observe at events. Football spectators support their home teams by attending games and cheering on individual players. Both prospectors and spectators are looking and waiting to see what will come next.

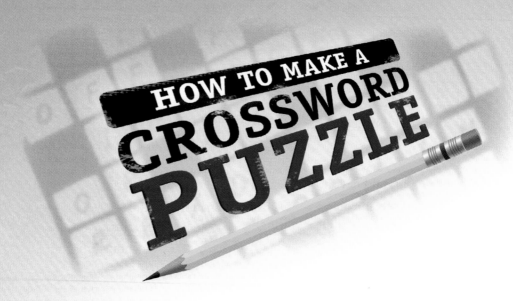

HOW TO MAKE A CROSSWORD PUZZLE

The crossword puzzle is based on a game called a word square. In a word square, words of the same length are written both across and down. Each word

5 appears twice. The oldest word squares were found in the ruins of Pompeii, an ancient Roman city.

The first "word-cross" was published in 1913 by the *New York*

10 *World*. It was an instant hit. If you follow the steps below, you can make your own crossword puzzle.

Step 1: Choose the words and write the clues.

Pick six to eight words.

15 Include a mix of shorter and longer words. Write a simple clue for each word. Don't worry about how to arrange the clues. Just write a clue that fits each word.

A Word Square

T	A	N
A	P	E
N	E	T

STEP 1

My words
triangle
feather
weather
cattle
apple
example
title

Words & clues
triangle= three-sided shape
feather= what a bird has
weather= rain and shine
cattle= group of cows
apple= red fruit
example= for instance
title= a book's name

Step 2: "Cross" the words.

20   Use grid paper to figure out how the words will fit together. Start by writing one word that goes across the grid. Then write another word that
25 goes down. One letter in the second word should cross a letter in the first word. Add the remaining words, one at a time. Each word should cross at least
30 one letter in another word. Use a pencil. You may need to erase a word and find another position for it.

STEP 2

Step 3: Number the words.

      After all of the words are in
35 place, number them. Start with the word at the top. Number the words from top to bottom and from left to right.

STEP 3

Step 4: Number and sort the clues.

Number the clues the same
40 way you numbered the words.
For example, let's say that the
word "triangle" is number 1
in the puzzle. The clue for
"triangle" should also be
45 number 1. Then sort the clues
into two groups: Across and
Down.

STEP 4

Across
3. what a bird has
6. for instance
7. red fruit

Down
1. three-sided shape
2. group of cows
4. a book's name
5. rain and shine

Step 5:

Make a blank puzzle.
Draw a dark
outline around the
50 shape of your puzzle.
Then make a blank
version of it. Be sure to
include the numbers.

STEP 5

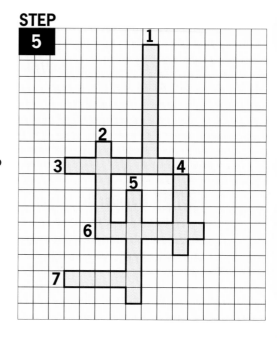

Step 6: Finish the puzzle.
Write the clues under
55 the puzzle. Then give your
crossword to someone else
to solve.

STEP 6

Across
3. what a bird has
6. for instance
7. red fruit

Down
1. three-sided shape
2. group of cows
4. a book's name
5. rain and shine

A COLLECTION OF PUZZLING TALES

Around the world, people like to tell and hear stories. We especially like stories that give us puzzles to solve. Puzzling stories satisfy our natural **curiosity**. For centuries, in many different cultures such tales have been
5 told. Often, these stories become folktales. Folktales are stories that usually have a message. They appeal to young and old alike. They are passed down orally from one generation to the next.

Today, modern mystery writers puzzle us with their
10 stories. A mystery story presents us with some kind of confusing event. At the beginning of the mystery, we don't know what made the event happen. We read the mystery for clues. The clues often reveal the truth. From ancient times until today, we love stories that puzzle us.

15 Four puzzling tales follow. The challenge is to figure out what happened and how it happened. Each story is different. **Visualize** the characters. Imagine the settings. Think about the events. Listen and read each story carefully. Look for the clues that will help you solve each puzzle!

curiosity
desire to know or learn

visualize
to imagine

The Sticks of Truth
—A Tale From India

20 Long ago in India, judges traveled from village to village. One day, a judge stopped at an inn to rest. The innkeeper who greeted the judge was very upset. Someone had just that day stolen his daughter's gold ring. The judge told the innkeeper not to worry because he would find out
25 who the thief was. The judge had all the guests gather in one room so that he could question them. Their answers to

his questions did not reveal the thief, so the judge decided to use some old magic. He told all the guests he was going to give them the sticks of truth.

30   "These are magic sticks," he explained, "that will catch the thief."

He kept a stick for himself and gave each guest a stick to keep under the bed during the night.

"The stick belonging to the thief will grow two inches 35 during the night. At breakfast we will compare sticks, and the longest stick will be the thief's."

The next morning the judge had the guests assemble at his table and hold their sticks up to his to see if the sticks had increased in length. But one after another, the sticks 40 were the same length.

At last, there was only one woman left to show her magic stick. She held her stick carefully up to the judge's stick. The judge looked at it and then called out, "This is the thief! Her stick is shorter than all the rest."

confessed

admitted; disclosed

45   Once caught, the woman **confessed** she was the thief and returned the ring. But all the guests were confused about the sticks of truth. The judge had said the longest stick would belong to the thief, but instead she had the shortest stick. Why?

ᴄhe ᴄʟᴇᴠᴇʀᴇsᴛ sᴏɴ
—ᴀ Tale Fʀom Eᴛhiopia

50   Once there lived an old man who had three sons. When he grew old and ill and knew that he soon would die, he gathered his three sons in his room.

"There is no way I can divide the house and farm to support all three of you. The one who proves himself the

inherit

to receive something from an ancestor

55 cleverest will **inherit** the house and farm. There is coin on the table for each of you. The one who can buy something that will fill this room will inherit all I own."

The eldest son took his coin, went straight to the 60 marketplace, and filled his wagon full of straw. The second son thought a bit longer and then also went to the marketplace, where he bought sacks and sacks of feathers.

The youngest son thought and then quietly went to a little shop. He bought two small things and tucked them into
65 his pocket.

That night the father asked his sons to show him what they had bought. The eldest son spread his straw on the floor, but it filled only a portion of the room. The second son dumped out his sacks of feathers, but they filled only
70 two corners of the room. Then the youngest son smiled, pulled the two small things out of his pocket and filled the room with them from corner to corner.

"Yes," said the father, "you are indeed the cleverest and have filled my room when the others could not. You shall
75 inherit my house and farm."

What had the youngest son bought and with what did he fill the room?

which flower?
—A Tale From the Middle East

Once long ago there lived two rulers named the Queen of Sheba and King Solomon. They were from different
80 lands and were both famed for their wisdom. King Solomon paid a visit to the Queen of Sheba, and she decided to test King Solomon's wisdom by a series of tests and riddles. He passed each one with ease until she led him to a room filled with flowers of every shape and color. The queen had
85 directed the finest craftsmen and magicians in her land to **construct** the flowers so that they looked exactly like the real flowers from her garden.

"The test," she told King Solomon, "is to find the *one* real flower among all the **artificial** ones."
90 King Solomon carefully looked from flower to flower and back again, searching for even the smallest of differences. He looked for any sign of wilted leaves or petals but found lifelike leaves and petals on every flower. And fragrance was no help, because the room was filled with
95 fragrances.

construct
to put together; assemble

artificial
man-made; not natural

"Please," said King Solomon. "This room is so warm. Could we open the curtains and let in the breeze? The fresh air will help me think more clearly."

The Queen of Sheba agreed. Within minutes after the
100 curtains were opened, King Solomon leaned over, picked the one real flower, and handed it to the queen.

How did he discover it?

Love and Pumpkins
—A Tale From the Philippines

When the king announced he was going to marry, stories of the bride quickly spread through the palace.
105   "She's beautiful," said one servant.

"With the voice of a bird," said another.

"More than that," said the third. "She can do anything! When the king dared her to get a large pumpkin inside a narrow-necked jar without cutting the pumpkin or
110 breaking the jar, she did it. My cousin was there when the king broke open the jar."

"That's impossible. Your cousin tells lies," said a servant just joining the group.

"No, it's true," said another. "I heard the king announce
115 it myself."

How did the bride do it?

Tales reprinted from *Stories to Solve: Folktales from Around the World* by George Shannon

Solution to "The Sticks of Truth": The thief, worried about being caught, cut off two inches of her stick during the night in an effort to hide its growth. But since the sticks were not magical, her stick was the only short one.

Solution to "The Cleverest Son": He bought a match and a candle and filled the room with light.

Solution to Which Flower?: A bee flew in the window and immediately went to the real flower.

Solution to Love and Pumpkins: Since the king did not say she had to start with a large pumpkin, the bride placed a tiny pumpkin inside the jar, then let it grow while it was attached to the vine.

Answer It

1. Describe how the judge found the thief in "The Sticks of Truth."

2. Plan a modern-day solution to the problem presented in "The Cleverest Son."

3. Summarize the problem in "The Cleverest Son."

4. Explain how a bee helped King Solomon pass the test in "Which Flower?"

5. Compose a different title for the folktale "Love and Pumpkins."

THE DISAPPEARING man

by Isaac Asimov

I'm not often on the spot when Dad's on one of his cases, but I couldn't help it this time.

I was coming home from the library that afternoon, when a man dashed by me and ran full speed into an alley
5 between two buildings. It was rather late, and I figured the best thing to do was to keep on moving toward home. Dad says a nosy fourteen-year-old isn't likely to make it to fifteen.

But in less than a minute, two policemen came
10 running. I didn't wait for them to ask. "He went in there," I said.

One of them rushed in, came out, and shouted, "There's a door open. He went inside. Go 'round to the front."

They must have given the alarm, because in a
15 few minutes, three police cars drove up, there were plainclothesmen on the scene, and the building was surrounded.

I knew I shouldn't be hanging around. Innocent bystanders get in the way of the police. Just the same, I was
20 there when it started and, from what I heard the police saying, I knew they were after this man, Stockton. He was a **loner** who'd pulled off some pretty spectacular jewel robberies over the last few months. I knew about it because Dad is a detective on the force, and he was on the case.

loner

a person who prefers to be alone

25   "Slippery fellow," he said, "but when you work alone, there's no one to double-cross you."

    I said, "Doesn't he have to work with someone, Dad? He's got to have a fence—someone to **peddle** the jewels."

    "If he has," said Dad, "we haven't located him. And why
30 don't you get on with your homework?" (He always says that when he thinks I'm getting too interested in his cases.)

    Well, they had him now. Some jeweler must have pushed the alarm button.

    The alley he ran into was closed on all sides but the
35 street, and he hadn't come out. There was a door there that was open, so he must have gone in. The police had the possible exits guarded. They even had a couple of men on the roof.

    I was just beginning to wonder if Dad would be
40 involved, when another car came up, and he got out. First thing he saw me and stopped dead. "Larry! What are you doing here?"

    "I was on the spot, Dad. Stockton ran past me into the alley."

45   "Well, get out of here. There's **liable** to be shooting."

    I backed away, but I didn't back off all the way. Once my father went into the building, I got into his car. The driver knew me, and he said, "You better go home, Larry. I'm going to have to help with the search, so I can't stay here to
50 keep an eye on you."

    "Sure, you go on," I said. "I'll be leaving in a minute." But I didn't. I wanted to do some thinking first.

    Nobody leaves doors open in New York City. If that door into the alley was open, Stockton must have opened it.
55 That meant he had to have a key; there wasn't time to pick the lock. That must mean he worked out of that building.

peddle	to sell things

liable	likely; probably going to

I looked at the building. It was an old one, four stories high. It had small businesses in it, and you could still see the painted signs in the windows in the fading light.

60 On the second-floor window, it said, "Klein and Levy, Tailors." Above that was a theatrical **costumer**, and on the top floor was a jeweler's. That jeweler's made sense out of it.

If Stockton had a key to the building, he probably worked with that jeweler. Dad would figure all that out.

65 I waited for the sound of shots, pretty scared Dad might get hurt. But nothing happened. Maybe Stockton would see he was cornered and just give in. I hoped so. At least they didn't have to evacuate the building. Late on Saturday, I supposed it would be **deserted**.

70 After a while, I got tired of waiting. I chose a moment when no policemen were looking and moved quickly to the building entrance. Dad would be hopping mad when he saw me, but I was curious. I figured they had Stockton, and I wanted to see him.

75 They didn't have him.

There was a fat man in a vest in the lobby. He looked scared, and I guess he was the watchman. He kept saying, "I didn't see *any*body."

Policemen were coming down the stairs and out of the
80 old elevator, all shaking their heads.

My father was pretty angry. He said, "No one has anything?"

A police sergeant said, "Donovan said no one got out on the roof. All the doors and windows are covered."

85 "If he didn't get out," said my father, in a low voice that carried, "then he's in the building."

costumer

a person who makes costumes

deserted

left empty; abandoned

"We can't find him," said the sergeant. "He's nowhere inside."

My father said, "It isn't a big building—"

90 "We had the watchman's keys. We've looked everywhere."

"Then how do we know he went into the building in the first place? Who saw him go in?"

There was a silence. A lot of policemen were **milling**
95 about the lobby now, but no one said anything. So I spoke up. "I did, Dad."

Dad whirled and looked at me and made a funny sound in the back of his throat that meant I was in for it for still being there. "You said you saw him run into the alley," he
100 said. "That's not the same thing."

"He didn't come out, Dad. There was no place else for him to go."

"But you didn't actually see him go in, did you?"

"He couldn't go up the side of the buildings. There
105 wouldn't have been time for him to reach the roof before the police—"

But Dad wasn't listening. "Did *anyone* actually see him go in?"

Of course no one said anything, and I could see my
110 father was going to call the whole thing off, and then when he got me home I was going to get the talking-to of my life.

The thought of that talking-to must have stimulated my brain, I guess. I looked about the lobby desperately, and said, "But, Dad, he *did* go into the building, and he
115 didn't disappear. There he is right now. That man there." I pointed, and then I dropped down and rolled out of the way.

There wasn't any shooting. The man I pointed to was close to the door—he must have been edging toward
120 it—and now he made a dash for it. He almost made it, but a policeman who had been knocked down grabbed his leg and then everyone piled on him. Later they had the jeweler, too.

I went home after Stockton was caught, and when my
125 father got home much later, he did have some things to say

milling

moving around randomly; wandering

about my risking my life. But he also said, "You got onto that theatrical costume bit very nicely, Larry."

I said, "Well, I was sure he went into the building and was familiar with it. He could get into the costumer's if
130 he had to, and they would be bound to have policemen's uniforms. I figured if he could dump his jacket and pants and get into a policeman's uniform quickly, he could just walk out of the building."

Dad said, "You're right. Even after he got outside, he
135 could pretend he was dealing with the crowd and then just walk away."

Mom said, "But how did you know which policeman it was, Larry? Don't tell me you know every policeman by sight."

140 "I didn't have to, Mom," I said. "I figured if he got a policeman's uniform at the costumer's, he had to work fast and grab any one he saw. And they wouldn't have much of an assortment of sizes anyway. So I just looked around for a policeman whose uniform didn't fit, and when I saw one
145 with trouser legs stopping above his ankles, I knew he was Stockton."

Asimov, Isaac. 1985. "The Disappearing Man," from *The Disappearing Man and Other Mysteries*. New York: Walker. Reprinted by permission of the Estate of Isaac Asimov c/o Ralph M. Vicinanza, Ltd.

Answer It

1. Summarize what the police knew when they arrived on the scene.

2. The police knew that the thief had run into the building. Design a strategy the police could have used for finding the thief.

3. Explain how Larry identified the thief.

4. Make a generalization about Larry's personality.

5. Compose a short newspaper article reporting the arrest of Stockton, the jewelry thief.

Puzzle People

The Spanish word for jigsaw puzzle, *rompecabezas*, literally translated means "broken heads." And no wonder! The mental challenges presented in puzzles can be so difficult—and entrancing—that they can make our brains, well . . . ache.

But, in fact, puzzles are good for our brains. Puzzles challenge our wits. We must concentrate intensely, think **logically**, and make connections by sorting through layers of information. And, once we solve them, puzzles make us feel proud and smart, too. There's a lot of satisfaction in that "Aha!" moment when we finally crack the code of a puzzle we've been laboring over for hours.

If it takes a determined person to solve a puzzle, what sort of person does it take to design a puzzle in the first place? Who are some of the people behind the puzzles?

logically
with reason; sensibly

Crossword Craze

In 1913, the crossword puzzle made its **debut** in print as the "word-cross." In no time at all, the country was hooked on this new form of amusement. During the 1920s, most of the major newspapers began publishing crossword puzzles. In 1924, the first published book of crossword puzzles sold nearly half a million copies in its first year.

debut
the first appearance

Margaret Farrar was one of the editors of that first book of puzzles. She helped to develop many of the modern rules of the crossword puzzle, including the rule that a puzzle's pattern must look identical right side up and upside down. (This rule is usually applied only to advanced crossword puzzles.)

Farrar became the first crossword editor at *The New York Times*, one of the nation's most highly respected newspapers. There, Farrar instituted the tradition of making puzzles become gradually more difficult over

the course of the week, a tradition that continues today. Monday's puzzle is the easiest, and Saturday's puzzle, as Farrar once explained, is "a two-cups-of-coffee puzzle."

35 When asked if mistakes ever appeared in the famous newspaper's crossword puzzles, Farrar replied, "Oh dear, yes!" She recalled that the *Times* once constructed a puzzle that asked for the defining characteristic of a famous character in the novel *Moby Dick*. The *Times* mistakenly

40 assumed that the answer was "wooden leg." But an eight-year-old boy wrote in to point out that the character in *Moby Dick* had an artificial leg fashioned from ivory, not from wood. Farrar explained, "Perfectly true, but I couldn't help wondering, rather testily, what an eight-year-old was

45 doing reading *Moby Dick*!"

The Cube Loved Round the World

The best-selling puzzle in history is a colorful cube made of plastic, known as Rubik's Cube. The Cube is made up of 26 brightly colored smaller cubes, which can be rotated. The objective is to **align** the smaller cubes so that

50 each side of the Cube is all one color.

This puzzle looks deceptively simple—almost like a child's toy. But, in fact, the Cube is extremely difficult to solve. The Cube can be rotated into 43 quintillion possible configurations—only one of which is correct.

55 The Cube's difficulty adds to its **allure**. During the peak of the Cube's popularity in the early 1980s, people all over the world became obsessed with solving the colorful puzzle. Some people even developed "Rubik's wrist," an injury developed from the **repetitive** motion involved in

60 rotating parts of the cube.

Even the inventor of the Cube, a Hungarian named Enro Rubik, was stunned when he realized how difficult it was to solve his own puzzle. Here's how he describes his first experience trying to solve the Cube:

65 "It was wonderful to see how, after only a few turns, the colors became mixed. . . . It was tremendously satisfying to watch this color parade. Like after a nice walk when you have seen many lovely sights you decide to go home, after a

align

to place objects in a line

allure

attractiveness; temptation

repetitive

done again and again

while I decided it was time to go home, let us put the cubes
70 back in order. And it was at that moment that I came face
to face with the big challenge: What is the way home?"

Maize Mazes

Most of the time, we do everything we can to keep
ourselves from getting lost. We ask for directions. We travel
with maps. Some of us even travel with a GPS (Global
75 Positioning System), which uses satellites to tell us our
exact location on the planet. On the other hand, sometimes
we go to great lengths to become lost—very lost—just for
fun in the winding paths of mazes.

Mazes have been around for centuries. Recently,
80 though, they have made a comeback in an unexpected
place: cornfields. Viewed from above, these maize mazes
appear as intricate patterns, and some are even designed
to represent images. One maze was designed to look like
Oprah Winfrey! But from the inside of a corn maze at
85 ground level, little can be seen at all. Walls of corn stalks
tower on all sides and **envelop** those who dare to wander
inside. The challenge is to first get lost and then find the
way out. What makes getting lost in a corn maze so fun?

Ask Adrian Fisher, who helped design one of the
90 first corn mazes. He has since built over 400 mazes in 21
countries. According to Adrian Fisher, one the world's
premier maze designers, the challenge—and fun—of mazes
is in the numerous decisions required to find the way out.
He says, "A roller coaster . . . will give you a great number
95 of . . . thrills, but the only decision you make is to stand in
line for 28 minutes and then be strapped in. Here, you're
making choices all the time."

A Puzzle From Behind the Iron Curtain

When Alexey Pajitnov invented the computer game
Tetris, he might not have foreseen how successful his game
100 would become, but he certainly had an understanding of
how addictive the game can be. While writing its code,
Pajitnov says he spent many hours "testing the system."

envelop
to surround;
enclose

In the game of Tetris, different geometric shapes fall from the top of the screen and pile up at the bottom.

105 Players have a second or two to rotate the shapes to fit them together. Rows disappear if there are no gaps between the shapes. But if there are gaps, the screen quickly begins to fill up with jumbled shapes, and in short order, the player loses.

Pajitnov invented Tetris in the Soviet Union in 1985,
110 at the end of the Cold War, a period of tense relations between the Soviet Union and Western countries, including the United States. By that year, the Soviet Union's leader, Mikhail Gorbechev, had begun loosening trade restrictions with the United States and Europe. Tetris was exported
115 to other countries and marketed as "the first game from behind the Iron Curtain."

Tetris began to gross millions of dollars, but Pajitnov did not at first profit from his own invention. In the Soviet Union, the government, not individuals, owned inventions.
120 Pajitnov did not begin to make money from Tetris until 1996, when the game's license was renewed. Pajitnov has no regrets, however. "You could always make a little more, but I never seriously think about this stuff. I live as I live." More than 70 million copies of his game have now been sold.

125 What will the next great puzzle sensation be? Who knows? Could you or someone you know be the one to create the next world-challenging puzzle?

Think About It

1. Why did Margaret Farrar refer to Saturday's *New York Times* crossword puzzle as a "two-cups-of-coffee puzzle"?

2. Explain the objective of Rubik's Cube.

3. Describe Enro Rubik's reaction to his own puzzle the first time he tried to solve it.

4. Summarize Adrian Fisher's statement about mazes and roller coasters.

5. Compare Tetris and Rubik's Cube.

6. If you were to invent a puzzle, what type of puzzle would it be? Why?

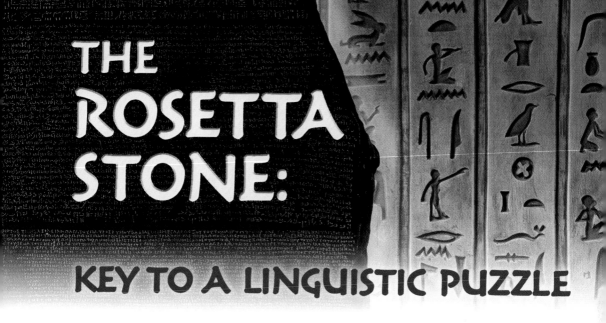

THE ROSETTA STONE:
KEY TO A LINGUISTIC PUZZLE

The Discovery

In 1798, Napoleon and his army landed in Egypt.
They were there to conquer Egypt for the glory of France.
Napoleon brought soldiers with him. He also brought
biologists, **linguists**, mathematicians, and archeologists.
5 He brought these scholars to study and record everything
about Egypt. In 1799, French soldiers were working to
restore a fort in the small port of Rosetta (el-Rashid). They
unearthed a large flat piece of stone. It was made of black
basalt. The stone was inscribed with three bands of **script**.
10 As soon as Lieutenant Bouchard, the officer in charge, saw
the stone, he realized that it was an important discovery.
He had the soldiers pack the stone carefully. It was
transported to French scholars in Cairo. There the stone
would undergo further study.
15 Everyone was excited when they saw the stone. The
French scientists knew almost immediately that the Rosetta
Stone was the key. It was the key to unlocking one of
history's most **tantalizing** linguistic puzzles—how to read
ancient Egyptian hieroglyphs. They knew this because
20 they could read the bottom band of writing. This writing
was in Greek. Part of the Greek said that each of the three
inscriptions on the rock was the same text. The top part
of the stone contained hieroglyphs. The middle part of the

linguists
people who study
languages

script
handwriting; a col-
lection of symbols

tantalizing
teasing; tempting

The Rosetta Stone was inscribed with three bands of writing.

Hieroglyphs

Demotic Script

Greek

stone was written in demotic script. Demotic script was
25 a cursive version of hieroglyphic writing. The appearance
of these three sets of writing together seemed to suggest a
straightforward way to solving the mystery of how to read
Egyptian hieroglyphs. However, it would be twenty-three
more years before anyone would finally unlock this puzzle.

The Puzzle

30   Before the discovery of the Rosetta Stone, scholars
in Europe had worked for centuries to decipher ancient
Egyptian hieroglyphs. They had met with limited success.
The writing was made up of pictures. It appeared on
Egyptian monuments, tombs, buildings, vessels, and
35 other items. It also appeared on papyrus, a type of paper.
It fascinated many scientists and linguists. They knew
the writing held the key to understanding this ancient
civilization, which had **flourished** for thousands of years.
    Ancient Egyptians used hieroglyphs for writing as
40 early as 3100 BC. The last hieroglyphic inscription dates
from AD 394. After that time, the knowledge of how to
write or read hieroglyphs was lost for over 1,500 years.
Egyptian hieroglyphs are made of pictures. The pictures
are of the animals, plants, and household items that ancient
45 Egyptians saw around them every day. In the following
centuries, people tried to decipher the pictures as symbols

flourished

thrived; prospered

of objects. For example, a circle would represent the sun, and so on. But the system of language behind hieroglyphs was much more complicated. Thus, the early attempts of 50 deciphering the code failed. However, early scholars did understand that there was a connection between ancient hieroglyphs and the later phases of Egyptian writing.

Phases of Ancient Egyptian Writing. Ancient Egyptian writing passed through several distinct phases. 55 The oldest version dates to around 5,000 years ago. This version consisted of what appear to be pictographs. Clearly, this form of writing required a tremendous amount of time to do. As a result, an easier cursive form of writing, known as hieratic, was developed.

60 **Hieratic.** In hieratic writing, the letters corresponded to the original picture-type symbols of the earlier script. However, hieratic writing simplifies the hieroglyphic signs so that they can be written much more quickly. Both hieroglyphic and hieratic writing were used from 65 3,000 to 600 BC. Hieroglyphs were often reserved for the inscriptions of names and messages on monuments and buildings. Hieratic writing was primarily used on papyrus documents.

Demotic. Demotic script derived from hieratic writing. 70 It first appeared about 600 BC. It was an even more cursive style than hieratic. It was used primarily for business documents. Hieratic writing continued to be used for religious and literary purposes. The middle portion of the Rosetta Stone contains demotic script.

Unlocking the Puzzle

75 In 1801, the French began their surrender in Egypt to British and Turkish forces. In doing so, the French also surrendered the Egyptian antiquities they had collected. The Rosetta Stone, along with many other artifacts, was sent to the British Museum. Prints and copies of the stone 80 were sent to scholars in Europe and America. It was hoped that someone would solve the puzzle of what was written on it. The demotic text looked more like words than pictures. That helped some scholars start to identify word groups.

Jean-François Champollion.

bilingual

in two languages

thesis

a proposed explanation; theory

The frequently repeated name of a king written on the
85 Rosetta Stone lent an important clue. Scholars identified
the Greek royal name *Ptolemaios* in the demotic text.
Then, in 1816, an Englishman named Thomas Young
compared that name with a word written in hieroglyphs.
The word appeared within an oval called a cartouche.
90 This oval was used to surround royal names. He
concluded that the name *Ptolemaios* as written in Greek
(PTΩLΞMΔΦΩS) was the same as that in the hieroglyphic
writing. Young correctly concluded that the royal
name was written alphabetically. This means each sign
95 represents a sound. However, he still incorrectly believed
that the other hieroglyphs were symbolic.

The man credited with the final decipherment is the
French linguist Jean-François Champollion. Champollion
had mastered many Eastern languages at a very young
100 age. When he was 16 years old, he presented a paper tying
the Coptic language of contemporary Egypt with the
language of ancient Egypt. He traveled to Egypt. He took
voluminous notes. He had access to additional **bilingual**
writings on other artifacts and monuments. From Young's
105 work, Champollion realized that all hieroglyphs could be
phonetic, not just those contained in the cartouches. He
used his knowledge of Greek, demotic, and Coptic words
as guides. Champollion solved the puzzle of hieroglyphic
writing. Again working with names, he matched the
110 signs in "Ptolemy" on the Rosetta Stone to the name that
he found on another monument. He let the hieroglyphs
represent *sounds*, rather than *symbols*. In this way, he was
able to read: **? + l + e + o + p + a + t/d + ? + a.**

He guessed correctly that the second name was
115 *Cleopatra.* He continued to successfully translate other
hieroglyphs on the Rosetta Stone. He also translated
hieroglyphs on other Egyptian artifacts. In 1822, he
presented his **thesis** . He proposed that hieroglyphs were
a combination of phonetic and nonphonetic signs. His
120 thesis opened up the way for us to understand the Ancient
Egyptian world.

The Hieroglyphic Puzzle Solved

Today we know that in hieroglyphic writing there are about 800 commonly used hieroglyphic signs. These signs are called glyphs. Most common are the 24 glyphs that
125 represent single consonant sounds. Hieroglyphic signs can be divided into four categories. First, as alphabetic signs, they can represent a single sound. This sound is usually a consonant sound. Second, as syllabic signs, they can represent a combination of two or more consonants. Third,
130 as word-signs, they are the pictures of objects. In this case they are used as the words for those objects. And fourth, as determiners, they are used in relationship to other hieroglyphs to explain their meanings.

Breaking the code of a written language is like breaking
135 any other code. First, the basis of the code must be found. For centuries, scholars had presumed that hieroglyphic writing was based on a pictographic code. After all, pictures of familiar objects were used in the writing. But

Champollion proposed that hieroglyphs were a combination of phonetic and nonphonetic signs.

as every scientist knows when trying to solve a puzzle, all
140 possibilities must be examined. In this case, the code was
primarily alphabetic. It was much like the kind of code we
use in English today.

Jean-François Champollion, Thomas Young, and
dozens of other linguists, historians, and Egyptologists
145 were persistent. They never gave up in their pursuit of
cracking the code. Their hard work made it possible for the
Rosetta Stone's hieroglyphs to be decoded. Today, the term
"Rosetta Stone" is used as a metaphor to refer to anything
that is a critical key to figuring out a difficult problem. The
150 Rosetta Stone sits in the British Museum in London. It is
on view to the world, as the solution to one of the greatest
language puzzles of all time.

Think About It

1. Describe the appearance of the Rosetta Stone.

2. The bottom band of script on the Rosetta Stone
   was in Greek. How did this help linguists unlock the
   puzzle of the Rosetta Stone?

3. Compare and contrast hieratic and demotic scripts.

4. Trace the history of the Rosetta Stone from the time
   it was discovered until it reached the British Museum.

5. Early scholars of hieroglyphic writing made an
   incorrect assumption about the writing, which
   prevented them from breaking its code. Summarize
   that assumption.

6. Explain the significance of understanding the
   Egyptian hieroglyphic writing.

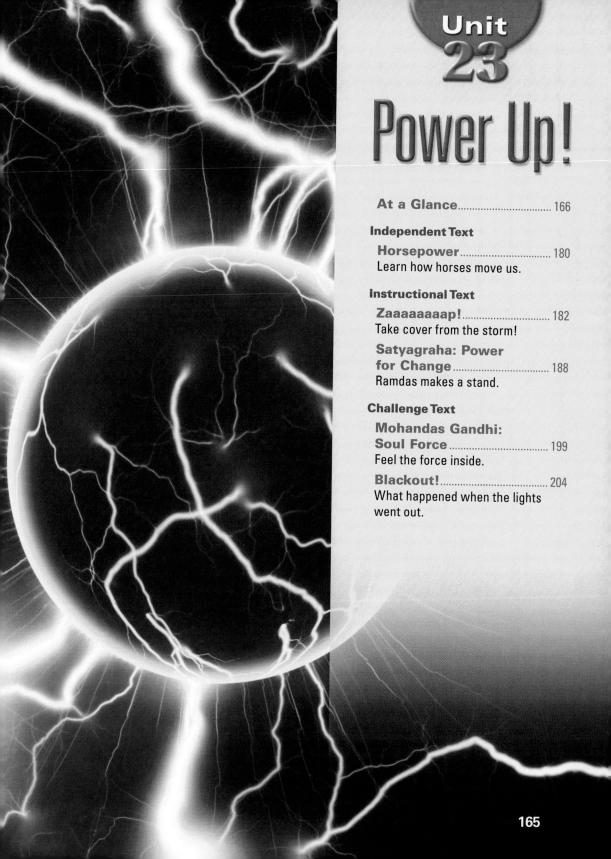

Unit
23

Power Up!

STEP

1

Phonemic Awareness and Phonics

Unit 23 introduces the vowel diphthong syllable type.

Syllables

Review: Words are made up of **syllables**.

- A syllable is a word, or word part, that has one vowel sound.
- A syllable's type is determined by the syllable's vowel sound.

  A **closed syllable** ends with a consonant and has a short vowel sound.

  An **r-controlled syllable** has an **r-controlled** vowel sound.

  An **open syllable** ends with a vowel and has a long vowel sound.

  A syllable that ends with vowel + consonant + **e** is a **final silent e syllable**.

  A syllable with a vowel digraph is a **vowel digraph syllable**.

  A final syllable that ends in a consonant followed by **le** is a **final consonant + le syllable**.

Vowel Diphthong Syllables

A syllable that contains a vowel diphthong is a **vowel diphthong syllable**.

- The speech sound represented by the vowel diphthong is a glide. Moving from one vowel position to another produces a gliding speech sound.
- The vowel diphthongs each have two vowel combinations: **oi**/**oy** and **ou**/**ow**.

Go to the **Vowel Chart** on page A3. Find the vowel diphthongs and the cue words for the sounds they represent on the chart:

  Find oi and oy for / *oi* /. Find the cue words **oil** and **boy**.
  Find ou and ow for / *ou* /. Find the cue words **out** and **cow**.

Word Recognition and Spelling

Prefixes

We can expand words and change meaning by adding **prefixes**. These word parts are added to the beginnings of words. Example: **per** + form = perform

(See Step 3: Vocabulary and Morphology for links to meaning.)

> **Unit 23 Prefix**
> **per-**

Suffixes

We can expand words and change meaning by adding **suffixes**. These word parts are added to the ends of words. Example: human + **ize** = humanize

(See Step 3: Vocabulary and Morphology for links to meaning.)

> **Unit 23 Suffixes**
> **-ate, -ize**

Roots

We can build words using roots. Roots carry the most important part of a word's meaning. We usually attach a prefix or suffix to make the root a word. Example: per + **fect** = perfect

> **Unit 23 Roots**
> **fac/fact/fec/fic; ject**

Essential Words

Unit 23 Essential Words

courage	herb	honor
debt	honest	hour

Spelling Lists

The Unit 23 spelling lists contain three categories:

1. Words with the vowel diphthongs <u>oi</u>/<u>oy</u> and <u>ou</u>/<u>ow</u>

2. Essential Words (in italics)

3. Words with prefixes, roots, and suffixes

Spelling Lists

Lessons 1–5		Lessons 6–10	
courage	however	aloud	factories
debt	loyal	approximate	memorize
drowned	noise	defects	perfectly
enjoy	point	difficult	perform
herb	pounds	disappointed	rejected
honest	power	downtown	thousand
honor	without	escaped	underground
hour		estimate	

Vocabulary and Morphology

Unit Vocabulary

Sound-spelling correspondences from this unit and previous units make up this unit's vocabulary.

- What do these words mean?
- Do some of them mean more than one thing? Which ones?

UNIT Vocabulary

oi	loyal	found	shout	downtown
avoid	oyster	fountain	sour	drown
boil	royal	ground	south	drowsy
coin	soy	hound	stout	eyebrow
disappoint	toy	house	thousand	flower
exploit		loud	trousers	growl
join	**ou**	mound	trout	however
joint	account	mount	underground	howl
moist	aloud	mountain	without	meow
noise	amount	mouse		owl
point	around	mouth	**ow**	plow
poison	blouse	noun	allow	powder
soil	bound	outcome	anyhow	power
spoil	boundary	output	bow	shower
toilet	cloud	outside	brown	towel
	compound	playground	browse	tower
oy	couch	pouch	clown	town
annoy	counselor	pound	cow	vowel
boy	count	profound	coward	
destroy	encounter	proud	crowd	
enjoy	farmhouse	round	crown	
joy	flour	scout	download	

Word Relationships

Synonyms are words that have the same or similar meanings.
Examples: power/strength; joy/happiness; poisonous/toxic

Meaning Parts

Prefixes

Review: Prefixes can add to or change the meanings of words. The
prefix **ex-** means "out of, from." Examples: **ex**port, **ex**it

Review: A prefix often assimilates to the root or base word to which
it is attached. In **assimilation**, the spelling of the prefix changes to
make pronunciation easier, but the meaning of the prefix does not
change. Examples: **ex-** changes to **e-** before **mit** to create **emit**;
ex- changes to **ef-** before **fect** to create **effect**.

The Unit 23 prefix has the following meanings.

Unit 23 Prefix	Meanings	Examples
per-	through, thoroughly, throughout	perfect, perform, permit

Suffixes

Suffixes can add to or change the meanings of words. Some suffixes
indicate verb form. When added to a base word or root, they can also
change the base word or root to an adjective.

Unit 23 Suffixes	Meanings	Examples
-ate	cause to be, having the quality of	illustrate, operate, considerate
-ize	cause to be, become, resemble	legalize, memorize, humanize

Roots

A root is the basic meaning part of a word. Roots of English words often come from another language, especially Latin. A root usually needs a prefix or suffix to make it into a word.

Example: per + fect = perfect (per = thoroughly, **fect** = made, perfect = made thoroughly)

Unit 23 Roots	Meanings	Examples
fac	to make, do	facsimile, faculty
fact	to make, do	factory, benefactor, satisfactory
fec	to make, do	affect, defector, disinfect
fic	to make, do	difficult, significant, insignificantly
ject	to throw	reject, object, projectile

Challenge Morpheme

Root	Meanings	Examples
lumen	to light	illuminate, illuminator, luminous

Grammar and Usage

Pronouns

Review: **Pronouns** are function words that are used in place of nouns. Different pronouns have different functions. Most pronouns have **antecedents**—nouns to which they refer. Example: *Ken* is on the football team. **He** plays fullback. (**He** refers to *Ken*.)

Indefinite pronouns do not refer to definite people or things. They refer to unspecified or unknown people or things. Indefinite pronouns do not have antecedents.

> **Indefinite Pronouns**
>
> Ramdas believes that **someone** with an injury should not play.
>
> In this sentence **someone** is an indefinite pronoun. It does not refer to a specific person or thing.

Indefinite Pronouns

all	both	few	no one	several
another	each	many	nothing	some
any	either	most	one	somebody
anybody	everybody	neither	ones	someone
anyone	everyone	nobody	other	something
anything	everything	none	others	

Prepositions and Prepositional Phrases

Review: **Prepositions** show the **positions** or **relationships** of nouns or pronouns. Prepositions often show a position in space or time or both; this is indicated by the base word of preposition, **position**.

Prepositional phrases begin with a preposition and usually end with a noun or pronoun. The noun or pronoun at the end of the phrase is the **object of the preposition**. A prepositional phrase can appear at the beginning, middle, or end of a sentence. It can act as an adjective or an adverb. Example: **despite the power loss**

Prepositions in Unit 23

beneath	besides	despite	unlike

Phrasal Verbs

Review: A **phrasal verb** consists of a verb and a word whose form looks like a preposition. But the second word does not function as a preposition. Instead, it is part of the meaning of the phrasal verb. The meaning of the phrasal verb is usually different from the meanings of its individual words.

Example: She **pointed out** the streaks of light in the sky. (**Point out** is a phrasal verb meaning "show or indicate.")

Phrasal Verbs in Unit 23

blow up	leave out	switch off
do over	point out	take down
dust off	put on	throw away
give away	set up	turn down

Linking Verbs

Review: Verbs are words that describe actions (point, plow, organize, speculate) or a state of being (is, were).

Review: Some verbs can act as main verbs or helping verbs. Forms of **be** belong to this group of verbs. Helping verbs combine with the main verb to form a verb phrase. The helping verb signals the time. Examples: The light **is flashing** across the sky. She **was illustrating** the story about storms. They **will be speculating** about the amount of rain this spring.

- When the verb **be** is the main verb, it acts as a linking verb. Linking verbs connect, or link, the subject of the sentence to a word in the predicate.

- A noun that follows a linking verb renames, or tells more about, the subject. This noun is called a **predicate nominative**. The subject and the predicate nominative name the same person, place, thing, or idea. Example: *Gandhi* **was** a *leader.* The verb **was** links the subject *Gandhi* to the noun *leader.*

- An adjective that follows a linking verb describes the subject. This adjective is called a **predicate adjective**. The predicate adjective describes the subject. Example: *Gandhi* **was** *nonviolent.* The verb **was** links the subject *Gandhi* to the adjective *nonviolent.*

Sentence Patterns

Review: **Conjunctions** join words, phrases, or clauses in a sentence. Any sentence part can be joined by conjunctions to create a compound component.

Review: Predicate nominatives, predicate adjectives, and direct objects can be compounded with the conjunctions **and**, **or**, or **but**.

Sentence Part	Compound Examples
Predicate Nominative	Ramdas was a *student* **and** the coach's *assistant*.
Predicate Adjective	Gandhi was *nonaggressive* **but** *powerful*.
Direct Object	Ramdas used *patience* **and** *nonviolence* to overcome Bill's aggression.

Punctuation

Quotation Marks

Review: We use **quotation marks** in text to record the exact words a person has spoken. Quotation marks are placed before the first word and after the last word spoken. Usually there are words before or after the quotation that indicate who is speaking. Example: "Get down from there!" yelled Mriel.

Colons and Semicolons

The **colon** and **semicolon** are punctuation marks that have several uses. One use for the colon is after the greeting in a business letter.

> **Colons in Business Letters**
> Dear Coach Conner:

One use of the semicolon is to combine two related sentences.

> **Semicolons**
> The gym will be closed on Monday; we will practice on the outside courts instead.

Listening and Reading Comprehension

Informational Text

- Some **informational text** is nonfiction material about a specific topic, event, experience, or circumstance. It is typically found in content area text. Textbooks, biographies, and essays are examples of informational text.

  Some informational text uses graphs, charts, or pictures to visually illustrate facts. In this unit, **"Horsepower"** uses a graph to display information.

Vocabulary in Context

- **Context clues** help us understand new vocabulary. Pronoun referents, meaning signals, and visuals, such as charts and graphs, provide meaning links.

Signal Words

- Different types of sentences can help us think about new information in different ways.

  Some sentences require us to assemble or reorganize elements into a new pattern or structure. These sentences ask us to **Create It**. They use specific **signal words**.

  > **Signal Words for Create It**
  > hypothesize, revise

Literary Terms and Devices

📖 **Genres** are types or categories of literature. Unit 23 features two genres, fiction and science fiction.

- **Fiction** is a literary genre that includes imaginary stories. Fiction is sometimes based on real people, places, or events. **"Satyagraha: Power for Change"** is an example of fiction.

- **Science fiction** is a particular type of fiction that features settings and people that are futuristic or fantastic. Science fiction often employs ideas, mechanisms, and devices that have not yet been invented or discovered. **"Zaaaaaaaap!"** is an example of science fiction.

Plot Analysis

- **Plot** refers to a pattern of events in a narrative or drama. The plot guides the author in composing the work. It helps the reader follow the story.

- **Characters** and **setting** are two components of plot analysis. The characters, which can be people, animals, or things, take part in the story. The setting is the story's time and place. Together these two components make up the introduction in the plot's development.

- To understand how a plot develops, we must first identify a story's main **problem** and its **solution**.

- After we become proficient in identifying a story's main problem and solution, we will learn how a plot develops and apply plot development to our writing.

- Plot development usually consists of five elements:

  Introduction (setting and characters);

  Conflict (rising action);

  Climax (turning point);

  Resolution (falling action);

  Conclusion (the situation at the end of the story, with a look to the future).

STEP

6

Speaking and Writing

Signal Words

- Some sentences ask for information. Other sentences require us to assemble or reorganize elements into a new pattern or structure. They use specific **signal words**.

> **Signal Words for Create It**
>
> Make a **hypothesis** about how Maitn and Josha know each other.
>
> **Revise** the prediction you made earlier of how the story would end.

Paragraph Organization

- Some paragraphs describe. A **descriptive** paragraph creates a mental image. It paints a picture with words. Through the use of sensory information, examples, and comparisons, a descriptive paragraph helps the reader form a picture in the mind.

Plot Analysis

- Fiction includes characters created by the author. During prewriting, the author thinks about **character traits**. In good writing, each character must become distinct. Some character traits a writer may consider include: the character's personal appearance, personality, relationships with other characters, reactions to various situations, and means of coping with difficulties. Anything that distinguishes a character might be a character trait.

- Good writers usually include information about characters in the plot's introduction. This is because the reader needs to know the characters in order to follow the plot. Good writers can tell the reader about a character by including:

    A description of the character in simple narrative form;

    An incident during which the character interacts with others;

    A dialog in which the character is speaking to others.

More About Words

- **Bonus Words** use the same sound-spelling correspondences that we have studied in this unit and previous units.

- **Idioms** are common phrases that cannot be understood by the meanings of their separate words—only by the entire phrase.

- **Why? Word History** explains the origin of the word **perfume**.

UNIT Bonus Words

oi	foil	**oy**	county	**ow**
adjoin	foist	boycott	devour	bow-wow
adroit	groin	convoy	doghouse	brow
android	hoist	corduroy	dour	chow
anoint	loiter	coy	douse	chowder
appoint	midpoint	decoy	flounder	cower
asteroid	ointment	employ	foul	downsize
broil	pinpoint	envoy	greenhouse	downstream
charbroil	poise	loyalist	grouch	flowerpot
checkpoint	recoil	ploy	groundhog	frown
conjoin	rejoinder		loudspeaker	glower
despoil	sirloin	**ou**	outfield	gown
devoid	spoilsport	arouse	pout	prowl
doily	tabloid	astound	roundup	sow
embroider	tenderloin	battleground	scour	sunflower
enjoin	thyroid	birdhouse	spouse	touchdown
flashpoint	trapezoid	bout	spout	uptown
foible	void	countdown		vow
				wow

Idioms	
Idiom	**Meaning**
be a fly in the ointment	be a detrimental detail; a drawback
be in the doghouse	be in great disfavor or trouble
be out at the elbows	be poorly dressed; lacking money
bring down the house	get overwhelming audience applause
have your head in the clouds	be unaware of the facts of a situation
keep your ear to the ground	pay attention to everything that is happening around you and to what people are saying
make a mountain out of a molehill	exaggerate a minor problem
paint the town red	go on a spree; go out and have a good time
pound the pavement	travel the streets on foot, especially in search of work
put your house in order	organize your affairs in a sensible, logical way

Word History

Perfume—Per- is a prefix that came into English from Latin. **Per-** means "through." And **fume**, from the Latin *fumus*, meant "smoke." So how can we explain today's meaning of **perfume**? It surely doesn't mean "through the smoke." But centuries ago, in Italy, that's exactly what it meant: "to fill with smoke."

When English borrowed the word, it meant "fumes produced by burning a substance, such as incense." We know this from the work of early English writers. For example, in 1650, a writer wrote, "she dyed of the plage and they *perfumed* the house with the graines of juniper." Another writer, offering advice about an ailing horse, wrote, "take a wreath of Pease-straw or wet hay," light it, and "hold it under the Horse's nose so as they smoke may ascend up into his head, then being thus *perfumed.*"

Gradually, the ideas of burning and smoke were left behind and a perfume came to mean "a pleasant aroma."

HORSE POWER

We can measure length by using a ruler. We can measure heat and cold with a thermometer. We can measure how fast a car is going with a speedometer. But what if we want to measure a car's power? What would we 5 use? Believe it or not, we would use horses.

Cars are often described as having "horsepower." Why do we compare the power of cars to the power of horses? The rise of many civilizations throughout the world has happened with the help of horses. Approximately 50,000 10 years ago, some of the earliest people kept horses for food. When early humans started farming, they tamed the horse. They used the horse for riding. They also used it to pull carts and plows. The first draft horses appeared in the Near East between 3,000 and 2,000 BC. For centuries, people 15 have used horses to move things. They used horses for war. They used them for travel. Horses were used to pull plows. They were used to pull mills. These mills ground grain into flour. In many places, horses became the key to food. They

also became the key to money and power. The number of
20 horses that people owned could make them important in
the eyes of others.

James Watt was the first person to coin the term
"horsepower." He invented a new kind of steam engine in
the 18th century. When he was ready to sell it, he wanted a
25 way to say how much power the engine had. He wanted to
say that the engine could do the work of so many horses. To
do this, he had to figure out the power of one horse doing
a task. By watching a horse pull a mill, Watt calculated
that one horse could pull 33,000 pounds, one foot, in one
30 minute. This became the definition for "horsepower."

Today, we talk about how much horsepower a car has.
We can measure the car's horsepower by hooking its engine
up to a dynamometer. The device places a load on the
engine. It measures the amount of power the engine can
35 pull against the load.

We now measure the power of cars, lawn mowers,
vacuums, and many other machines using horsepower. And
today, people still love the power of horses. They also love
the horsepower of their cars. But it's funny today to see cars
40 pulling trailers carrying horses. As we progress into the
future, we are still taking horses for a ride.

Horsepower Produced

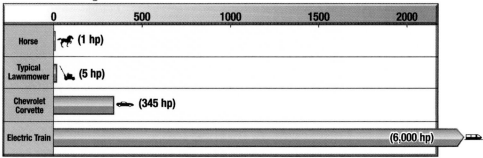

hp = horsepower

Zaaaaaaaap!

a science fiction story

Prologue

The year is 2160. Thirteen-year old Maitn and her family are living at the end of "The Dark," a period of history when the world faced a serious energy **crisis**. Many factors contributed to this dark period. Fossil fuel supplies on Earth
5 suddenly ran out in 2080. At the turn of the century, a severe drought in the Northern Hemisphere limited the use of hydroelectric power. Alternative energy sources—such as solar, wind, and ocean wave power—were in development but not ready for powering whole cities. To respond to the
10 crisis, many nuclear power plants were built as quickly as possible. A massive earthquake in the Pacific Ocean in 2152 damaged nuclear power plants in several countries and exposed thousands of people to unhealthy doses of radiation. Maitn's best friend, Josha, suffers from radiation exposure.
15 However, this time period has not been all dark. Scientists have made advances in medical research as a result of a whole new field of study called "**organic** engineering." Organic engineering of some kinds of fruit has raised the hope of finding a cure for radiation sickness and
20 some types of cancer. This cure is still being tested, however, and is not ready for public use.

A major breakthrough in energy generation has also made it possible to harness the power of lightning. The system isn't perfect, but, overall, it seems to be much
25 safer than nuclear power. But watch out when a lightning storm comes!

Zaaaaaaaap!

Maitn shimmied up the branches of the pear tree, her feet feeling for a firm hold. She saw what she was looking for almost ten feet farther above. The fruit glimmered

---

crisis

an emergency

---

organic

produced from living things

---

30 huge and welcoming, a feat of organic engineering and the world's next miracle cure.

The pear was for Josha, so the fact that picking it from the tree was illegal meant little to her. Josha was close enough to be family. He had been getting weaker. On his
35 last trip to the clinic, the doctor had told his family that his exposure to radiation eight years earlier was slowly killing him. Josha had been visiting a friend near the Powell Nuclear Power Plant when the accident happened. The earthquake damaged the plant's cooling system, and the
40 radiation leak made many people in the area sick, including Josha. Ironically, both of his parents now worked at the same plant although no power had been produced by it since the accident. Josha's parents were part of a team responsible for assisting in the cleanup after the nuclear
45 accident.

Lost in thought, Maitn didn't see the cracked branch above her. As her left hand went to grasp it, the branch split, and she skittered almost halfway down the trunk. Intent on her goal, Maitn **deftly** climbed back up to the
50 pear. She picked the ripened fruit off the branch and dropped it into the duffel bag that hung at her side.

deftly
skillfully; quickly

The task complete, she sighed and looked off to the west. There was a storm brewing; the clouds on the horizon hung dark and heavy. In the distance, she could see the
55 flashes that could only be lightning. The lightning meant that her mom would be working this evening. Her mom had a job at the new Lightning Power Corral.

Maitn looked toward the lightning corral that was right next to the experimental orchard. It consisted of a
60 huge web of thin metal wires. Thousands of thin metal wires connected to the web were lifted into the sky. The wires were held up by small weather balloons that sent meteorological data to the power plant operators on the ground. Just before the lightning was right above the corral,
65 Maitn's mother would flip the vacuum switch. The energy from the lightning bolts would funnel down the wires to be stored in giant batteries and then doled out and shipped to the surrounding counties.

"Hey!" a voice yelled.

70 Maitn glanced down. It was her brother, Mriel.

"Get down from there! A storm is coming!"

Maitn let gravity take her down the branches until she hung just five feet above the ground. Then she dropped and dusted off her pants.

75 "What're you doing? Trying to get killed?"

Maitn pointed to the duffel bag. "For Josha."

Mriel let out a sound that was half smug, half **aggravated**.

aggravated
irritated; annoyed

"That won't do him any good. Don't you know that

80 radiation poisoning is **irreversible**?"

"I know that," Maitn said, shuffling her feet. "But at least he'll have some hope. At least that's something he can hold on to."

irreversible
not able to be changed; permanent

"You're a saint, you know that? Come on, Mom's getting

85 ready to go to work, and she said she has permission for us to go with her and watch."

They made it home just before the warning siren sounded. It **reverberated** off the buildings surrounding the corral. A friendly voice advised them, "Stay indoors or

90 don a rubber suit. Leave all electrical appliances on standby for the duration of the storm."

reverberated
echoed

Mom was leaving the house. Maitn and Mriel ran after her. The three of them mounted the four-seater trike and pedaled to the corral. The wind started picking up as they

95 neared Demante Avenue, and now it blew dust in their eyes and rustled in their jackets.

They parked the trike and hurried toward the building. Her mother used a key card to get into power plant next to the corral. Mriel followed closely behind her, but Maitn

100 stopped and turned. Her eyes fell on the same pear tree she had climbed earlier that bordered the station. As they were pedaling, she thought she had seen someone in that tree. "Mom!" she shouted, above the wind.

But Mom and Mriel were now locked inside the

105 power plant. As a safety precaution, the doors locked automatically when a storm was very close.

The flashes of lightning grew brighter. The clouds loomed darker overhead. It wouldn't be long before her Mom had to activate the switch so that the storm's energy 110 was sucked down into the power corral.

Maitn ran over to the tree and strained to see through the wind-whipped branches. There was someone up there, all right, and it didn't take long to see who it was. Quickly, Maitn climbed up the tree.

115   "My sleeve is stuck!" Josha yelled when he saw her.

His eyes were sunken and his face was pale, but in his hands he held a pear even larger than the one Maitn had picked.

"Great minds think alike," she muttered.

120   Josha started to speak, but she waved him to be quiet. She had heard a sound that made her stomach lurch. It was the loud hum of the vacuum switching on. In less than a minute, more than a billion volts of electricity would be spewing through the atmosphere, striking the spiderweb's 125 wires helter-skelter. Though not many volts would stray, some would, and a tree 40 feet tall would be a great bull's-eye.

Maitn climbed above Josha and ripped his jacket loose from the branch that held it tight.

130   "Hurry up!" she screamed, pulling at him as she went down. Another flash of lightning lit up the sky and painted

spots in front of her eyes. As her heart pounded in her throat, she jumped from the tree, pulling Josha with her.

Their landing was rough, but necessity jerked them
135 instantly to their feet. Suddenly, the air changed texture. The hairs on the back of Maitn's neck stood on end. It was coming. The incredible power was coming.

The pair ran as fast as they could, the sound of crackling electricity filling their ears. They spotted a
140 concrete drainage pipe 20 yards from the tree, and dived into it. They lay there while the storm crashed around them, breathing heavily and watching the spectacular fireworks as the corral collected the lightning's power.

Then, after what seemed like an eternity, the storm
145 moved on, and the hum of the wires died down. The plant's workers emerged to inspect the corral. The captured energy would soon be transported to the hundreds of thousands of people in the state who needed it.

Josha took a huge bite from his prize pear, and offered
150 one to Maitn, his way of thanking her for his rescue. She took the bite willingly, and tucked her smaller pear into his pocket for later. Energized by the power of hope, the two headed home.

Adapted from "Zaaaaaaaap!" By Jennifer A. Ratliff

Lightning Power

It's often stated that the average lightning bolt, which contains a billion volts at 3,000 amps, or 3 billion kilowatts of power, contains enough energy to run a major city for months. However, National Oceanic and Atmospheric Administration (NOAA) meteorologist Thomas Schlatter says:

- The energy input in a typical 3-mile-long lightning channel is estimated to be one billion to ten billion joules. One hundred joules of energy will keep a 100-watt light bulb going for one second. One billion joules will keep the light bulb lit for 116 days.

- If all the energy associated with a bolt of lightning could be captured and used, it would keep a house going for somewhere between half a month and five and a half months.

- The total energy in a lightning strike is partitioned in several ways. Energy is radiated away in the brilliant flash of light. Some energy heats the air in the immediate vicinity of the lightning channel, and some generates the low-frequency sound waves we hear as thunder. The remainder, electrical energy, is only a small fraction of the total. To be fair, we should consider only the electrical energy available at the bottom of the stroke for capture and storage. For an average stroke that is probably less than ten million joules.

Capturing and using the energy in lightning has been the subject of many imaginative proposals over the years, but there are practical reasons for not trying it.

Answer It

1. Make a hypothesis about how Maitn and Josha know each other.

2. Revise the prediction you made earlier of how the story would end.

3. Summarize the factors that contributed to the energy crisis during the era of "The Dark."

4. Assess the level of danger that Josha and Maitn are exposed to during the storm.

5. Paraphrase Maitn's explanation of how a pear can help Josha.

SATYAGRAHA: Power for Change

by Alden R. Carter

Ramdas Bahave met me at the sidelines. "In what part of the body are you wounded, Kenneth?" he asked.

"Hand," I gritted.

"The smallest finger again?"

5   "Yeah."

"Let me see it, please."

I held out my right hand, the dislocated little finger already twice normal size and rapidly turning purple.

Rollin Acres, my best buddy and the team's fullback,
10 made a barfing sound. "Jeez, I wish you'd stop messing up that finger, Ken. It's disgusting."

"Just watch the game, Rollin."

"Sure. But, you know, if you had a little more vertical you could catch a pass like that."

15   "I've got more vertical than you do."

"You're supposed to. You're a tight end. Who ever heard of a fullback with vertical leap?"

Ramdas interrupted. "Would you like me to correct this problem now?"

20   "Yeah, do it," I said.

Ramdas took my pinkie in his strong, slender fingers and pulled. Pain shot up my arm and my eyes teared. Dang! This time he really was going to pull it out by the roots. Then there was a pop and sudden easing of the pain. He felt

25 gently along the joint. "It is back in place. Are you all right? Feel faint, perhaps?"

"I'm okay. Just tape me up and get me back in."

He made a disapproving sound but started buddy-taping my pinkie and ring fingers. Out on the field we'd
30 covered the punt and held Gentry High to four yards on two running plays. Still time to win if we could hold them on third down. "Come on, Patch," I yelled. "Now's the time."

"Please hold your hand still, Kenneth," Ramdas said.

The Gentry quarterback dropped back to pass as Bill
35 Patchett, our all-conference defensive end, bull-rushed their left tackle. Bill slung the kid aside, leaped a shot at his ankles by the fullback, and buried the quarterback. The ball popped loose and Bill dove on it, but the ref signaled no fumble, down by contact. Bill jumped up and started yelling
40 at the ref, but a couple of the other seniors pulled him away before he got a flag.

Ramdas handed me a bag of ice. "Here. Sit down. Rest."

"I can't sit down. We're getting the ball back."

While Gentry set up to punt, Coach Carlson strolled
45 down the line to me. "Finger again?"

"Yes, sir."

"Can you play?"

"Yes, sir."

Coach looked at Ramdas, who shrugged. "It is a
50 dislocation like the other times. I think he should keep ice on it."

Coach looked at me. "Right hand?"

I nodded.

"Hard for you to hold on to a football, then. I'll put in
55 Masanz."

So that was it for me for that game. We got the ball back on our thirty with two minutes to go. Marvin Katt, our quarterback, got two quick completions against their prevent defense but couldn't connect on the big pass
60 downfield. Final score: 16–10. Yet another loss for ol' Argyle High.

Bill Patchett spent his usual five minutes bashing his fists, forearms, and head into lockers. At six four, 240, that's

a lot of frustration on the loose, and the rest of us stayed
65 out of his way. "Hey, Bauer," he yelled at me. "Where were
you on that last series?"

I held up my bandaged hand. "Dislocated a finger."

"And so little doc Ramdas wouldn't let you play, huh?"

"It wasn't like that, Bill."
70 He didn't listen. Instead he grabbed a roll of tape and
fired it at Ramdas, who was straightening up the training
room, his back to us. The roll of tape flew through the
open door and did a three-cushion bank shot around the
room. Ramdas jumped out of the way and looked at us in
75 confusion.

"Hey, Ramboy!" Bill yelled. "Your job is to get people
back in, not keep them out!"

Ramdas didn't answer, only stared. That just made Bill
madder, and he started for the door, fists balled. "The idea
80 is to win. No matter what it costs. So unless a guy's got an
arm ripped off, you get him back in!"

Rollin stepped in front of him. "Come on, Bill. We all
feel terrible about losing. You played—"

"He doesn't feel terrible! He doesn't care one way or the
85 other as long as he gets to play with his bandages and his
ice packs."

"Yeah, yeah, sure, Bill," Rollin said. "Just let it alone
now. Go take a shower. You'll feel better."

Bill **stalked** back to his corner, smashing another
90 locker door, and started pulling off his uniform.

I got into the passenger seat of the Toyota pickup
piloted by my **liberated**, non-committed, female friend,
Sarah Landwehr. (You can call her my girlfriend if you've
got the guts. I don't.) "Tough loss," Sarah said.
95   "Aren't they all? A couple more, and we'll have to start
replacing lockers."

"Billy Patchett took it out on poor, defenseless
inanimate objects again, huh?"

"Yep. He got after Ramdas too. Rollin broke it up."
100   "What's with Bill, anyway? It's not Ramdas's fault you
guys lost."

stalked

walked in an angry
way

liberated

independent; freed
from influence or
control by others

inanimate

lifeless; non-living

"Well, Ramdas would rather sit a guy down than risk making an injury worse. Bill doesn't think that's the way to win football games."

105 Sarah snorted. "So he thinks you should risk permanent injury just to win a stupid game?"

"Something like that. Let's go to Mac's. I'm hungry." I started fiddling with the radio dial, hoping she'd let the subject drop.

110 She didn't, which is pretty typical of her. "I still don't get it. There's got to be more to it than that."

I sighed. How to explain? "Ramdas doesn't seem to care if we win or lose. And that drives Bill nuts. I mean, look at it from his standpoint. Here he is, the best player on a lousy

115 team. He's been all-conference, but he could have been all-state if he'd played in a winning program. And all-state means a scholarship and the chance to play for a Division One or a Division Two school. All-conference doesn't guarantee anything."

120 "None of that **justifies** being mean to Ramdas."

"No, but it explains it a little."

She harrumphed, unimpressed. "So what's going to happen next? Is Bill going to start punching him?"

"I don't think it'll come to that."

125 "Well, I think it might! And I think you'd better do something about it, *team captain.*"

"Only one of four."

"Still—"

"I know, I know. I'll keep an eye on things."

130 She glared at me. "You should do a heck of a lot more than that, Kenny."

Maybe she was right, but I didn't plan on doing anything. If Ramdas felt there was a big problem, he should go to Coach Carlson. Me, I was going to ignore the whole

135 thing as long as possible.

We didn't have practice Monday, and I didn't see anything of Ramdas or Bill until Tuesday morning.

justifies
explains; gives
reasons for

Rollin and I were coming down the east corridor maybe twenty feet behind Bill when Ramdas turned the corner.

140 Bill took a step to his left and put a shoulder into him. Ramdas bounced off the lockers, skidded on the slippery floor, and only just managed to keep his balance. Bill didn't even look back.

"Oh-oh," I said. "I hope Bill doesn't make a habit of that."

145   "He already has," Rollin said. "Started yesterday morning. Every time he sees Ramdas, *wham*, into the lockers."

"Wow, did you say anything to him?"

"To Bill?"

150   "Yeah."

"I said something. Asked him why. He says he's gonna get Ramdas's attention one way or another."

"I don't think getting his attention is the problem."

"Neither do I, but are you going to argue with someone

155 as big and ornery as Billy Patch?"

No, and it wouldn't do any good if I did. Besides, I had a couple questions of my own for Ramdas.

At noon I found him sitting by himself in the cafeteria, a textbook open beside his tray. I sat down across from

160 him. "Hey, Ram," I said.

"Hello, Kenneth." He marked his place, closed the book, and looked at me expectantly.

"Why do you always use people's full names?"

He smiled, shrugged slightly. "I like their sound. I do

165 not like to use contractions either. I like the full words."

"It makes you sound like a professor or something."

"Sorry."

"Uh, well, not a problem. But, look, you've got to do something about this thing between you and Bill Patchett."

170 "What would you suggest?"

"For starters you could act like you care if the team wins or loses."

"But I do not care. Football is a lot of pointless violence as far as I can see."

175 "Then why'd you volunteer to be a trainer?"

"To help with the wounded."

I shook my head. "Well, maybe you could at least stop being so passive about everything."

He laughed. "You would have me fight William 180 Patchett?"

"Well, not exactly, but—"

"Because I will not fight. It goes against everything I believe."

"I don't expect you to fight him, but you can stand up to 185 him in other ways."

"But I am."

"How's that?"

"By not reacting with force. Force is never justified."

"Well, maybe not in this case, but—"

190 "No, Kenneth, in all cases. Never, no matter how good the cause."

"Oh, come on. How else are we supposed to keep other people or other countries from taking what's ours? Sometimes you've got to use force."

195 He sighed. "I guess that is what a lot of you Americans believe. But I believe that you can **resist** in another way. Mahatma Gandhi called it *satyagraha*, to stand firmly for truth and love without ever resorting to force."

I stared at him in disbelief. I mean, Bill was about to 200 turn him into a smear of jelly and Ramdas was talking about some dead holy man! "Well, that may be very cool, Ram, but—"

"You have heard of Gandhi, have you not?"

> **resist**
> to oppose; be against

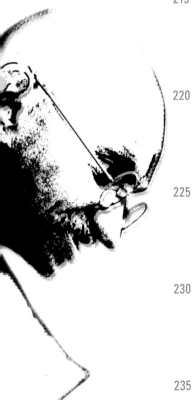

"Sure. I mean, the name, anyway. And I'd love to hear
more. But right now I think you'd better tell me what you're
planning to do about Bill Patchett."

"I am telling you. The Mahatma used *satyagraha* to
free all of India from the British. I think I can use it to
control Mr. William Patchett."

Oh, sure. But I bet Gandhi never had to face down six
foot four, 240 pounds of crazed defensive end. "Ram, listen—"

He interrupted gently. "Let me tell you a story. Under
British rule it was illegal for Indians to make their own
salt. Everyone had to buy expensive government salt, and
that was very hard on the poor. Three thousand of the
Mahatma's followers went to protest the law at a place
called the Dharasana Salt Works. They stepped four at
a time up to a line of soldiers, never lifting a hand to
defend themselves, and let the soldiers beat them down
with bamboo clubs. Those who could got up and went
to the back of the line. All day they marched up to the
soldiers until the soldiers were so tired they could not lift
their arms."

"What did that prove?"

"It proved that the Mahatma's followers were willing to
suffer for what they believed without doing hurt to others.
Their example brought hundreds of thousands of new
recruits to the struggle for independence. Eventually, the
jails were full and the country did not work anymore and
the British had to leave."

It was my turn to sigh, because this had gotten a long
way from football or figuring out a way to keep Bill from
turning Ramdas into an ooze of pink on a locker door.
"Look, Ramdas, that might have worked in India, but in this
country—"

"Your Martin Luther King made it work in this country."

"Okay, point taken, but what are you going to do about
Bill?"

"Just what I am doing. I am going to answer his violence
with *satyagraha*. Someday, his arms will get tired."

"If he doesn't kill you first."

Ramdas smiled faintly. "There is always a risk."

Ramdas didn't get it. OK, he was Indian, had moved here with his family only a couple of years ago. But
245 somehow he must have gotten this *satyagraha* thing wrong. No way could it work. During study hall I went to the library, figuring I could find something that would prove it to him. All the Internet computers were busy, so I went to the shelves. I found a thick book with a lot of
250 photographs of Gandhi and sat down to page through it. And . . . it . . . blew . . . me . . . away. Here was this skinny little guy with thick glasses and big ears wandering around in sandals and a loincloth, and he'd won! And I mean big time: freed his country without ever lifting his hand against
255 anybody. Incredible.

Now, I'm not the kind who tosses and turns half the night worrying about things. I'm a jock. I need my sleep. When I hit the pillow, bam, I'm gone. But that night I lay thinking until well past midnight. Hadn't Jesus said
260 to turn the other cheek? Ramdas was living that, and he was a Hindu or something, while most of the guys I saw in church on Sunday would prefer to beat the other guy to a pulp. Man, oh, man, I didn't need this. Let Sarah and Ramdas talk philosophy; I was just a jock. But like it
265 or not, I was going to have to do something or feel like a **hypocrite** forever.

Wednesday morning I went to see Coach Carlson with my plan. He didn't like it. "Look, I'll get Patchett's attention," he said. "I'll tell him to quit giving Ramdas a
270 hard time."

"Coach, I really want to do this. For a lot of reasons."

We talked some more and he finally agreed, though he still didn't like it much.

Next I talked to Rollin. He shook his head. "Man, you
275 could get hurt. And I mean *bad*."

"I'll take that chance. Just tell the other guys not to step in. And if Ramdas starts, you stop him."

Finally, I told Sarah. She studied me for a long minute. "You're not really doing this for Ramdas, are you?"
280 "I'm not sure."

> **hypocrite**
> a person who claims to believe one way, but acts differently

"Can I shoot Bill with a tranquilizer dart if things get out of hand?"

"I guess that wouldn't be too bad an idea. But I don't think they will. He's big, but I'm pretty big too."

285 Bill Patchett takes everything seriously, which makes it all the scarier practicing against him. Bill is, by the way, not a moron. He maintains a 4.0 in a full load of honors classes and is the only kid in school with the guts to carry a briefcase. On the football field, he studies an opponent,
290 figures out his moves, and then pancakes him or blows by him. Believe me, I know; I've been practicing against him for years. But as I'd reminded Sarah, I'm big too, and I'd seen all his moves.

We lined up for pass rushing/blocking drill. The center
295 hiked the ball to Marvin Katt, who was back in the shotgun. Billy Patch hit me with a straight bull rush. I took it, letting him run over me. When I got up and took my stance for the next play, he gave me a funny look. "Ready this time?"

"Yep," I said, and set my feet to make it just as hard as
300 possible for him.

Cat Man yelled, "Hut, Hut, HUT!" and there was the familiar crash of helmets and shoulder pads. Bill hit me so hard my teeth rattled. Every instinct told me to bring up my arms to defend myself, but I just took the hit. I landed
305 flat on my back, the air whooshing out of my lungs.

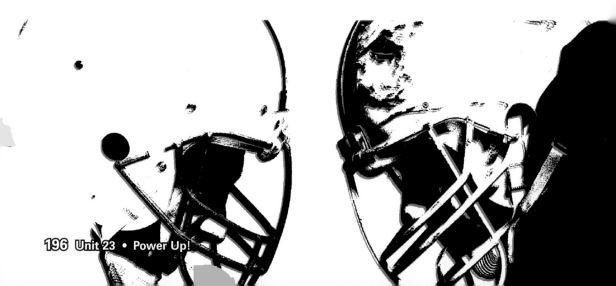

He glared down at me. "C'mon, Bauer. Get with the program, huh?"

He must have figured I was trying to sucker him, because the third time he took a step to the right, as if he expected me to come at him hard. Instead, I took a step to my left to get in front of him and let him run me down.

After that play he didn't talk and he didn't try to go around me. He just came at me as hard as he could. After a while the other players stopped practicing and just watched. Cat Man would yell, "Hut, Hut, HUT!" and the same thing would happen again. I lost count how many times Bill decked me. Finally, he hit me so hard my ears rang and the back of my helmet bounced two or three times on the turf. I just lay there, almost too stunned to move, as he stalked off toward the locker room. But it wasn't quite enough. Not yet.

Somehow I managed to stumble to my feet. "Hey, Bill, I can still stand, Bill. Can still stand up to you." He turned and came at me with a roar. And it was the hardest thing I'd ever done in my life to take that hit without trying to protect myself. He hit me with every ounce of his 240, drove me into the turf, and the world flashed black and then back to light.

We lay a yard apart, panting. "Okay," he gasped. "I give up. What's this all about?"

"It's about standing up without fighting back."

"Don't give me puzzles, man. I'm too tired."

"It's about Ramdas. He doesn't want to fight."

"The little weasel should stand up for himself."

"He is, just like I did now. He calls it *satyagraha*. I don't know if I'm even pronouncing it right, but it means standing firm without using force. He won't fight no matter what you do."

"That's dumb."

"It's what he believes. I think he's got a right to that."

We sat up, still breathing hard. Bill took off his helmet and wiped sweat from his face. "You were driving me crazy. This was harder than a game. I'm whipped."

I took a breath. "Ramdas told me a story." I told him
345 about the three thousand guys who'd walked up to the
soldiers at the Dharasana Salt Works and let themselves get
beaten down with clubs.

Bill listened. "And that worked, huh?"

"Yeah, it did."

350 He shook his head. "I couldn't do that. I don't have
the guts." He struggled to his feet and plodded toward the
sidelines where Sarah, Ramdas, Coach Carlson, and most
of the team were watching. Passing Ramdas, he laid a hand
briefly on his shoulder. It wasn't much, but a start maybe.

355 Ramdas met me halfway to the sideline. "In what part
of the body are you wounded this time, Kenneth?"

"All over, but nothing special."

"Your hand. It is all right?"

"Fine."

360 He hesitated. "And your spirit? How is it?"

I looked at him, saw his eyes shining with something
that might have been laughter or maybe a joy I didn't quite
understand but thought I recognized from the old black-
and-white pictures of Gandhi and his followers.

365 "Feeling not too bad," I said. "Not bad at all."

Answer It

1. Make a generalization about Bill Patchett.

2. Explain Ramdas' response to Bill Patchett.

3. Hypothesize why Kenneth changes his mind about
   the best way to deal with Bill Patchett.

4. Summarize Kenneth's approach to using *satyagraha*
   on the football field.

5. Compose an alternate ending to the story.

Mohandas Gandhi: SOUL FORCE

In 1947, India overcame 200 years of British rule. Though many countries, such as the United States, won their revolutions with long, bloody wars, India won its independence using an entirely different kind of power.

5 According to Mohandas K. Gandhi, the man who led the struggle for India's independence, it was the combined powers of courage, nonviolence, and truth that won freedom from Great Britain.

If a war is fought with nonviolence, then what are the

10 weapons? In India, with Gandhi's leadership, the weapons were ordinary things like spinning wheels and a pinch of salt.

Gandhi would never have frightened anyone passing him in a dark alley. He was a slight man with a bald head.

15 He wore round, wire-rimmed glasses. He covered his body with only a couple pieces of homespun cloth. He often carried a walking stick.

Born in Porbandar, a small town on the west coast of India, on October 2, 1869, Gandhi was a very timid little

20 boy. He was afraid of the dark and insisted on sleeping with the lights on. According to his religious tradition, Gandhi was married when he was 13 years old. Even though Gandhi did poorly in his studies, his uncle thought he might **excel** as a lawyer, and so when Gandhi was 19 years old, he

25 departed for London, where he enrolled in law school.

In Great Britain, Gandhi tried hard to look and behave like a successful man. Not only did he acquire flawless

> "*You* must be the **change** *you wish to see in the* **world.**"
>
> — Mohandas Gandhi

excel
to perform better than others

impression

an idea; effect

English, he wore fancy clothes, rented rooms that were beyond his means but gave the **impression** of wealth, and
30 even learned to dance the fox trot.

After awhile, though, he realized that none of these affectations made him any happier, and so he began discarding them. He started cooking for himself, and he returned to his religious tradition of being a vegetarian.
35 Rather than taking expensive taxis, he walked to his destinations. Gandhi felt a little better living more simply, and he managed to pass his law exams.

Returning to India, he began to practice law. Unfortunately, his severe shyness had not disappeared, and
40 so he experienced great difficulty appearing and speaking in court. His career suffered as a result, and so again, his family stepped in to provide assistance. This time, they found him a job practicing law in South Africa.

Gandhi was shocked when he experienced the
45 prejudiced ways that Indians were treated in South Africa. One time, when he was riding in the first-class section of a train, another passenger demanded that he move to third class. Gandhi possessed a first-class ticket and refused to move, and so the passenger fetched a steward who threw
50 him off the train in the middle of the winter night. Gandhi spent that long, cold night reflecting on what had happened to him, especially wondering how Indian people who were subjected to this kind of racism could fight back.

Gandhi lived in South Africa for over 20 years and
55 become a leader in the Indian community there. Though some people might have planned wars or violent uprisings after experiencing injustice, Gandhi **devised** another kind of power. He called it *satyagraha*.

devised

created; developed

In practicing *satyagraha*, a person never gives in to
60 violence when trying to resolve conflicts; instead, he or she uses nonviolent resistance. Translated as "soul force," *satyagraha* means holding fast to truth or firmness in a righteous cause. Gandhi wrote, ". . . determined spirits fired by an **unquenchable** faith in their mission can alter
65 the course of history." He dedicated the rest of his life to demonstrating how *satyagraha* worked.

unquenchable

impossible to suppress or destroy; cannot be stopped

When he returned to India, one of Gandhi's biggest goals was Indian independence. Surely millions of Indians could overtake the handful of British ruling India! Why not stage a forced revolution and win back the country? According to Gandhi, not only did violence fan the flames of hatred, but war always led to more war. Gandhi believed in the power of nonviolent resistance to overcome corrupt systems.

So instead of war, Gandhi thought up creative ways to resist unfair British laws. For example, Indians were forced to buy cloth made in English factories. Gandhi organized a mass movement in which the people throughout India used spinning wheels to make their own homespun cloth and sew their own clothes. The British could no longer make money selling their factory-made cloth to Indians, and even better, the Indians were learning **self-sufficiency**.

self-sufficiency
independence

There were also severe laws against Indians making their own salt. In hot India, salt is a very important part of the people's diet, but with the salt laws in place, Indians were forced to buy expensive salt from the British. Again, Gandhi suggested using the power of resistance. In 1930, he began a 240-mile walk to the sea. As he walked, spreading the word about resisting this unjust British law, thousands of people left their villages and joined him. When they reached the ocean, Gandhi bent down and pinched up a bit of salt from the beach.

Gandhi and his followers walked 240 miles to protest salt laws.

The British arrested him for breaking their salt laws, but they knew they were losing their grip on the Indian
100 people. How could they stop people from making their own clothes and salt? Even better, these simple acts of resistance empowered the Indian people, giving them control over their own lives.

Even so, Indian society was not free from its own
105 conflicts. An ancient caste system in India divided people into categories of importance, with the priests at the top and a group called the "untouchables" at the bottom. Not only were the "untouchables" not allowed to enter temples or use wells, but people in other castes literally would
110 not touch them. Gandhi knew that even if India gained independence from Great Britain, it would not be a free country if a group of people were treated with inequality and cruelty. He gave the "untouchables" the name *Harijan*, or "people of God," and throughout his life, he used
115 techniques of nonviolent resistance to gain rights for the *Harijan*.

One of the biggest obstacles in the struggle for Indian independence was the conflicts between the Hindu and Muslim people in that country. Each group was
120 worried that the other would have more power in a newly independent India. On several occasions, violent fighting broke out between the Hindus and Muslims. To stop the violence, Gandhi would go on a fast, refusing to eat so long as there was violence. Many people on both sides of this
125 conflict, Hindu and Muslim, respected and loved him. They did not want Gandhi to die, and so they promised to keep the peace. By this time, Gandhi's followers were calling him Mahatma, which means "great soul."

Gandhi used fasting with the British, as well. Many
130 times they threw him in prison for his acts of resistance, and there he would quit eating. The British knew that if the Mahatma died in prison, chaos would break out in India, and so time and again, they released him from prison and gave in to his requests.

135 In 1947, when India finally won its independence from Great Britain, most people celebrated, but Gandhi's heart

was broken. The Muslim and Hindu people had not been able to forge a working **alliance**, and so India was divided into two countries: Pakistan was Muslim, while the rest of
140 India was Hindu.

alliance

a group of people joined for a purpose

On January 30, 1948, Gandhi walked to his evening prayer meeting. Each night hundreds, sometimes even thousands, of people joined him for prayer. As he was walking to the meeting place, a man rushed up to him and
145 dropped to his knees in front of Gandhi, as if he were about to pray. Instead, this Hindu man, who didn't like Gandhi's attempts to bring peace between Hindus and Muslims, pulled out a gun and fired.

Gandhi died right away, but no one could kill his spirit.
150 His deep belief in the powers of courage, nonviolence, and truth has continued to inspire people around the world. A few years later, Dr. Martin Luther King Jr. used those powers to lead the nonviolent movement for African American civil rights in the United States. Gandhi's
155 *satyagraha* also inspired Nelson Mandela, who led the anti-apartheid movement in South Africa.

Gandhi once said, "You must be the change you wish to see in the world." The power of his "soul force" lives on in those who use nonviolent means for positive change.
160 Dedicated to truth and armed with courage, they strive to make the world a better place for us all.

Think About It

1. Explain why Gandhi was thrown off a train in South Africa.

2. Define *satyagraha* in your own words.

3. Summarize Gandhi's plan for resisting Britain's rule through the use of spinning wheels.

4. Explain why Gandhi gave the "untouchables" the name *Harijan*.

5. Summarize the way that Gandhi used fasting to bring about change.

6. Gandhi once said, "You must be the change you wish to see in the world." Put that message into your own words.

BLACKOUT!

On August 14, 2003, people all over the northeastern
United States were powering up for ordinary activities. In
Cleveland, Ohio, David turned on his computer to write
his final paper for summer school. In New York City, Julian
5 plugged in the vacuum cleaner because he had promised
his mom he'd vacuum the apartment before she got home
from work. In Detroit, Consuelo happily climbed into the
seat of a Ferris wheel next to her best friend.

The activities of David, Julian, and Consuelo were all
10 **dependent** on one thing: electricity as power. Probably
none of them even thought about this at the time. But when
David's computer suddenly shut down, Julian's vacuum
cleaner died, and Consuelo's Ferris wheel stopped in midair, they probably all knew they'd lost electricity. What they
15 didn't know was why they'd lost electricity.

In fact, on that day in the summer of 2003, power went
out over a region covering eight American states and parts
of Canada. Roughly 50 million people lost power. What
happened?

How Power is Produced

20 To understand what causes a power failure of this
kind, it helps to know how electricity is produced. In 1882,
Thomas Edison built the first electrical generating plant;
it used steam power to generate electricity to light parts of
New York City. By 1896, electricity created by the force of
25 water turning **turbines** at Niagara Falls was transmitted to
the city of Buffalo, 20 miles away.

For almost 100 years, the same basic system was used.
Power plants were built next to the cities where the demand
was highest. Electricity was distributed from these local

dependent
reliant upon

turbines
machines that
produce power

30 plants across transmission lines that connected the power
plants to the cities. Today the system is much more complex.
In an effort to serve more and more customers, power plants
cooperate to serve areas that cover many thousands of
square miles. They form an **interconnected** system that
35 supplies power to millions of buildings and homes.

   So how does electricity get from this complex system to
David's computer, Julian's vacuum cleaner, and Consuelo's
Ferris wheel? First, electrical power is created by generators
in power plants. The generators must turn in order to
40 produce electricity, and this is done in many different ways.
Some power plants use hydroelectric dams or nuclear
reactors; others use large diesel engines, gas turbines, or
steam turbines. Burning coal, oil, or natural gas is another
way to power generators.

45   Once the electrical power is generated, it is distributed
through transmission lines. These are the tall metal
structures often built along highways with wires strung
between them. These lines are connected to power
substations, which lead out to other poles and lines, and
50 eventually are connected to the power poles that run down
roads and streets. The lines then run from the power poles
straight into buildings and homes. (Some neighborhoods
now have their power lines underground, so these lines
cannot be seen.) These wires run through the walls of the
55 buildings and are attached to the outlets—the places to
plug in appliances, such as David's computer or Julian's
vacuum cleaner. The electricity running Consuelo's
Ferris wheel traveled a similar path, only its end was an
amusement park rather than a home or an apartment
60 building.

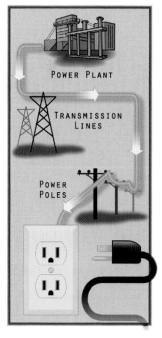

   Today, all of these parts—power plants, transmission
lines, substations, and power poles—are interconnected and
make up what is called the grid. In the United States, there
are three main grids. One serves most of the United States
65 and Canada east of the Rocky Mountains. Another serves
most of Canada and the United States west of the Rockies
(except Alaska and Hawaii). Texas has its own grid system.

Failures in the Grid

Small failures in these grids happen frequently. Tree
limbs can fall on power lines, knocking them out. Brush
70 fires can burn down power poles. Lightning can strike a
power line. A power line insulator has failed more than
once because a bird landed on it!

When part of the grid fails, other parts of the grid
take up the slack. For example, if a power plant in Ohio
75 shuts down, another one on the same grid in New York
or Michigan could take over and send power to the same
customers. Small failures in the grid usually go unnoticed
as a result of this interconnected system. However, when
several breaks or disturbances occur at once, the rest of the
80 grid is put under pressure. When too much pressure is put
on an **isolated** part of the grid, it will overload and shut
down. Before long, cascading failures result, like a chain
reaction, and an entire area loses power. This is called
a blackout.

isolated

separated

What Happened on August 14, 2003?

85   The biggest blackout in North American history
began with a series of failures that caused a massive chain
reaction. A joint U.S.-Canadian government investigation
into the outage blamed an Ohio utility company for
starting the chain reaction.

90   First, the company's computer system failed, preventing
it from being fully aware of the problem as it began.
Second, workers hadn't trimmed some overgrown tree
limbs that were too close to key transmission lines. When
these lines became overloaded, they sagged on the tree
95 limbs and shorted out. Finally, when the utility did become
aware of the problem, they should have reduced the load of
the remaining lines by cutting off power for a short time
period to some customers. They also should have notified
other power plants on the grid so they could **compensate**
100 by producing more power. The Ohio company didn't take
these steps, and so more overloaded lines tripped off, and
soon the chain reaction was out of control.

compensate

to provide some-
thing else; provide
an alternate action

With more and more of the grid out, enormous amounts of power were trying to travel through fewer lines. Shortly after 4:10 p.m., huge power surges swept through Michigan and then into New York, knocking out power from Manhattan to Toronto to Detroit. These surges overwhelmed the system, and generators in the U.S. and Canada began automatically shutting down to avoid damage. By the evening commute, 263 power plants had gone offline.

Elevators didn't work, so workers in New York and in many other cities had to walk down dozens of flights of stairs to exit their buildings. The stairwells were dark and crowded, so the going was very slow in some places. Once on the streets, there were no trains or subways running. Some people had to walk many miles to get home. Electric pumps didn't work in some areas, so drinking water wasn't available either.

There were many heroes during the Blackout of 2003. Volunteers stood in busy intersections and directed traffic. Folks who had cars ferried as many walkers home as possible. At least one ice cream store owner gave away as many free ice cream cones as he could before his ice cream melted. People gathered with their neighbors on that hot August night, lit candles, and shared what food they had in their warming refrigerators.

What happened to David, Julian, and Consuelo? David had to write his paper out by hand and type it into the computer the next day. Julian couldn't vacuum for his mom. He waited for her in the dark and was happy when she finally arrived after walking all the way home from work. After some nerve-wracking moments, Consuelo and her friend were rescued off the Ferris wheel.

During the Blackout of 2003, people had to walk many miles to get home.

The Future of Power

135   The need for electrical power—to run our televisions, refrigerators, computers, heating systems, lighting, and much more—is not likely to decrease in the future. Many people are asking if our existing grid system can continue to meet increasing demand.

140   Other forms of generating electrical power could be used to reduce the strain on the existing grid. For example, fuel cells convert chemicals such as oxygen and hydrogen into water to produce electricity. Wind turbines use wind to make electricity. These and other **alternative** sources
145 of power could be installed locally. They could serve as backup power sources when the grid goes down.

       Before Thomas Edison invented the electric light and built the first electrical generating plant a little more than a century ago, people went about their business without
150 electricity. But Edison's inventions led to a new and more productive world. The Blackout of 2003 reminds us how dependent we are on electrical power and how much we take for granted that it will always be there. The Blackout of 2003 should remind us to use this resource wisely so that our
155 future remains bright.

Adapted from "Blackout!" By Kathiann M. Kowalski

alternative
different; additional

Think About It

1. Compare how power is produced today to how it was produced a hundred years ago.

2. Explain what a grid is and how its parts are interconnected to help bring electrical power into homes and businesses.

3. List two things that can cause part of a power grid to fail.

4. Explain how the problems of one utility company in Ohio could lead to power outages in places as far away as New York and Canada.

5. Describe the effects of the Blackout of 2003.

6. Imagine you are in charge of a national task force set up after the Blackout of 2003. What are some things you would do ensure that a blackout of such magnitude does not occur again?

Have a Dream

STEP
1

Phonemic Awareness and Phonics

Unit 24 reviews the seven syllable types.

Syllable Types

Review: Words are made up of syllables.

- A syllable is a word or word part that has one vowel sound.
- Every word has at least one syllable.
- The syllable type is determined by the syllable's vowel sound.
- There are seven syllable types.

Syllable Type	Pattern	Vowel Sound	Diacritical Mark/Symbol
Closed	A syllable that ends with a consonant sound. (**dig, trans-mit**)	The vowel sound is short.	ă
r-Controlled	A syllable that has a vowel followed by **r**. (**car, mar**-ket)	The vowel sound is r-controlled: / âr /, / ôr /, or / êr /.	âr
Open	A syllable that ends with a vowel sound. (**she, my, o**-pen)	The vowel sound is long.	ā
Final silent e	A syllable that ends in a final silent **e** (**made**, in-**flate**)	The vowel sound is long.	ā_e
Vowel digraph	A syllable that contains a vowel digraph. (r**ai**n, pl**ay**)	The vowel sound is usually long.	ā
Final consonant + le	A final syllable that ends in a consonant followed by **le**. (puz**zle**)	The vowel sound is schwa. /zəl/	ə
Vowel diphthong	A syllable that contains a vowel diphthong. (**oi**l, b**oy**; **ou**t, c**ow**)	The vowel sound is a glide, sounding like two sounds.	oi, ou

STEP

2

Word Recognition and Spelling

Prefixes, Suffixes, and Roots

We can expand words and add meaning by adding **prefixes** and **suffixes**.

- Prefixes are added to the beginnings of words.

- Suffixes are added to the ends of words.

- Roots are the basic meaning part of words. We usually attach a prefix or suffix to make the root a word.

Refer to page A16 for a list of prefixes, roots, and suffixes, and their meanings.

Prefix Review

con-	ex-	mid-	over-
condense	example	midline	overflow
conduct	exchange	midmorning	overhear
confess	exclaim	midtown	overlay
confiscate	exclusive	midway	overload
conform	**fore-**	midweek	overplay
constraint	foreclose	**mis-**	**per-**
construct	foreground	misapply	perfectly
de-	foretell	misbehave	permanent
deactivate	forethought	miscount	perpendicular
debrief	forewoman	mishandle	**pro-**
decay	**in-**	mislead	proclaim
declassify	inaccurate	**non-**	profile
depart	indignify	noncommittal	profuse
dis-	ineffective	nondescript	provider
disable	insensitivity	nonmetal	
disagree		nonstandard	
disarray		nonviolent	
displease			
disqualify			

Suffix Review

-able
accountable
advisable
forgivable
payable

-ate
appropriate
culminate
deactivate
filtrate

-en
deepen
sharpen
widen

-er
entertainer
trainer
waiter

-ful
painful
purposeful
successful

-ist
artist
medalist
motorist

-ize
symbolize
vocalize
winterize

-less
effortless
formless
jobless
powerless

-ment
fulfillment
requirement
wonderment

-ness
bitterness
bluntness
cleverness

-or
actor
administrator

conductor
navigator
projector

-ous
enormous
famous
joyous
tremendous

-y
antsy
bulky
grainy

Root Review

dic/dict
dedicate
dictate
predictable
unpredictably

duc
educable
educate
reeducate
uneducated

duct
deductibility
induct
reproductive
semiconductor
unproductive

fac/fact
artifacts
benefactress

facsimile
matter-of-fact
satisfactory

fec
affected
defector
effectively
imperfectness
perfectly

fic
difficulties
insignificantly
pontificate
significant

form
conformity
deformity
informative

nonconformist
uninformed

ject
adjective
injector
interjectory
objectiveness

port
import
portfolio
reportable
supportable
transportable

spect
inspective
respectable
respectfully
spectacles

scrib
ascribes
describable
inscriber
scribal
subscriber

script
conscripting
oversubscribe
typescript

tract
attractable
contractor
distractive
intractable
protractor

Essential Words

Unit 24 Essential Words

half	listen	tambourine
limousine	pour	villain

Spelling Lists

The Unit 24 spelling lists contain three categories:

1. Words with the seven syllable types

2. **Essential Words** (in italics)

3. Words with prefixes, roots, and suffixes

Spelling Lists

Lessons 1–5

cuticle	*limousine*
details	*listen*
dream	*pour*
flowers	preamble
friends	slowly
half	*tambourine*
hours	*villain*
joined	

Lessons 6–10

actor	flammable
antsy	forgivable
beagle	ineffective
building	midmorning
conduct	misbehaved
departed	perfectly
disposable	winterize
famous	

Vocabulary and Morphology

Unit Vocabulary

Sound-spelling correspondences from this unit and previous units make up this unit's vocabulary.

- What do these words mean?
- Do some of them mean more than one thing? Which ones?

UNIT Vocabulary

adequate	died	integrity	semiprivate
administrator	dinner	intermediate	seventeen
aggregate	dream	joined	shelter
agony	elder	liquid	shouted
ambiguous	enclose	meteoroid	shown
anthropoid	entitle	midst	skirt
bible	entity	mischief	slowly
bitter	exasperate	nuclear	spontaneous
callous	excuse	orchard	stir
capitol	expense	perform	subsequent
classify	fabulous	plains	subtitle
clever	female	poet	supper
compromise	flowers	pounds	syllables
consequent	friends	preamble	temper
coordinate	hinder	preserve	thorn
copper	hours	professorial	tidy
corporate	hypothesis	propagandize	tied
correspond	immense	qualitative	upper
counterpoint	immigrate	raised	utilize
cried	implicate	razor	waste
curl	indicate	reached	wheels
curse	inform	ruler	whisper
curve	inquire	satisfactory	
cuticle	instruments	scorn	
details	integrate	sediment	

Word Relationships

Synonyms are words that have the same or similar meanings.
Example: **Save** and **preserve** are synonyms.

Antonyms are words that have opposite meanings.
Example: **Sweet** and **bitter** are antonyms.

Meaning Parts

Prefixes

Prefixes can add to or change the meanings of words.
A prefix + a base word or root = a new word with a new meaning.
Examples: **ex** + port = export; **de** + tract = detract

Suffixes

Suffixes can change the meaning or function of words.
Examples: verb to noun: require + **ment** = requirement;
noun to adjective: color + **ful** = colorful;
verb to adjective: retract + **able** = retractable

Roots

A **root** is the basic meaning part of a word. It usually needs a prefix
or suffix to make it into a word. Roots of English words often come
from other languages, especially Latin.
Example: in + **spect** + or = inspector (in = into, **spect** = look, **or** = the
person who does something. Inspector = the person who looks into
something)

Refer to page A16 for a list of prefixes, roots, and suffixes and their
meanings.

STEP 4

Grammar and Usage

Nouns

Review: **Nouns** are words that:

- Name a person, place, thing, or idea. An idea is a thought; it cannot be touched or seen.

- Function as subjects, direct objects, indirect objects, objects of a preposition, or predicate nominatives.

Adjectives

Review: **Adjectives** describe nouns. They answer: **Which one? How many?** and **What kind?**

Adjectives

A **single inspired** man **from the south** changed many lives.

Which one?	**from the south** (prepositional phrase that acts as an adjective)
How many?	**single** (single word that acts as an adjective)
What kind?	**inspired** (past participle that acts as an adjective)

Tense Timeline

Review: **Verbs** describe an action or a state of being. Verbs also convey time. The **Tense Timeline** shows the relationship between time and verb form.

Yesterday	Today	Tomorrow
Past	Present	Future
-ed		

Irregular Verbs

Some verbs signal time through irregular past forms.

Unit 24 Irregular Verbs

Base Verb	Past Tense	Past Participle
buy	bought	bought
spread	spread	spread
steal	stole	stolen
teach	taught	taught
throw	threw	thrown
weave	wove/weaved	woven/weaved

Action Verbs

Review: Some verbs show action. Examples: dribble, speak, throw

- A noun or pronoun that follows an action verb tells who or what receives the action. This noun is called a **direct object**. Example: Dr. King inspired many *people*. The noun *people* tells whom Dr. King inspired.

Linking Verbs

Review: Some verbs can act as main verbs or helping verbs. Forms of **be** belong to this group of verbs. Helping verbs combine with the main verb to form a verb phrase. The helping verb signals the time. Examples: He is playing basketball. The speech was inspiring the people. She will be investigating the idea.

- The verb **be** can also act as a **linking verb**. Linking verbs connect, or link, the subject of the sentence to a word in the predicate.

- A noun that follows a linking verb renames, or tells more about, the subject. This noun is called a **predicate nominative**. The subject and the predicate nominative name the same person, place, thing, or idea. Example: *Dr. King* **was** a *leader*. The verb **was** links the subject *Dr. King* to the noun *leader*.

- An adjective that follows a linking verb describes the subject. It is called a **predicate adjective**. Example: *Dr. King* was *inspiring*. The verb **was** links the adjective *inspiring* to the subject *Dr. King*.

Sentence Patterns

Form: N/LV/N   **noun/linking verb/noun**

Function: S/P/PN   **subject/predicate/predicate nominative**

Dr. King **was** a leader.

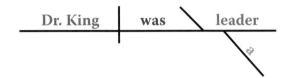

Form: N/LV/ADJ   **noun/linking verb/adjective**

Function: S/P/PA   **subject/predicate/predicate adjective**

Dr. King **was** inspiring.

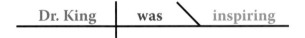

Form: N/V/N   **noun/verb/noun**

Function: S/P/DO   **subject/predicate/direct object**

Dr. King inspired many people.

Listening and Reading Comprehension

Informational Text

- Some informational text is nonfiction material about a specific topic, event, experience, or circumstance. It is typically found in content area text. Textbooks, biographies, and essays are examples of informational text.

- Much informational text is organized by main ideas and supporting details. **"Dreaming the Night Away"** provides an example of this type of text organization.

Vocabulary in Context

- **Context clues** help us understand new vocabulary. Pronoun referents, meaning signals, and visuals, such as charts and graphs, provide meaning links.

Signal Words

- To comprehend what we read and hear, we have to understand many different types of questions. Different types of questions can help us think about new information in different ways.

  Remember It questions ask us to recall information.
  Signal words: recognize, state, list, locate, choose, name, recall, retrieve, repeat, describe

  Understand It questions ask us to put facts together to build meaning. Answers to these questions require a new organization of information.
  Signal words: predict, conclude, illustrate, define in your own words, tell, summarize, paraphrase, identify, sort, classify, categorize, match, discuss, explain, compare, contrast

  Apply It questions ask us to use information or procedures. Answers to these questions must explain or use information to do something.
  Signal words: generalize, infer, use, show

  Analyze It questions ask us to break down information and see how the parts relate in patterns and structures. Answers to these questions require an organization of information to show the relationship of parts.
  Signal words: distinguish, select, organize, outline, arrange

Evaluate It questions ask us to make judgments based on criteria and standards.
Signal words: assess, justify, critique, judge

Create It questions ask us to put elements together to form a whole or to reorganize elements into a new pattern or product.
Signal words: plan, design, compose, hypothesize, revise

Refer to page A18 for a chart of the signal words for each type of question.

Literary Terms and Devices

📖 **Genres** are types or categories of literature. Unit 24 features the genre **fiction**. Fiction is based on a plot.

- **Fiction** is a literary genre that includes stories that are not true. Fiction is sometimes based on real people, places, or events. **"Dream Team"** is an example of fiction.

- **Plot** is a literary term referring to the pattern of events in a narrative or drama. **"Dream Team"** provides an example of plot development.

Plot Analysis

- **Plot** refers to a pattern of events in a narrative or drama. The plot guides the author in composing the work. It helps the reader follow the story.

- **Characters** and **setting** are two components of plot analysis. The characters, which can be people, animals, or things, take part in the story. The setting is the story's time and place. Together these two components make up the introduction in the plot's development.

- To understand how a plot develops, we must first identify a story's main **problem** and its **solution**.

- After we become proficient in identifying a story's main problem and solution, we will learn how a plot develops and apply plot development to our writing.

- Plot development usually consists of five elements: introduction (characters and setting), conflict (rising action), climax (turning point), resolution (falling action), and conclusion (the situation at the end of the story, with a possible look toward the future).

Speaking and Writing

Signal Words

- Some sentences ask for information. Other sentences require us to make judgments based on criteria and standards. They use specific **signal words**.

> **Sample Signal Words**
>
> **Explain** why dreams are unusual stories.
>
> **Justify** the author's concern about sleepwalking.
>
> **Hypothesize** why our muscles are immovable when we dream.

Paragraph Organization

- Some paragraphs are organized by **main ideas**. The content of these paragraphs includes the main idea, as well as supporting details. The supporting details provide examples, illustrations, and evidence for the main idea.

Plot Analysis

- Fiction includes characters created by the author. During prewriting, the author thinks about **character traits**. In good writing, each character must become distinct. Some character traits a writer may consider include: the character's personal appearance, personality, relationships with other characters, reactions to various situations, and means of coping with difficulties. Anything that distinguishes a character might be a character trait.

- Good writers usually include information about characters in the plot's introduction. This is because the reader needs to know the characters in order to follow the plot. Good writers can tell the reader about a character by including:

  A description of the character in simple narrative form;

  An incident during which the character interacts with others;

  A dialog in which the character is speaking to others.

More About Words

- **Bonus Words** use the same sound-spelling correspondences that we have studied in this unit and previous units.

- **Idioms** are common phrases that cannot be understood by the meanings of their separate words—only by the entire phrase.

- **Why? Word History** tells us about the origin of the word **nightmare**.

UNIT Bonus Words

abound	developed	impound	satellite
administer	diary	impulse	satire
arch	disloyal	indisposed	seeds
beagle	drizzle	jiggle	settled
bedspread	effect	jingle	shimmer
beginning	elements	juggle	slouch
bittersweet	empower	magazine	snuggle
bounty	entertainment	misinterpret	spleen
brownout	escrow	mucous	spreadsheet
bruise	establish	muffle	sprout
building	faculty	myrtle	standpoint
campground	feeble	nursery	stretch
candlestick	feeling	pity	sweatshirt
cape	fickle	popular	transfuse
capsule	fifteenth	porous	treadmill
card	forgetting	predispose	unplanned
carpetbagger	fowl	prominent	unsteady
clout	grader	repeated	usher
coil	griddle	reserved	valedictorian
cows	haste	reside	zenith
crumble	holy	retouch	
deploy	illegal	rubbish	

Idioms	
Idiom	**Meaning**
be a thorn in your side	be a constant annoyance or pain to you
be in the cards	be likely or certain to happen
live in a dream world	have unrealistic goals or expectations
make your toes curl	make you feel very embarrassed for someone; frighten or shock someone
stretch the rules	do something or allow someone to do something which is not usually allowed
stretch your legs	walk
throw a curve ball	surprise someone with something that is difficult or unpleasant to deal with
waste your breath	accomplish nothing after talking to someone
work like a dream	work very well
wouldn't dream of doing something	never do something because you think it is wrong or silly

 **Word History**

Nightmare—We all dream when we sleep, but sometimes we experience nightmares. We're not sure what causes these scary dreams, but we do know the history of the word **nightmare**. The first syllable is obvious—most of us do most of our sleeping at night. But what about the second syllable, *mare*?

In olden times, speakers of Old English used the word *mare* to mean "goblin." In Middle English, *nightmare* meant "a scary creature that pesters sleeping people." Today, we know that goblins don't exist, so the word no longer has that meaning. Instead, it means a dream that arouses fear, horror, or distress. We also use the word **nightmare** to describe an intensely distressing experience.

Dream While You Sleep

Sleep. Benjamin Franklin warned it could be a waste of time. Shakespeare disagreed. He called sleep the bath that heals the pains of work. He said that sleep soothes troubled minds. He called it the most nourishing food in life's feast.

5 It looks like Shakespeare was on the right track. Sleep is definitely not a waste of time. It's essential. We can't live without it. But it's not just the body that needs it. It's the brain!

During sleep, something fantastic happens. We dream. 10 Some people remember their dreams. Others say they never dream. But everybody does. We just don't always remember our dreams. Before we begin to understand dreams, though, we have to understand sleep.

What is Sleep?

What happens when we sleep? Our brains take a roller-15 coaster ride. Sleep has several stages. We cycle through these stages about four or five times per night. We drift. We sleep. We sleep deeply. We dream. We wake. We repeat the cycle.

The Stages of Sleep

Normally, we experience varying stages of sleep in several cycles during a typical night. During stages 1 through 4, sleep gets deeper. By the REM stage of sleep, our minds become more active.

Stage 1: We drift into slumber. We're in and out of sleep.

Stage 2: We are still easily awakened. But deep sleep is approaching.

Stage 3: Deep sleep has begun. We're difficult to wake now.

Stage 4: Sleep is deepest now. If we wake, we feel groggy. We're disoriented. Stages 3 and 4 heal the body. Wounds knit. The immune system goes to work.

REM Stage: Rapid eye movement, REM sleep, begins. Our eyelids are closed. But our eyes dart back and forth. Breathing is rapid. It's shallow. Our heart rates increase. Blood pressure rises.

The graph below represents how we cycle through the various stages of sleep in a typical eight-hour night.

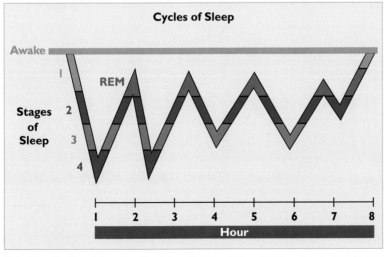

Color Key: ▪ = Stage 1 sleep ▪ = Stage 2 sleep ▪ = Stage 3 sleep ▪ = Stage 4 sleep ▪ = REM sleep
Source: http://faculty.washington.edu/chudler/sleep.html

What are Dreams?

Dreams can happen during any stage. But REM sleep is
40 prime time for dreaming.

During REM, the brain's nerve impulses increase.
The brain's logic centers take a nap. The limbic system
gets involved. Emotion and memory become active. The
"big sleep" of dreamtime happens in part of the brain's
45 cortex. The cortex controls logic. It controls planning
and sequential thinking. Maybe that's why dreams don't
make sense. And it's probably why our dreaming brains
don't care.

Shakespeare had it right. "Sleep," he wrote, "knits up
50 the raveled sleeve of care."

Adapted from "The Brain Never Sleeps," by Faith Hickman Brynie

"To sleep,
perchance to dream."

—William Shakespeare, 16th century playwright

Dreaming
the Night Away

by Judith Herbst

You have been asleep for perhaps an hour. Your muscles are relaxed. Your chest rises and falls with the slow, even rhythm of your breathing. There is a calm, almost angelic expression on your face. Silence and peace surround
5 you. The clock on your dresser ticks out the minutes to showtime. Four . . . three . . . two . . . one . . .

And suddenly the curtain is up! Your eyes are rolling back and forth, back and forth, back and forth behind your closed lids. This is it! This is REM, the amazing,
10 mysterious Rapid Eye Movement that signals a dream is in progress. You appear to be watching something, but your eyes are not looking at anything at all. Blind people also display REM.

REM begins quite early in our development as human
15 beings. It seems to be controlled by a part of the brain called the "pons," which is located in the brain stem. Research has shown that as soon as the brain stem develops in the fetus, there are signs of REM. So it looks as though we all start dreaming even before we're born, but what fetal
20 dreams are like is anybody's guess.

. . . back and forth, back and forth, back and forth . . .

This is the dance of REM. Somewhere deep inside your mind you are creating a little drama for an audience of one.

Your story, though, can hardly be called one of the year's
25 ten best. It's almost impossible to follow. The events are
confusing and disconnected. The characters come and go
for no apparent reason. The **dialogue** doesn't make any
sense. It's a mess, all right, but you don't seem to notice it.
On and on you dream, accepting even the most ridiculous
30 situations without question, thoroughly convinced that
it's all really happening. Furthermore, you are not just a
sleepy member of the audience, you're a participant, and
you react to everything that goes on. A frightening dream
in particular catches you like a hook, and you actually
35 experience fear.

OH MY GOSH! *You're in the back of a speeding car
and there's no driver! You try desperately to reach the
steering wheel, but you can't move. Crazily, the car swerves
off the road. The brake! You've got to reach the brake!*

40 Meanwhile, back in your bedroom, your heart is
thundering. Your breath is coming in quick, shallow bursts.
Beads of perspiration break out, soaking your pajamas and
pasting your hair to your forehead. Your blood pressure
has shot up, and the **adrenaline** is pumping, pumping,
45 pumping.

*Suddenly the car is on a high cliff. The speedometer
needle is climbing . . . 90 . . . 100 . . . 110 . . . You can see the
edge of the cliff just ahead. It's an endless drop to nowhere.
Do something! DO SOMETHING!*

50 Your terror in this dream is very real. You are not
pretending to be scared; you are scared, and all the
readouts in the sleep laboratories prove it. The readouts
also show something else. You are almost completely
paralyzed. With a few exceptions, your muscles have lost so
55 much tone, they are literally immovable. We do indeed toss
and turn and roll around quite a bit while we're sleeping
but not during a dream. During a dream we have about as
much ability to get up and walk around as our pillow does.
Scientists believe the purpose of this strange paralysis is to
60 prevent us from acting out our dreams.

dialogue

a conversation
between two or
more people

adrenaline

the hormone pro-
duced by the body
when frightened,
angry, or excited

Although sleepwalkers appear to be giving a dream performance, they are not. In fact, sleepwalkers are in an entirely different level of sleep. They are sound asleep but strangely **mobile**. No one knows why some people—
65 several million in North America alone—sleepwalk. This bizarre activity may begin at any time in a person's life and without any apparent cause. Sleepwalkers are completely unaware of what they are doing and usually remain ignorant unless they are told about it. And even then, they
70 will strenuously deny it. They'll insist they've been asleep all night, as, of course, they have. But while they've been snoozing upright, they have been involved in some very strange activities.

Like fleshy robots, they will suddenly open their eyes,
75 swing their legs over the side of the bed, and head off on some mysterious midnight errand. Talk to them and they won't answer. Wiggle your fingers in front of their eyes and they won't see you. They will, however, steer their way around furniture, take the dog for a walk, do their grocery
80 shopping, and even drive a car.

But sleepwalking is only funny in the cartoons. Some people have been injured during a walk because they managed to climb out onto window ledges thinking they were stepping onto the front porch. Members of the family
85 have been taken for intruders and attacked. It is a ridiculous myth that if you awaken a sleepwalker he or she will get lockjaw, die of a heart attack, or become paralyzed. The danger, instead, lies in what the sleepwalker is doing, since these people have been known to get themselves
90 into some pretty scary situations. Unfortunately, sleep-walking is as mysterious as dreaming, and science has not yet come up with a way to prevent a person from going on midnight strolls.

Of course, sleepwalkers dream, just like everybody else,
95 which makes for a pretty active night. They can return to bed, settle in, and slip easily into the next level of sleep. Before long, they are involved in more excitement, but this time their muscles are holding them prisoner. Now

mobile
capable of going from one place to another

Dr. Stephen La Berge.

phenomenon

a highly unusual
event

conscious

awake; alert; aware

illusion

a false thought
or idea

they have to be content to stay put while a whole series of
100 strange events unfolds before them in their dreams.

Sleep researcher Stephen La Berge has identified
something about our dreams that most of us experience
but few of us are aware of. La Berge calls the **phenomenon**
"lucid dreams." A lucid dream is one that you recognize as
105 a dream. You almost say to yourself, "Hey! Hold on, here.
This is a dream. All this stuff is fake. I'm dreaming!"

La Berge believes that once we know we are dreaming,
we have the ability to control the outcome of the dream on
a **conscious** level. We can change whatever we don't like.
110 He says he has learned to alter his dreams while he's asleep,
and he can teach others to do the same. But if dreams, as
they unfold naturally, are important in some way, perhaps
we shouldn't be fiddling with them. Perhaps we should let
nature take its course. Who knows? Maybe dreams are
115 serving a very definite purpose, whether we remember
them or not.

Dreams seem to be speeded-up versions of events, like
a movie run in fast forward, but actually, dreamtime often
parallels real time quite closely. If it takes you three seconds
120 to open a door in real time, that's how long it will take you
to open a door in your dream. The speed at which you do
things in a dream is only an **illusion**, because you edit the
scene. If you begin to walk across a bridge in your dream,
each step will match your waking steps, but you get to
125 the other side faster than normal because you have edited
out most of the steps. They are not necessary to the plot,
so to speak. That's why you are able to be in a wheat field
one minute and standing on a street corner the next. You
simply eliminate the travel time for the sake of the "real"
130 action.

You are also able to put your dream into slow motion.
You can slow down an attacking tiger to keep him from
grabbing you. If you're running through deep snow, you
can slow down the steps to make the event very frustrating.
135 Why you do this, however, is unclear, although it may have
to do with the purpose of the dream itself.

In our lifetime we will crank out about 125,000 dreams. No one knows why. . . . Most scientists today admit that dreams are far more complex bits of mind stuff than we

140 ever, well . . . than we ever dreamed. Nature has provided us with a truly bio amazing mechanism. Now, if we could just figure out what it's for. . . .

From *Bio Amazing: A Casebook of Unsolved Human Mysteries* by Judith Herbst

Answer It

1. The author compares dreams to stories. Explain why dreams are unusual stories.

2. Summarize what happens to our bodies when we dream.

3. Justify the author's concern about sleepwalking.

4. Assess why lucid dreaming is not necessarily a good thing.

5. Hypothesize why our muscles are immovable when we dream.

DREAM TEAM

by Ron Jones

*Based on a True Story

Every basketball coach hopes to encounter a "benny"
somewhere in their coaching career. A benny is one of
those special kids that come along once in a lifetime. A
kid that won't leave the gym until you've turned out the
5 lights and locked the door. And after it's locked will have
fourteen ways and nine friends ready to re-enter. They
possess all the natural skills and instincts of a great player.
A desire to work hard perfecting the most elementary
moves. And work even harder to help their teammates
10 experience success. Perhaps that's the invisible quality that
makes a benny. The unselfish willingness to share the art of
basketball with anyone that cares to listen or participate in
the game. Whatever that spirit is, it's the quality each coach
looks for. It's the thing to build around and learn from. It's
15 a winning season and perhaps a lot more.

At Cubberly High School in Palo Alto, where I was
basketball coach, the presence of a benny was extremely
unlikely. The students at Cubberly were white middle-class
children of professionally oriented parents. For the most
20 part, these kids mirrored their parents. They were striving

to become successful at something; what that something might be was never made clear. Without an objective in mind, the striving became all important. At Cubberly it meant getting in "advanced ability" groups, getting good
25 grades, getting accepted into a good university. Getting ahead. Getting through school. Getting. There was little time for intensity or giving to any one thing, especially a sport.

By a strange series of events it turned out I was wrong
30 about ever finding a benny at Cubberly. It started when school integration came to Palo Alto.[1] Black students volunteered to be bused across the freeway tracks. Cubberly High School as "host" school received its allotment of twenty-three "guest" students. As the basketball coach I
35 waited anxiously to see if any athletes might be a part of this transfer. Of course I was looking for a benny. Three days after the transfer students arrived I called the first basketball practice.

The turnout was excellent. Our basketball program had
40 been successful during the past few years and it gradually became known that if you turned out, you would get a chance to play. The prospect of gaining some new players from Ravenswood High School in East Palo Alto added to the tension and excitement of the first practice.

45 As the players came out onto the floor for the first time, I noted some familiar kids that had started on last year's team. In fluid movement they began the slow and graceful art of shooting their favorite shot. Dribbling a few steps and rearing up to take another shot. Rebounding
50 and passing out to a fellow player. Reliving past plays. Moving to the fantasy of future game-winning shots. Eyeing the new players.

At the baskets on each side of the central court the new players are assembled. They dribble the available
55 basketballs in place and watch the players moving on the center court. They don't talk much and look a little

---

[1] Until the 1960s, schools in many cities were segregated. In the early years of integration, students were often bused into different neighborhoods to achieve a better racial balance.

frightened. Then as if on cue they begin to turn and shoot at the available baskets. They too have a private shot and a move to the basket. Soon the entire gym is alive with
60 players outwitting invisible foes and arcing up game winning shots. Another season is beginning.

Midway into this first practice Cubberly High School basketball met Huey Williams. He came rushing into the gym. In fact he ran around the entire court three times. He
65 didn't have a basketball. He was just running. And smiling. Nodding his head to the dumbstruck players. He didn't speak a word. Just smiled and nodded hello. By his third lap, everyone knew we had our first black athlete.

Huey Williams wasn't exactly the transfer student
70 coaches dream about. He was short, about the shortest player on the club. With stocky frame and bowed legs and radar-like hair, he seemed like a bottle of soda water, always about to pop. His shots were explosions of energy that pushed the ball like a pellet. When he ran, he couldn't
75 stop. He'd race in for a layup and instead of gathering his momentum and softly placing the ball against the backboard, he raced straight ahead, full speed, ejecting the ball in midair flight like a plane letting go a rocket. The ball usually slammed against the backboard or rim and
80 careened across the gym. To say it simply, Huey was not a basketball player. He was something else.

Every player carries to the game a personality. That's part of what makes basketball so interesting. That personality is directly reflected in the way a person plays.
85 Now, Huey brought with him a personality I had never quite seen before. He loved life, people, school, anything and everything. "Mr. Jones, how are you today?" he'd say. "Fine I hope." You would have to agree with Huey. His view of the world was contagious. He always had a smile
90 that burst out when you least expected. "Mr. Jones, I didn't shoot too well did I?" He'd be smiling, getting ready to shoot again.

As the first black player on our team, Huey was well received. After all he didn't represent a threat to any of
95 the white players. If anything he was a puzzlement. How

could anyone try so hard, smile so much, and play so bad? Weren't all blacks supposed to be super athletes? How come he doesn't know his place, isn't solemn, and I like him?

You couldn't help but root for Huey and want to be around him. Carnegie and the make-you-feel-good folks could take lessons from Huey. He was a good human being that shared his optimism about life with anyone that ventured in his path. With a smile Huey started every practice with "We're going to win this whole thing, Mr. Jones. Just watch!"

I didn't share Huey's enthusiasm. It was the most unusual group of kids I had ever coached. In fact the team really constituted three distinct groups. Huey represented one of these groups. This was a collection of five kids who had never played before. They couldn't shoot or dribble, let alone jump. Passing was iffy. When they were on the court my greatest fear was that they might run into each other. Although lacking skill, they **personified** Huey's faith and willingness to work hard. My gosh how they tried.

A second group of kids on the team had all played together the past year. They were typical Palo Alto kids. I guess Chris Martin most exemplified the personality of this group. Chris was a class officer, good student, achievement oriented and serious about winning and of course playing. Chris just tolerated Huey and most everything else. His attention was on the future. Basketball at Cubberly was like the Pony League, Little League, and Junior League he had participated in so well. It was one more right step to some mythical big league called Hilton, or perhaps Standard Oil.

Chris knew all the lessons and skills of basketball. His jump shot was a picturebook example of perfection. He released the ball at the peak of his jump and followed through with his hands guiding the path of the ball as it slid into the basket. The closest parallel to Chris' behavior might be described as that of a little old man. He was "finicky" at the age of sixteen. If things weren't just right, his voice would stretch several octaves and literally squeak. For Chris things going just right meant a championship and of course a star role. I liked and felt sorry for Chris all

personified
described an object or idea as having human characteristics

at the same time. He reminded me of myself. A little selfish
135 and awfully conceited. Extremely insulated from feelings.

A third group of kids making up the team can best
be described as outlaws. Dave Warnock characterized
this group. Whereas Huey had a **reverence** for life and
Chris was busy controlling life, Dave seemed always on
140 guard and challenging the heck out of it. He was always in
trouble. Usually a team is composed of kids like Huey who
can't play and kids like Chris who have played throughout
childhood. Kids like Dave rarely show up on a team. To
have five kids like him on the same team was most unusual.
145 If not intolerable.

Dave's style of life and play was outside prediction.
Dave reminded me of a stork trying to play basketball.
His arms and legs flayed at the air as he stormed up and
down the court. His shots were what players call "watch
150 shots." He would crank up the ball without facing the
basket from some unexpected place and yet it would go
right in. Prompting the defensive player to say, "Look in the
other hand . . . you might find a watch." Dave was always
a surprise. A surprise if he showed up for practice and a
155 surprise that he stayed with it. In a strange way he was also
a breath of fresh air. He lived to the fullest. He didn't stop
to explain his actions. He just acted.

So there you have it. Not exactly a dream team.
Five kids charging around looking for the pass they just
160 dropped. Five kids straining for an expected championship.
And five kids who might not even show up for the game.
The entire team tilted on the verge of combustion. The kids
that centered around Chris and Dave openly hated each
other. Huey and his troop of warriors became the grease
165 that kept the team moving together. Happy and delighted
to be playing they were **oblivious** to the conflict. In their
constant attempt to mimic a Warnock pass or a Chris jump
shot they inevitably made the originals look ridiculous.
Huey with his intensity and honesty put everything in
170 perspective. It was simply impossible to get angry or serious
about yourself with Huey around. He had girlfriends to tell
you about, a cheer for a good play, a hand for someone who

reverence

great admiration;
respect

oblivious

unaware; not
noticing

had fallen, and a smile for everything. And if all that failed, he always had his "new shot" to show you.

175   It wasn't long before everyone was working to help Huey and the other inexperienced players. Chris was telling players about the right way to shoot. Dave was displaying one of his new trick passes. I was working hard to teach defense. If you don't have the ball, go get it. Don't wait for
180 someone to put it through the basket or even start a play. Go get the ball. Chase it. Surround it. Take it.

      We worked on how to press and trap a player with the ball. How to contest the inbound pass. Double team. Use the full court. Cut off the passing lane. Work together
185 with teammates to break over screens and sag into a help position. Work to keep midpoint vision. Block out. Experience the feeling of achievement without having the ball or scoring the winning point. Take pride in defense.

      The intensity and intricate working of defense was
190 something everyone on the team could do, and something new for everyone to learn. Defense is something most basketball teams just do not concentrate on. It's the unseen part of the game. Working hard on the techniques of team defense began to slowly draw the team together with a

195 common experience. As for offense, well, I taught the basic
passing pattern, but the shooting was up to whoever was on
the court. Chris and his group ran intricate patterns for the
layup or percentage shot. Dave with his team took the ball to
the hoop usually after three dribbles and a confederate yell.
200 Huey's team did their best just to get the ball up the court.

By the start of the season we had one spectacular
defense and three offenses. In fact I divided the team
into the three distinct groups. In this way everyone could
play. It confused the heck out of opponents. According to
205 basketball etiquette you're supposed to play your best five
players. We played our best fifteen. You are also supposed
to concentrate on scoring. We emphasized defense. Finally,
a good team has a mark of consistency. We were the most
inconsistent team you could imagine.

210 We would start each game with Huey's bunch. They
called themselves "the Reverends." With their **tenacity** for
losing the ball and swarming after it plus their complete
inability to shoot, they immobilized their opponents.
The starting fives they encountered couldn't believe the
215 intensity and madcaps of Huey's Reverends. By the time
they realized they were playing against all heart and very
little scoring potential, it was time to send in Chris' group.
Chris' team called themselves the "A Train." That they
were. They methodically moved down the floor, executed a
220 series of crisp passes, and scored. By this time in the game
Huey was smiling his all-knowing smile, and the coach
from the other team was usually looking over at our bench
in a state of confusion. Just as the other team adjusted
to systematic and disciplined play, we sent in Dave's "G
225 Strings." Dave's team played with reckless abandon. They
were always in places they weren't supposed to be. Doing
things that weren't in the book. Playing their game.

By the middle of the season we were undefeated. Oh, I
had to suspend Dave for breaking rules in the locker room
230 and once for smuggling a girl onto the travel bus. And
on occasion I had to remind Chris that I was the coach,
not him. But all in all the team was actually becoming
friends. It was a joy to witness this chemistry. Huey's group

tenacity

determination;
persistence

gradually improved. They started believing they could
235 beat anyone. The basketball still didn't go in the basket,
but in their minds and actions they were "starters." As
for Chris, he was actually beginning to yell for someone
besides himself. And Dave, well he didn't change much
in an outward way. He was still frantic on the basketball
240 court. It was off the court that he was becoming a little less
defensive. He started telling me of things he wanted in life.
Things not that much different than those securities and
accomplishments sought by others. In fact it was something
as simple as friendship.

245   Our first defeat of the year came not on the basketball
court but at the hands of the school superintendent. With
twelve games already played, the superintendent declared
that all transfer students were **ineligible** for interscholastic
sports. It was a knee-jerk reaction to other coaches in
250 the league who feared we might "raid" Ravenswood High
School of its top black athletes. No one worried about us
stealing away their intelligent students or class leaders, yet
that's just what we did. No one thought to ask the students
and parents how they felt. This was a coaches' decision.
255 Coaches who thought only about winning.

    The superintendent ordered Huey off the team
immediately. The announcement of this decision came
not in a telephone call or personal visit, but in a ten
word directive. "No transfer students will be eligible for
260 interscholastic athletic teams."

    The announcement came on a game day. The team was
already suited up waiting for the last minute game plan. I
read the superintendent's decision to the team. They were
stunned. And angry. Ideas and plots for Huey's survival
265 rang out against the white-tiled dressing room walls. Dave
slammed his shoe against a locker. "It's a bad decision."
Chris agreed. "We can appeal . . . let's go to the board
of education." Dave snapped. "When—in three weeks?"
Everyone joined the argument. "Let's give Huey a new
270 number." Yeah, but can we also change his color?" "We can
play against ourself . . . can't we?" "Let's make up our own
league." In the din my own thoughts were welling up.

ineligible
disqualified; cannot
participate

I didn't know when I started verbalizing my feelings, but I became aware of it as my whispers all of a sudden
275 were audible in the now silent locker room. As my personal decision became clearer so did my pronouncement of it. "Huey's dismissal is wrong. It's unfair to defer the decision or obey it. I think we should forfeit all our remaining games. Huey is a part of this team. If you are willing to
280 give other teams an automatic win over us in exchange for having Huey play . . . raise your hand." Fifteen players leaped to their feet. Dave was yelling, "Well, all right then, we've got a game to play!" It was unanimous.

The players streamed onto the floor to begin their
285 warm up. I could hear a few rebel yells and even that high pitched squeak of Chris'. Huey still brought gasps of surprise with his high velocity layup. When he did his latest new shot, a sweeping, running hook, the assembled fans roared approval. Huey grinned and promised more.
290 As the players finished their warmup, the school principal came by to remind me of the superintendent's decision. "Ron," he said, "I'm sorry about Huey, but he hasn't scored many points for you has he?" "No," I replied, "Huey hasn't scored a point." "Things will be different next year," he
295 confided. I agreed.

As the game was about to start they huddled for final instructions. "Any after-thoughts?" I asked. "There is still time." We were all bundled together in a knot. Hands thrust together in a tight clasp. Everyone looked up. Eyes
300 all met. Every single kid was smiling. My gosh, I've got fifteen Hueys.

The horn sounded calling for the game to start. I took the entire team to the scoring desk and informed the league official. "We formally forfeit this game." The opposing
305 coach from Gunn High School rushed over to see what the commotion was about. "What are you doing?" he asked. I told him of our decision. "That doesn't make sense. You guys are undefeated," he stammered. "We let two of *our* players go today." "It's our decision," I explained. "We're
310 here to play basketball, all of us."

And we did. All of us. Huey did his patented dash.
Chris his jump shot while Dave relied on surprise. It was
a combination hard to beat. We poured in twenty more
points than Gunn and, more importantly, displayed a
315 constant hustle. Players ran to shoot free throws. Ran
to take a place in the game. Ran off the floor on being
replaced. It reminded me of that first practice with this
strange kid running around the gym. Perhaps we had
learned more from Huey than we taught. At the close
320 of the game the Gunn coach stopped to comment,
"Congratulations, you've got quite a team there." I reminded
him that we had forfeited the game, that his team had won.
He turned, "No, your kids won. They're a bunch of bennys."
　　Dave Warnock was dead. Chris brought the message
325 to me. His father was a school official and he heard of
the news from the police. Dave had been at a party and
suffocated inhaling hair spray. Like a tape recorder erasing
its content I couldn't think or act. Then in forced flashes
I began to retread the past days. Searching for glimpses of
330 Dave. His face. His antics. Was there something there? A
warning? A plea? What did I miss?
　　The school community for the most part remained
ignorant of Dave's death and its self-destructive cause.
There were faculty murmurs, "That crazy kid." Other than
335 side glances at what had happened there was no marking
of Dave's death. Drugs and death are not part of the
curriculum. It was improper to alarm parents. The school
didn't stop its parade. Even for a moment of respect or
some such other platitude. Nothing. Everything as usual.
340 Including basketball.
　　The team gathered for practice out of habit. The season
actually had only a few days left. It had been a corrugated
course. Our protest to allow Huey the right to play had
sparked a boycott of all team sports. The boycott led to
345 a change in the rules allowing transfer students to play
with the condition that "due to the disruptions" no league
championship would be awarded. It was ok with us. We
declared ourselves champions. Actually it was Dave's idea.

Oh man, it didn't seem fair. Dave was a storm. He kicked
350 and dared the world. And lost. Or did he? I don't know.

One good thing about sports is that you can lose
yourself in physical exertion. Push yourself into fatigue. Let
the body take over the crying in the brain. I informed the
team that this would be our last practice. We would have a
355 game, full court scrimmage.

It was then that I realized Dave wasn't there. It's funny,
Dave was dead yet I expected him to come prancing into
the gym, the final trick on death itself.

Being short one player I joined in the scrimmage.
360 First Chris' bunch against Huey's team and then Dave's
group to play Chris'. I stood in for Dave. The play was
strangely conservative and sluggish. Perhaps this measured
play was in deference to Dave. Were we all letting our
thoughts wander? Just doing mechanical steps? Or was it a
365 subconscious statement that Dave's life was errant and not
to be **emulated**? Whatever, the play moved from one end
of the gym to the other like the arm of a ticking clock. Up
and down the floor.

It was Chris that broke the rhythm and silence.
370 Without warning he sliced across the floor, stole a pass,
dribbled the length of the court and slam dunked. Then
in an unexpected leap he stole the inbound pass. Taking
the ball in one hand he pivoted up a crazy sweeping hook
shot. It was a "watch shot" if I'd ever seen one. Out of the
375 blue as the ball cut through the net Chris erupted with a
shrill guttural yell that pierced the stillness. It was a signal.
The game tempo picked up, and became frantic. Everyone
pushed to their maximum. Straining for that extra effort.
Hawking the ball. Diving for a loose ball. Blowing tension.
380 Playing with relaxed abandon.

It felt wonderful. The game was fierce. Everything
learned in years of play was used. New moves were tried.
I crashed for a rebound, dived, elbows flying after a loose
ball and got it. Sprinted full tilt on a fast break. Yelled full
385 voice as I fed Huey with a behind-the-back pass that he
laid up for two. Everyone is moving as if driven by some

emulated

imitated

accelerating spell of power and will. Everything goes in. We can play forever. Play Forever.

The scrimmage raged on. The afternoon became
390 evening and still we played. The gym glowed in the yellow light, warm and wet. We were racing now back and forth. Exploding for shots. Playing the toughest defense. Jumping over a screen. Blocking out. Back for one more sensation of excellence.

395 My chest heaved for relief. Body throbbed. I couldn't stop playing. And didn't want to. Didn't Want To. Down the court. Set up. That's it. Feed the cutter. Fantastic. Now the defense. Keep low. No. Take it away. That's it. Steal the ball. Now go. Fly.

400 In a heap I collapsed. Legs simply buckled. I was shaking. Head not able to move. In slow motion the team centered around my crumpled form. I'm all right. The air is rushing back into an empty body. Giving life and movement. "I'm all right." Everyone is breathing hard,
405 pushing out air and taking it back in. Grabbing their knees and doubling over. Letting the body know it can rest.

Without any words everyone gathered themselves, then silently headed for the locker room and home. It's over. The scrimmage was ended. Practice finished. The season
410 complete.

I slowly shower and dress, waiting for the locker room to empty. Walking through the silenced place I stop to look and say goodbye. There is Chris' locker. A good kid. Hope his life goes well. He has changed and matured. Been a part
415 of other lives. Huey's locker is still open. Gosh, even his locker has a smile. What a person. I'll never forget. Dave's place. Empty. I hate you for leaving us. I love you.

I push up a twenty-five foot jump shot that is five feet beyond my range. It goes in. Rush to chase the ball. Try
420 again. Seek the magnificent feeling of doing the undone. The unplanned. The unexpected.

There is a sign that hangs over the exit from the locker room. It reads, "There Is No Substitute For Winning." Someone scratched out the word winning and replaced it.
425 "There Is No Substitute For Madness."

Adapted from "Winning" by Ron Jones

Answer It

1. What is a "benny"?

2. Describe the events that led Huey to attend Cubberly High School.

3. Justify the team's decision to forfeit the game.

4. Assess how Chris changed throughout the course of the story.

5. What was the coach's dream? Did it come true?

Pursuit *of a* Dream

The Dream

A woman stood over a developing tray. Gradually, black spots appeared in the shape of an X. Dr. Rosalind Franklin, an X-ray **crystallographer**, held the mystery of DNA in her hands. Yet, she didn't see it—not yet. She couldn't
5 know that it would lead to a Nobel Prize. A scientist, she was **methodical** in her experiments; she was confident that eventually the truth would become clear. This was her work. This was her dream.

In 1952, it was known that physical characteristics
10 were inherited. It was known that a genetic code was responsible for specific characteristics, such as the color of a child's eyes or the short tail of a Manx cat. It was strongly suspected that the code would be found buried in the molecule called DNA, or deoxyribonucleic acid. Yet no
15 one knew this with certainty because no scientist had yet unlocked the structure of DNA. What did the molecule look like? How was it organized? Once its structure was identified, a mystery would be solved. Many scientists dreamed of finding the structure of DNA. DNA's structure
20 held the keys to larger mysteries. It could potentially unlock the cause of hereditary diseases. But the story of the search for the structure of DNA became a mystery in itself, and Rosalind Franklin was one of the players in that mystery.

Oil and Water

Rosalind Franklin worked at King's College in London.
25 Franklin, an Englishwoman, was known for her success in using X-ray crystallography. The method uses X-rays to photograph molecules. Franklin had been hired to apply her method to the structure of DNA.

crystallographer
a person who studies the formation and structure of crystals

methodical
systematic; careful; in a step-by-step manner

Dr. Rosalind Franklin.

Maurice Wilkins, a British biophysicist who had begun
30 X-ray work on DNA, had been traveling when Franklin
arrived. He may have expected to **supervise** Franklin's
work, but she had assumed that she would be working
independently. She was a highly respected scientist who
had developed her own techniques. Franklin and Wilkins
35 quickly came to dislike one another. **Collaboration**
became impossible.

Rosalind Franklin wasn't afraid to argue. She was an
assertive woman who stood up for herself. Before arriving
in London, she had spent time at a lab in Paris where her
40 argumentative style was accepted and she got along well
with her colleagues.

In England, however, her frankness isolated her.
Though they came from similar backgrounds, Wilkins
and Franklin had somewhat opposite natures. He spoke
45 quietly and responded to her not with argument, but
with silence. The two were like oil and water. She kept to
herself; he interacted with others. Wilkins shared ideas
with other colleagues at King's College and with scientists
in Cambridge. Eventually, his decision to share Rosalind
50 Franklin's work—without her permission—would give him
a huge advantage.

Collaboration at Cavendish

Eighty kilometers away, at Cavendish Laboratory in
Cambridge, American scientist James Watson had begun
work with Francis Crick, a graduate student. They believed
55 that the Nobel Prize would belong to the first group to
publish the DNA structure, so they were determined to use
every available piece of information to help them build a
molecular model.

This is what they knew: It was a long molecule made
60 up of building blocks called nucleotides. The nucleotides
contained a sugar, a phosphate, and a base. The nucleotides
were probably combined in such a way that part of them
formed a backbone for support. Four different bases were
present: there were two purines, adenine and guanine,
65 and two pyrimidines, thymine and cytosine—called A, G,

T, and C, for short. They knew that these four bases were
flat molecules, and they learned from Austrian biochemist
Erwin Chargaff that the number of As was equal to the
number of Ts and that the number of Cs was equal to the
70 number of Gs. But they didn't know how all these pieces fit
together. What was the structure of the DNA molecule?

Clues from Crystallography

Rosalind Franklin's work began to expose many clues.
In November 1951, Watson attended a seminar during
which Franklin described her latest findings. Watson
75 didn't bother to take notes, but based upon what Watson
thought he had heard Franklin say at the seminar, he and
Crick rushed to produce a DNA model. Franklin, with the
group from King's College, went to Cavendish to look at
their model. She was quick to point out their errors. This
80 incident confirmed Franklin's conviction that guesswork
was no substitute for hard work.

Franklin continued her experiments by mounting a
piece of DNA on a platform and pointing a beam of X-rays
at it. When X-rays hit atoms in a molecule, they bounce
85 back. Atoms in crystalline material are arranged in regular
patterns, so when X-rays bounce back, they do so in regular,
predictable ways. They provide information about the
molecule's structure that is called a "diffraction pattern." It
can be captured on photographic paper, but X-rays are used
90 instead of visible light. X-rays are smaller than
the molecules, whereas the wavelength of visible
light is longer than molecules. Trying to see
molecules with visible light would be like trying
to measure a flea's leg with a yardstick!
95 Franklin worked with two forms of DNA,
which she called the A and B forms. Through
her photos, she had been the first to show that
there were two forms of DNA. The A form was
drier, and more crystalline. It gave more distinct
100 patterns than the B form, which was created
when she moistened the DNA and spun it into a thin fiber.
This gave a cloudier picture, but the spots were arranged

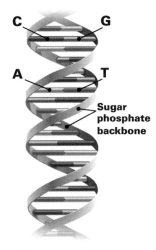

The structure of DNA resembles a twisted ladder.

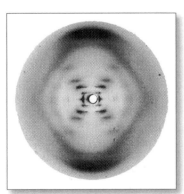

Rosalind Franklin's photograph of the B form of DNA.

in simpler patterns that were easier to interpret. It was Franklin's intention to learn as much as she could from the

105 A form first, before turning her attention to the B form.

At the end of February 1953, James Watson paid a visit to Maurice Wilkins. Watson wanted to get the latest news on Rosalind Franklin's work, and Wilkins showed him what he had obtained from Franklin a few days before, her photo

110 #51. Franklin had developed this photograph of the B form months earlier. Its X-shaped lines of spots spoke eloquently of a **helical** molecule, which Franklin clearly understood. However, because the A form didn't seem to show this pattern, she didn't want to draw conclusions until she had

115 done more work.

The moment he saw the photograph, Watson realized that Franklin had identified the missing piece of the puzzle. He took her findings back to his own lab. Using cardboard cutouts and metal rods, Watson and Crick built their model

120 and cracked the code. With its complementary double strands forming the sides of a twisting ladder, and its flat, tightly packed bases

125 forming the rungs, here was a molecule whose simplicity and **elegance** were worthy of its

130 function.

helical

spiral; circular

elegance

precision; neat, simple design

James Watson and Francis Crick with their DNA model.

Rosalind Franklin went to view the model. As a scientist, she took great pleasure in the beauty of the structural truth of DNA. She showed no disappointment because to her, it had been about the process of discovery.

135   Shortly afterward, Rosalind Franklin moved to Birkbeck College in London. Five years later, in 1958, she died of cancer at the age of 37. She never knew that Wilkins had shown Watson her photo. She never knew that it had been used by Watson and Crick to construct their model.

140   In 1962, four years after her death, the Nobel Prize was awarded for discovery of the structure of DNA. The Nobel Prize is not awarded to someone who has died or to more than three people for one discovery. Watson thought Franklin would have been included in the prize instead of

145 Wilkins if she had lived. The prize instead went to James Watson, Francis Crick, and Maurice Wilkins.

Adapted from "Out of Her Hands: The Woman Who Didn't Win the Nobel Prize" by Barbara Eaglesham

Think About It

1. In 1952, what aspect of DNA remained a mystery?

2. Describe some characteristics of Rosalind Franklin.

3. Explain how Maurice Wilkins helped Watson and Crick make the first accurate model of DNA's structure.

4. Who won a Nobel Prize for discovering the structure of DNA?

5. Do you think that Maurice Wilkins's actions were ethical? Why or why not?

6. Assess the author's point of view regarding the accomplishments of Watson and Crick.

Martin Luther King, Jr.:
The Freedom Dreamer

Martin Luther King, Jr., grew up in Atlanta, Georgia. Highly motivated, King worked hard at school. He skipped two grades and enrolled at Morehouse College at age 15. From Morehouse, he went to Crozer Theological Seminary.

5 He became a minister like his father and grandfather before him. Dr. King went on to head a congregation in Montgomery, Alabama.

In 1955, King gained national recognition. He employed nonviolent methods in the Montgomery Bus **Boycott**.

10 He led the Montgomery Improvement Association. The group had been formed to publicize and raise money to support the boycott. He took this opportunity to practice the principles of nonviolent protest. Gandhi had used nonviolent protest. It had helped win India's independence

15 from Great Britain in the 1940s. King had dreamed about the possibility of using Gandhi's "soul force." It was a way to attack racial segregation. King had the conviction and ability to inspire others. Many joined him. The peaceful boycott, under his guidance, changed the law that had

20 required African Americans to ride in the backs of buses.

After the success of the Montgomery Bus Boycott, Dr. King continued to use nonviolence. His efforts changed other discriminatory laws. Dr. King urged African Americans to use nonviolent sit-ins. They conducted

25 marches, demonstrations, and freedom rides. Their efforts

Boycott
the refusal to do business with a company

won greater freedom and equality. Dr. King was arrested for breaking discriminatory laws. He went to jail many times. He became a symbol around the world.

Others followed his example by protesting peacefully
30 and successfully against unjust laws. Churches formed the center of the African American community. It was no accident that black ministers stood at the forefront of the civil rights movement. Among them, King stood out. He was a brilliant **orator**. He held a strong belief that
35 Americans had a basic sense of decency. He believed they would respond to nonviolent protests. He understood the sheer force of moral right. He inspired others to follow him.

orator
a skilled public speaker

His movement had far-reaching success. Martin Luther King, Jr., spoke to television cameras as effectively
40 as to church congregations. Thousands of people—black and white, young and old, educated and uneducated— responded to his call. They risked losing their jobs, their homes, and their lives in the civil rights struggle. They looked to him as an inspiration. He became their beacon of
45 hope for a brighter future.

In the summer of 1963, King helped plan the March on Washington. About 250,000 people came to Washington to support civil rights legislation and the end of racial segregation in public schools. During the march, King
50 touched the heart of the nation. His "I Have a Dream" speech is now recognized as a classic. It is as esteemed as other famous speeches such as Lincoln's Gettysburg Address.

Time magazine named Dr. King the "Man of the Year"
55 for 1963. A few months later, the international community recognized his contributions to history. He won the Nobel Peace Prize. Martin Luther King was assassinated in 1968, but his legacy lives on. Each January, a national holiday honors the influence he exerted during this crucial time
60 in history.

The following is Dr. King's "I Have a Dream" speech. It was delivered August 28, 1963. Dr. King spoke on the steps of the Lincoln Memorial in front of a huge crowd during the March on Washington.

65   I am happy to join with you today in what will go down in history as the greatest demonstration for freedom in the history of our nation.

    Five score years ago, a great American, in whose symbolic shadow we stand today, signed the Emancipation
70 Proclamation. This momentous decree came as a great beacon light of hope to millions of Negro slaves who had been seared in the flames of withering injustice. It came as a joyous daybreak to end the long night of their captivity.

    But 100 years later, the Negro still is not free. One
75 hundred years later, the life of the Negro is still sadly crippled by the manacles of segregation and the chains of discrimination. One hundred years later, the Negro lives on a lonely island of poverty in the midst of a vast ocean of material prosperity. One hundred years later, the Negro
80 is still languished in the corners of American society and finds himself an exile in his own land. And so we've come here today to dramatize a shameful condition.

    In a sense we've come to our nation's capital to cash a check. When the architects of our republic wrote the
85 magnificent words of the Constitution and the Declaration of Independence, they were signing a promissory note to which every American was to fall heir. This note was a promise that all men—yes, black men as well as white men—would be guaranteed the unalienable rights of life,
90 liberty, and the pursuit of happiness.

    It is obvious today that America has defaulted on this promissory note insofar as her citizens of color are concerned. Instead of honoring this sacred obligation, America has given the Negro people a bad check, a check
95 that has come back marked "insufficient funds."

    But we refuse to believe that the bank of justice is bankrupt. We refuse to believe that there are insufficient funds in the great vaults of opportunity of this nation. And so we've come to cash this check, a check that will

100 give us upon demand the riches of freedom and security
of justice. We have also come to this hallowed spot to
remind America of the fierce urgency of now. This is no
time to engage in the luxury of cooling off or to take the
tranquilizing drug of **gradualism**. Now is the time to
105 make real the promises of democracy. Now is the time to
rise from the dark and desolate valley of segregation to
the sunlit path of racial justice. Now is the time to lift our
nation from the quicksands of racial injustice to the solid
rock of brotherhood. Now is the time to make justice a
110 reality for all of God's children.

It would be fatal for the nation to overlook the urgency
of the moment. This sweltering summer of the Negro's
legitimate discontent will not pass until there is an
invigorating autumn of freedom and equality. Nineteen
115 sixty-three is not an end but a beginning. Those who
hoped that the Negro needed to blow off steam and will
now be **content** will have a rude awakening if the nation
returns to business as usual. There will be neither rest
nor tranquility in America until the Negro is granted his
120 citizenship rights. The whirlwinds of revolt will continue to
shake the foundations of our nation until the bright day of
justice emerges.

But there is something that I must say to my people
who stand on the warm threshold which leads into the
125 palace of justice. In the process of gaining our rightful
place we must not be guilty of wrongful deeds. Let us not
seek to satisfy our thirst for freedom by drinking from the
cup of bitterness and hatred. We must forever conduct
our struggle on the high plane of dignity and discipline.
130 We must not allow our creative protest to degenerate
into physical violence. Again and again we must rise to
the majestic heights of meeting physical force with soul
force. The marvelous new militancy which has engulfed
the Negro community must not lead us to a distrust of all

gradualism
the practice of
reaching a desired
result by making
slow and small
steps

content
satisfied; pleased

135 white people, for many of our white brothers, as evidenced by their presence here today, have come to realize that their destiny is tied up with our destiny. And they have come to realize that their freedom is inextricably bound to our freedom. We cannot walk alone.

140   And as we walk, we must make the pledge that we shall always march ahead. We cannot turn back. There are those who are asking the devotees of civil rights, "When will you be satisfied?" We can never be satisfied as long as the Negro is the victim of the unspeakable horrors of police

145 brutality. We can never be satisfied as long as our bodies, heavy with the fatigue of travel, cannot gain lodging in the motels of the highways and the hotels of the cities. We cannot be satisfied as long as the Negro's basic mobility is from a smaller ghetto to a larger one. We can never

150 be satisfied as long as our children are stripped of their selfhood and robbed of their dignity by signs stating "for whites only." We cannot be satisfied as long as a Negro in Mississippi cannot vote and a Negro in New York believes he has nothing for which to vote. No, no we are not

155 satisfied and we will not be satisfied until justice rolls down like waters and righteousness like a mighty stream.

   I am not unmindful that some of you have come here out of great trials and tribulations. Some of you have come fresh from narrow jail cells. Some of you have come from

160 areas where your quest for freedom left you battered by storms of persecution and staggered by the winds of police brutality. You have been the veterans of creative suffering. Continue to work with the faith that unearned suffering is redemptive.

165   Go back to Mississippi, go back to Alabama, go back to South Carolina, go back to Georgia, go back to Louisiana, go back to the slums and ghettos of our northern cities, knowing that somehow this situation can and will be changed.

170   Let us not wallow in the valley of despair. I say to you today my friends—so even though we face the difficulties of today and tomorrow, I still have a dream. It is a dream deeply rooted in the American dream.

I have a dream that one day this nation will rise up
175 and live out the true meaning of its **creed**: "We hold these
truths to be self-evident, that all men are created equal."

I have a dream that one day on the red hills of Georgia
the sons of former slaves and the sons of former slave
owners will be able to sit down together at the table of
180 brotherhood.

I have a dream that one day even the state of
Mississippi, a state sweltering with the heat of injustice,
sweltering with the heat of oppression, will be transformed
into an oasis of freedom and justice.

I have a dream that my four little children will one day
185 live in a nation where they will not be judged by the color of
their skin but by the **content** of their character.

I have a dream today.

I have a dream that one day down in Alabama, with its
vicious racists, with its governor having his lips dripping
190 with the words of interposition and nullification—one day
right there in Alabama little black boys and black girls will
be able to join hands with little white boys and white girls
as sisters and brothers.

I have a dream today.

195 I have a dream that one day every valley shall be
exalted, and every hill and mountain shall be made low,
the rough places will be made plain, and the crooked places
will be made straight, and the glory of the Lord shall be
revealed and all flesh shall see it together.

200 This is our hope. This is the faith that I go back to the
South with. With this faith we will be able to hew out of
the mountain of despair a stone of hope. With this faith
we will be able to transform the jangling discords of our
nation into a beautiful symphony of brotherhood. With
205 this faith we will be able to work together, to pray together,
to struggle together, to go to jail together, to stand up for
freedom together, knowing that we will be free one day.

This will be the day, this will be the day when all of
God's children will be able to sing with new meaning "My
210 country 'tis of thee, sweet land of liberty, of thee I sing.

Land where my fathers died, land of the Pilgrim's pride, from every mountainside, let freedom ring!"

And if America is to be a great nation, this must become true. And so let freedom ring from the prodigious
215 hilltops of New Hampshire. Let freedom ring from the mighty mountains of New York. Let freedom ring from the heightening Alleghenies of Pennsylvania.

Let freedom ring from the snow-capped Rockies of Colorado. Let freedom ring from the curvaceous slopes of
220 California.

But not only that; let freedom ring from Stone Mountain of Georgia.

Let freedom ring from Lookout Mountain of Tennessee.

Let freedom ring from every hill and molehill of
225 Mississippi—from every mountainside.

Let freedom ring. And when this happens, and when we allow freedom to ring—when we let it ring from every village and every hamlet, from every state and every city, we will be able to speed up that day when all of God's
230 children—black men and white men, Jews and Gentiles, Protestants and Catholics—will be able to join hands and sing in the words of the old Negro spiritual: "Free at last! Free at last! Thank God Almighty, we are free at last!"

Adapted from "1929–1968 Timely Leader" by Jim Haskins;
"Five Leaders of Freedom" by Peter Roop; and "To the
Promised Land: The Civil Rights Years" by Sylvia Whitman

Think About It

1. Explain the meaning of the term "soul force" used in lines 16 and 132–133.

2. Describe how Dr. King worked to change discriminatory laws.

3. According to Dr. King, list what the Constitution guarantees Americans. (Lines 89–90)

4. Explain what Dr. King meant when he said, "Let us not seek to satisfy our thirst for freedom by drinking from the cup of bitterness and hatred."

5. Describe the dream that Dr. King had for his own four children.

6. Discuss the purpose of Dr. King's speech.

Appendix

English Consonant Chart

(Note the voiceless/voiced consonant phoneme pairs)

Mouth Position

Type of Consonant Sound	Bilabial (lips)	Labiodental (lips/teeth)	Dental (tongue between teeth)	Alveolar (tongue behind teeth)	Palatal (roof of mouth)	Velar (back of mouth)	Glottal (throat)
Stops	/p/ /b/			/t/ /d/		/k/ /g/	
Fricatives		/f/ /v/	/th/ /<u>th</u>/	/s/ /z/	/sh/ /zh/		/h/[1]
Affricatives					/ch/ /j/		
Nasals	/m/			/n/		/ng/	
Lateral				/l/			
Semivowels	/ʰw/ /w/[2]			/r/	/y/		

1   Classed as a fricative on the basis of acoustic effect. It is like a vowel without voice.

2   /ʰw/ and /w/ are velar as well as bilabial, as the back of the tongue is raised as it is for /u/.

Adapted with permission from Bolinger, D. 1975. *Aspects of Language* (2nd ed.). Harcourt Brace Jovanovich, p. 41.

English Vowel Chart

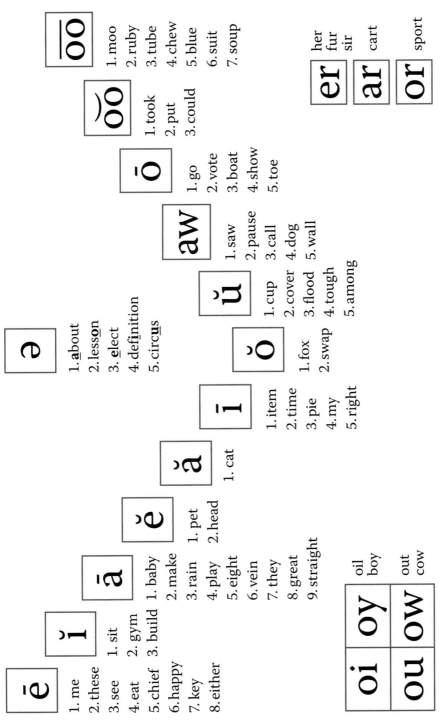

ē
1. me
2. these
3. see
4. eat
5. chief
6. happy
7. key
8. either

ĭ
1. sit
2. gym
3. build

ā
1. baby
2. make
3. rain
4. play
5. eight
6. vein
7. they
8. great
9. straight

ĕ
1. pet
2. head

ă
1. cat

ī
1. item
2. time
3. pie
4. my
5. right

ə
1. about
2. lesson
3. elect
4. definition
5. circus

ŏ
1. fox
2. swap

ŭ
1. cup
2. cover
3. flood
4. tough
5. among

aw
1. saw
2. pause
3. call
4. dog
5. wall

ō
1. go
2. vote
3. boat
4. show
5. toe

o͞o
1. moo
2. ruby
3. tube
4. chew
5. blue
6. suit
7. soup

o͝o
1. took
2. put
3. could

er
her
fur
sir

ar
cart

or
sport

oi
oil

oy
boy

ou
out

ow
cow

Note: The order of spelling examples reflects the relative frequency of incidence for that spelling of the phoneme.

Vowel Chart based on Moats, L.C. (2003). *LETRS: Language Essentials for Teachers of Reading and Spelling,* Module 2 (p. 98). Adapted with permission of the author. All rights reserved. Published by Sopris West Educational Services.

abandon	ambiguous	attend	believe	break
able	among	attract	below	breakfast
abound	amount	avail	beneath	breastbone
abroad	ample	avoid	benefit	breath
account	amuse	await	between	breathe
accurate	analyze	away	bias	breeze
accuse	android	axle	bible	bridle
accustom	angle	babble	birdhouse	brief
achieve	animal	bacon	birthday	bristle
address	ankle	bait	bitter	brittle
adequate	annoy	banana	bittersweet	broil
adjoin	annual	barley	bleed	brow
adjust	anoint	barnacle	blouse	brown
administer	anthropoid	battle	blow	brownout
administrator	anyhow	battlefield	boast	browse
admire	apart	battleground	boat	bruise
adroit	appeal	bay	boggle	bubble
advocate	apple	beach	boil	buckle
afford	appoint	beagle	borrow	buffalo
afraid	approach	beak	bottle	bugle
against	arch	beam	bound	build
aggregate	around	bean	boundary	building
agony	arouse	beast	bounty	buildup
agree	arrest	beat	bout	built
ahead	article	beautiful	bow / $b\bar{o}$ /	bundle
aid	ashamed	beauty	bow / bou /	business
ail	aside	beaver	bowl	busy
aim	asleep	bedspread	bow-wow	cable
alarm	assemble	bee	boy	calendar
alike	asteroid	beech	boycott	callous
alley	astonish	beef	braid	camel
allocate	astound	beetle	braille	camera
allow	atomic	beginning	brain	campground
aloud	attain	belief	bread	canal

candle	coat	correspond	curse	details
candlestick	coax	couch	curtain	determine
cape	cocoa	counselor	curve	developed
capitol	coddle	count	custom	devoid
capsule	coffee	countdown	cuticle	devour
captain	coil	counterpoint	daily	dial
carbon	coin	country	daisy	diamond
card	collapse	countryside	dangle	diary
carpenter	colleague	county	day	die
carpetbagger	colony	couple	daytime	died
cattle	combine	couplet	dazzle	diesel
chain	comfort	courage	dead	different
charbroil	compensate	course	deaf	difficult
charcoal	compete	cousin	deal	dimple
cheap	complain	cow	dealt	dinner
cheat	component	coward	death	disappoint
checkpoint	compound	cower	debt	discreet
cheek	compromise	cows	decay	disease
cheese	concurrent	coy	decoy	disgruntle
chief	confer	crackle	decrease	disloyal
chimney	confine	cradle	decree	display
chow	conform	crayon	deed	doe
chowder	confuse	cream	deep	doghouse
chuckle	conjoin	creek	defeat	doily
classify	consequent	creep	definite	dollars
clay	consider	cried	degree	domain
clean	consonant	cripple	delay	domestic
clever	constrain	critical	delicate	dominant
cloak	contain	croak	delivery	dominate
cloud	contradict	crow	democrat	donkey
clout	converse	crowd	demonstrate	double
clown	convoy	crown	deploy	dour
coach	coordinate	cruel	deposit	douse
coal	copper	crumble	despoil	download
coast	corduroy	cultivate	destroy	downsize
coastal	corporate	curl	detail	downstream

downtown
drain
dread
dream
dribble
driveway
drizzle
drown
drowsy
each
eager
eagle
ease
east
easy
eat
eel
effect
effort
elbow
elder
elements
eleven
embroider
employ
empower
enable
enclose
encounter
endeavor
enemy
enjoin
enjoy
entertain
entertainment
entitle

entity
envoy
escrow
establish
esteem
estimate
evident
example
exasperate
excuse
expense
explain
exploit
external
extra
extraordinary
eyebrow
fable
fabulous
factories
factory
faculty
faint
faith
family
farmhouse
favorite
feast
feather
federal
fee
feeble
feed
feedback
feel
feeling

feet
fellow
female
festival
fickle
fiddle
field
fifteen
fifteenth
finally
flashpoint
flee
fleet
float
flounder
flour
flow
flower
flowerpot
flowers
foe
foible
foil
foist
follow
forgetting
formal
forthcoming
foul
found
fountain
fowl
freckles
free
freehand
freeze

frequent
friend
friends
frizzle
frown
funeral
gable
gaggle
gain
gait
gamble
gargle
giggle
glee
glow
glower
goad
goal
goat
gobble
gown
grader
grain
grammar
grapple
gray
grease
great
greed
green
greenhouse
greet
griddle
groan
groin
grouch

ground
groundhog
grow
growl
grumble
guarantee
guard
guess
guest
guild
guilt
guilty
hail
half
handkerchief
handle
hassle
haste
hay
head
headquarters
heal
health
heap
heat
heather
heaven
heavy
heel
herb
hesitate
hinder
history
hobble
hockey
hoe

hoist	ingrain	label	loyalist	misinterpret
holiday	innovate	ladle	lullaby	moan
hollow	inquire	laid	magazine	model
holy	inroad	lain	mail	modest
homestead	instant	language	mailbox	modify
honest	instead	lay	mainland	moist
honey	instruments	layer	mainstay	molecule
honor	integrate	lead / *lēd* /	maintain	money
horizon	integrity	lead / *lĕd* /	maize	monkey
hospital	intermediate	leaf	manual	moral
hound	internal	leak	maple	mound
hour	interval	lean	marble	mount
hours	iron	leap	maximize	mountain
house	isolate	least	may	mouse
however	jail	leather	maybe	mouth
howl	jay	leave	meal	mucous
huddle	jeans	leopard	mean	muffle
humble	jeep	lessen	meanwhile	multiple
hypothesis	jiggle	lesson	medical	multiply
idle	jingle	level	meek	museum
illegal	join	liberal	meet	mustard
illustrate	joined	lie	melody	muzzle
imitate	joint	lifeboat	memory	myrtle
immediate	journal	limousine	meow	mystery
immense	journey	liquid	merchant	nail
immigrate	joy	listen	mercury	need
implicate	juggle	little	meteoroid	needle
important	jumble	lizard	microscope	neglect
impound	jungle	load	middle	nibble
impulse	justify	loaf	midpoint	nineteen
increase	keel	loan	midst	noble
indeed	keen	loiter	mingle	nobleman
indicate	keep	loud	minimize	noise
indisposed	kettle	loudspeaker	minimum	noun
industry	key	low	minnow	nozzle
inform	kitchen	loyal	mischief	nuclear

nuisance
numeral
nursery
oak
oat
oath
oboe
obtain
occupy
octopus
offend
ointment
opposite
orchard
organize
outcome
outfield
outside
oven
overcoat
owe
owl
own
oyster
paddle
pain
paint
panda
particular
pay
pea
peach
peacock
peanut

peasant
pebble
peculiar
peek
peel
peep
peeve
perform
permanent
pickle
pie
pillow
pimple
pineapple
pinpoint
pity
plains
play
playground
pleasant
plow
ploy
poet
point
poise
poison
popular
porous
potato
pouch
pound
pounds
pour
pout
powder
power

practical
praise
pray
preach
preamble
predispose
prefer
preserve
president
priest
probably
professorial
profound
prominent
propagandize
protocol
proud
prowl
puddle
purple
puzzle
qualitative
queen
radical
rail
railroad
rain
raincoat
raindrop
raise
raised
ramshackle
rattle
rattlesnake
ray
razor

reach
reached
ready
real
realize
really
realm
rebuild
recognize
recoil
recommend
rectangle
redeem
reed
reef
referee
refresh
regret
regular
regulate
rejoinder
relay
release
relevant
relief
relieve
remain
remainder
remedy
repeated
reproach
republican
reserved
reside
restaurant
restrain

retain
retire
retouch
retreat
reveal
riddle
rifle
ripple
rival
road
roadside
roadway
roast
round
roundup
row
rowboat
royal
rubbish
rubble
ruffle
ruler
sable
sacred
saddle
sail
sailboat
sailor
saint
salary
sample
satellite
satire
satisfactory
say
scorn

scour	shouted	spontaneous	subway	thousand
scout	show	spouse	sunflower	thread
scream	shower	spout	supper	threaten
screech	shown	sprain	supple	three
screen	shuffle	spray	sustain	throat
scribble	shuttle	spread	sweat	throttle
scuffle	similar	spreadsheet	sweater	throw
sea	simple	sprinkle	sweatshirt	thyroid
seal	single	sprout	sweep	tickle
season	sirloin	squeak	sweet	tidy
sediment	sixteen	squeal	syllable	tie
see	skirt	squeeze	syllables	tied
seed	sleep	stable	sympathy	timetable
seedling	slouch	stain	table	title
seeds	slow	standpoint	tabloid	toad
seek	slowly	staple	tackle	toast
seem	snail	startle	tail	toe
seen	sneeze	statistic	tailor	toilet
seldom	snow	stay	tambourine	topple
semiprivate	snuggle	steady	tangle	touch
senator	soak	steak	tattle	touchdown
separate	soap	steal	tea	towboat
settle	soil	steel	teach	towel
settled	sorrow	steep	tee	tower
seventeen	sour	steeple	teen	town
several	south	stifle	teeth	toy
shadow	southern	stimulate	telegram	trail
shallow	sow / sō /	stir	temper	train
sheep	sow / sou /	stout	temple	trample
sheepskin	soy	street	tenderloin	transfuse
sheet	spectacle	streetcar	terminate	trapezoid
shelter	speech	stretch	theater	travel
shield	speed	struggle	thermometer	tray
shimmer	spleen	stumble	thief	tread
shingle	spoil	subsequent	thirteen	treadmill
shout	spoilsport	subtitle	thorn	tree

tremble	uncle	valentine	way	widespread
trial	underground	valley	wealth	widow
triangle	underneath	vehicle	weapon	wiggle
trifle	uniform	ventricle	weather	window
trouble	universe	vertical	weave	without
troublemaker	unplanned	villain	weed	witness
troublesome	unsteady	violent	week	wobble
trousers	upkeep	vitamin	weekend	women
trout	upper	void	weep	wow
tumble	uptown	vow	wheel	yellow
turkey	usher	vowel	wheels	young
typical	utilize	waist	whisper	zenith
ultimate	vain	wait	whistle	
umbrella	valedictorian	waste	wicked	

Consonants

p	**p**u**p**, ra**pp**ed, **p**ie	zh	vi**s**ion, trea**s**ure, a**z**ure
b	**b**o**b**, e**bb**, **b**rother	h	**h**at, **h**ere, **h**ope
t	**t**ire, jump**ed**, hur**t**	ch	**ch**ur**ch**, ma**tch**, bea**ch**
d	**d**ee**d**, ma**d**, file**d**	j	**j**udge, en**j**oy, **j**ell
k	**c**at, **k**i**ck**, **c**ut	m	**m**op
g	**g**et, **g**ill, ma**g**azine	n	**n**ot
f	**f**lu**ff**, rou**gh**, **ph**oto	ng	si**ng**
v	**v**al**v**e, e**v**ery, ele**v**en	l	**l**and
th	**th**in, **th**ree, ma**th**		
<u>th</u>	**th**is, **th**ere, mo**th**er	w	**w**ith, **w**agon, **w**est
s	**s**od, **c**ity, li**s**t	r	**r**amp
z	**z**ebra, ha**s**, bee**s**	y	**y**ard, **y**es, **y**ellow
sh	**sh**ip, **s**ugar, ma**ch**ine		

Vowels

ē	**b**ee**t**	(bēt)	ō	**b**oa**t**	(bōt)
ĭ	**b**i**t**	(bĭt)	o͝o	**p**u**t**	(po͝ot)
ā	**b**ai**t**	(bāt)	o͞o	**b**oo**t**	(bo͞ot)
ĕ	**b**e**t**	(bĕt)	oi	**b**oi**l**	(boil)
ă	**b**a**t**	(băt)	ou	**p**ou**t**	(pout)
ī	**b**i**te**	(bīt)	î	**p**ee**r**	(pîr)
ŏ	**p**o**t**	(pŏt)	â	**b**ea**r**	(bâr)
ô	**b**ou**ght**	(bôt)	ä	**p**a**r**	(pär)
ŭ	**b**u**t**	(bŭt)	ô	**b**o**re**	(bôr)
ə	**r**a**bb**i**t**	(ră' bət)	û	**p**ea**rl**	(pûrl)

The definitions that accompany the readings relate to the context of the readings. They are provided to help students understand the specific reading selection. For complete definitions of these words, consult a dictionary. Pronunciations are taken from the *American Heritage® Dictionary of the English Language*, Fourth Edition.

accurate (ăk'yər-ĭt)—precise; without error

adrenaline (ə-drĕn'ə-lĭn)—the hormone produced by the body when frightened, angry, or excited

aggravated (ăg'rə-vāt'ĭd)—irritated; annoyed

align (ə-līn')—to place objects in a line

alliance (ə-lī'əns)—a group of people joined for a purpose

allure (ə-lōōr')—attractiveness; temptation

alternative (ôl-tûr'nə-tĭv)—different; additional

antiquity (ăn-tĭk'wĭ-tē)—very old, ancient times

artificial (är'tə-fĭsh'əl)—man-made; not natural

audacity (ô'dă'sə-tē)—shameless boldness; overconfidence

bedevil (bĭ-dĕv'əl)—to annoy or harass; torment

bilingual (bī-lĭng'gwəl)—in two languages

blurred (blûrd)—indistinct; unclear

boycott (boi'kŏt')—the refusal to do business with a company

cables (kā'bəlz)—covered bundles of wire

caloric intake (kə-lôr'ĭk ĭn'tāk')—the eating or consuming of calories

cellists (chĕl'ĭsts)—musicians who play the cello

charisma (kə-rĭz'mə)—personal charm and appeal

collaboration (kə-lăb'ə-rā'shən)—the effort of two or more people working together to achieve the same goal

communications (kə-myōo'nĭ-kā'shənz)—ways of exchanging information

compensate (kŏm'pən-sāt')—to provide something else; provide an alternate action

complacency (kəm-plā'sən-sē)—happiness or satisfaction with the way things are

confessed (kən-fĕst')—admitted; disclosed

conscious (kŏn'shəs)—awake; alert; aware

construct (kən-strŭkt')—to put together; assemble

content (kən-tĕnt')—*adj.* satisfied; pleased

content (kŏn'tĕnt')—*n.* meaningful part

convenient (kən-vēn'yənt)—useful; easy to use

costumer (kŏs'tōom'ər)—a person who makes costumes

creed (krēd)—a formal statement of beliefs

crisis (krī'sĭs)—an emergency

crystallographer (krĭs'tə-lŏg'rə-fēr)—a person who studies the formation and structure of crystals

cuisine (kwĭ-zēn')—food; French for "food" and "kitchen"

curiosity (kyōōr'ĕ-ŏs'ĭ-tē)—desire to know or learn

debut (dā-byōō')—the first appearance

deftly (dĕft'lē)—skillfully; quickly

dependent (dĭ-pĕn'dənt)—reliant upon

deserted (dĭ-zûr'tĭd)—left empty; abandoned

devised (dĭ-vīzd')—created; developed

dialogue (dī'ə-lôg')—a conversation between two or more people

dignity (dĭg'nĭ-tē)—respect; worthiness

disdain (dĭs-dān')—contempt; the feeling that someone deserves no respect

disoriented (dĭs-ôr'ē-ĕnt'ĭd)—confused

distribution (dĭs'trə-byōō'shən)—the passing out of goods over a wide area

egocentric (ē'gō-sĕn'trĭk)—selfish; self-centered

elaborate (ĭ-lăb'ər-ĭt)—complex; detailed

elegance (ĕl'ĭ-gəns)—precision; neat, simple design

eloquent (ĕl'ə-kwənt)—persuasive, powerful expression

emulated (ĕm'yə-lāt'ĭd)—imitated

enormity (ĭ-nôr'mĭ-tē)—great evil; outrage

entranced (ĕn-trănst')—enchanted; fascinated

envelop (ĕn-vĕl'əp)—to surround; enclose

exalted (ĭg-zôlt'ĭd)—praised highly, honored

excel (ĭk-sĕl')—to perform better than others

exuberant (ĭg-zōō'bər-ənt)—high-spirited; enthusiastic

flourished (flûr'ĭsht)—thrived; prospered

frigid (frĭj'ĭd)—extremely cold; freezing

gesture (jĕs'chər)—a thoughtful action

glumly (glŭm'lē)—sadly; unhappily

gradualism (grăj'ōō-ə-lĭz'əm)—the practice of reaching a desired result by making slow and small steps

harmonious (här-mō'nē-əs)—in agreement; working well together

helical (hē'lĭ-kəl)—spiral; circular

heredity (hə-rĕd'ĭ-tē)—the passing of genes from parent to child

heritage (hĕr'ĭ-tĭj)—beliefs, traditions, and history passed from one generation to the next

hypocrite (hĭp'ə-krĭt')—a person who claims to believe one way, but acts differently

illusion (ĭ-lōō'zhən)—a false thought or idea

impression (ĭm-prĕsh'ən)—an idea; effect

inanimate (ĭn-ăn'ə-mĭt)—lifeless; non-living

indignantly (ĭn-dĭg'nənt-lē)—angrily; discontentedly

indolently (ĭn'də-lənt-lē)—lazily

ineligible (ĭn-ĕl'ĭ-jə-bəl)—disqualified; cannot participate

inherit (ĭn-hĕr'ĭt)—to receive something from an ancestor

inheritance (ĭn-hĕr'ĭ-təns)—the property received when someone dies

inherited (ĭn-hĕr'ĭ-tĭd)—passed from parent to child

innate (ĭ-nāt')—born with; possessed at birth

integrity (ĭn-tĕg'rĭ-tē)—strong morals; honesty

interconnected (ĭn'tər-kə-nĕk'tĭd)—linked to each other; joined together

interpret (ĭn-tûr'prĭt)—to translate; figure out

irreversible (ĭr'ĭ-vûr'sə-bəl)—not able to be changed; permanent

isolated (ī'sə-lā'tĭd)—separated

jouncing (jouns'ĭng)—bouncing; moving with bumps or jolts

justice (jŭs'tĭs)—fairness

justifies (jŭs'tə-fīz')—explains; gives reasons for

lethargy (lĕth'ər-jē)—a lack of energy; sluggishness

liable (lī'ə-bəl)—likely; probably going to

liberated (lĭb'ə-rā'tĭd)—independent; freed from influence or control by others

linguistic (lĭng-gwĭs'tĭk)—connected with the study of language

linguists (lĭng'gwĭsts)—people who study languages

logically (lŏj'ĭ-klē)—with reason; sensibly

loner (lō'nər)—a person who prefers to be alone

luxurious (lŭg'zhoŏr'ē-əs)—extremely enjoyable; self-indulgent

mannerisms (măn'ə-rĭz'əmz)—behaviors or expressions

matriarch (mā'trē-ärk')—the female head of a family

maturation (măch'ə-rā'shən)—becoming fully grown

metamorphosis (mĕt'ə-môr'fə-sĭs)—a change; transformation

methodical (mə-thŏd'ĭ-kəl)—systematic; careful; in a step-by-step manner

milling (mĭl'ĭng)—move around randomly; wandering

mind (mīnd)—to take care of; look after

mobile (mō'bəl)—capable of going from one place to another

musings (myoō'zĭngz)—deep thoughts

oblivious (ə-blĭv'ē-əs)—unaware; not noticing

opponent (ə-pō'nənt)—a person who takes the opposite side in a game or contest

optics (ŏp'tĭks)—the science of light; vision; lenses

orator (ôr'ə-tər)—a skilled public speaker

organic (ôr-găn'ĭk)—produced from living things

passive (păs'ĭv)—accepting without resistance or struggle

pathos (pā'thŏs)—quality that brings out feelings of kindness, understanding, or sadness

pedagogue (pĕd'ə-gŏg')—demanding teacher

peddle (pĕd'l)—to sell things

personified (pər-sŏn'ə-fīd')—described an object or idea as having human characteristics

phenomenon (fĭ-nŏm'ə-nŏn')—a highly unusual event

predominates (prĭ-dŏm'ə-nāts')—overshadows or overpowers others

prodigy (prŏd'ə-jē)—a genius; someone of great ability

promote (prə-mōt')—to support or encourage

pulses (pŭls'əz)—bursts of movement; vibrations

recipient (rĭ-sĭp'ē-ənt)—one who receives

recital (rĭ-sīt'l)—a formal performance in front of an audience

reiterated (rē-ĭt'ə-rāt'ĭd)—repeated

reluctantly (rĭ-lŭk'tənt-lē)—hesitantly; unwillingly

repetitive (rĭ-pĕt'ĭ-tĭv)—done again and again

resist (rĭ-zĭst')—oppose; be against

reverberated (rĭ-vûr'bə-rāt'ĭd)—echoed

reverence (rĕv'ər-əns)—great admiration; respect

righteous (rī'chəs)—right; justified

rummaged (rŭm'ĭjd)—searched

savored (sā'vərd)—enjoyed the taste of

script (skrĭpt)—handwriting; a collection of symbols

segregated (sĕg'rĭ-gāt'ĭd)—separated or isolated

self-sufficiency (sĕlf' sə-fĭsh'ən-sē)—independence

serene (sə-rēn')—very calm; peaceful

signals (sĭg'nəlz)—sounds, images, or messages that are sent or received

signify (sĭg'nə-fī')—to show; indicate

stalked (stôkt)—walked in an angry way

stamina (stăm'ə-nə)—ability to do something for a long time; endurance

subject (sŭb'jĭkt)—1. likely to; expected to 2. prone; having a tendency toward

supervise (soo'pər-vīz')—to oversee; manage

tantalizing (tăn'tə-līz'ĭng)—teasing; tempting

tenacity (tə-năs'ĭ-tē)—determination; persistence

tenement (tĕn'ə-mənt)—a low-rent apartment building

tentatively (tĕn'tə-tĭv-lē)—shyly; hesitantly

thesis (thē'sĭs)—a proposed explanation; theory

turbines (tûr'bĭnz)—machines that produce power

uncivilized (ŭn-sĭv'ə-līzd')—primitive; barbarous; without basic services or humanity

unquenchable (ŭn-kwĕn'chə-bəl)—impossible to suppress or destroy; cannot be stopped

verdant (vûr'dnt)—covered with green plants

visualize (vĭzh'oo-ə-līz')—to imagine

Prefixes, Roots, and Suffixes (Units 13–24)

Prefix	Meanings	Examples
anti-	opposite; against	antimatter, antitoxic
con-	with, together	conflict, contribute
de-	from	decode, deduct
dis-	not, absence of, apart	disgust, disinterest, discuss
ex-	out, from	excavate, expand
fore-	before, in front of	foretell, forehand
in-	not; into, toward	inactive, ingrained, income
inter-	between, among	interact, interstate
mid-	middle	midsummer, midterm
mis-	wrongly, badly, not	misfile, misprint, misunderstand
non-	not, without	nonstop, nonsense
over-	beyond, above, too much	overdue, overpass, overslept
per-	through, thoroughly, throughout	perfect, perform, permit
pre-	before	preregister, preset
pro-	forward, in front of	progress, protect
re-	back, again	return, revisit
sub-	below, beneath, under	subcompact, submarine
super-	above, over; superior	supersonic, superhero
trans-	across, through	transfer, transport
un-	not, do the opposite of	unlike, unplug
under-	below, less	underpass, undersized

Root	Meanings	Examples
dic/dict	to say, tell	indicate, predict
duc/duct	to lead	educate, conduct
fac	to make, do	facsimile, faculty
fact	to make, do	factory, benefactor
fec	to make, do	affect, defector
fic	to make, do	difficult, significant

form	to shape	reform, transform
ject	to throw	reject, projectile
lumen	to light	illuminate, luminous
pel/puls	to drive, push	compel, repulse
pend/pens	to hang, pay, weigh	pendulum, compensate, pensive
port	to carry	deport, export
rect/reg	right, straight	correct, direct, regal
scrib/script	to write	inscribe, transcript
spect	to look at, see, watch	inspect, prospector, spectator
tract	to pull	extract, retract

Suffix	Meanings	Examples
-able	capable of, can do	dependable, lovable
-ate	cause to be, having the quality of	illustrate, considerate
-dom	state or condition of being	freedom, stardom
-en	to become, made of, caused to be or have	deepen, stiffen, widen
-er	someone who, something that	entertainer, trainer
-ful	full of, characterized by	colorful, painful
-ist	someone who	artist, medalist
-ize	cause to be, become, resemble	legalize, memorize, humanize
-less	without, lacking	spotless, helpless
-ly	how something is done	quickly, softly
-ment	state, act, or process of	agreement, ailment
-ness	state, quality, condition, degree of	lateness, sweetness, thickness
-or	someone who, something that	director, donor
-ous	full of, having, characterized by	humorous, rigorous, nervous
-some	characterized by	lonesome, tiresome
-y	characterized by, consisting of, the quality or condition of	funny, stormy, tricky

Signal Words Based on Bloom's Taxonomy

Category	Meaning	Location
Remember Units 7–8	Retrieve relevant knowledge from long-term memory	
list	state a series of names, ideas, or events	Unit 7
locate	find specific information	
name	label specific information	
recognize	know something from prior experience or learning	
state	say or write specific information	
describe	state detailed information about an idea or concept	Unit 8
recall	retrieve information from memory to provide an answer	
repeat	say specific infomation again	
retrieve	locate information from memory to provide an answer	
Understand Units 9–12	Construct meaning from instructional messages, including oral, written, and graphic communication	
conclude	arrive at logical end based on specific information	Unit 9
define in your own words	tell the meaning of something in one's own words	
illustrate	present an example or explanation in pictures or words	
predict	foretell new information from what is already known	
tell	say or write specific information	
identify	locate specific information in the text	Unit 10
paraphrase	restate information in somewhat different words to simplify and clarify	
summarize	restate important ideas and details from multiple paragraphs or sources	

Category	Meaning	Location
categorize	place information into groups	Unit 11
classify	organize into groups with similar characteristics	
discuss	talk about or examine a subject with others	
match	put together things that are alike or similar	
sort	place or separate into groups	
compare	state the similarities between two or more ideas	Unit 12
contrast	state the differences between two or more ideas	
explain	express understanding of an idea or concept	
Review **Remember** and **Understand** levels		Unit 12
Apply Units 13–15	Carry out or use a procedure in a given situation	
generalize	draw conclusions based on presented information	Unit 13
infer	draw a logical conclusion using information or evidence	
use	apply a procedure to a task	
show	demonstrate an understanding of information	Unit 14
Review **Apply** level		Unit 15
Analyze Units 16–18	Break material into its constituent parts and determine how the parts relate to one another and to an overall structure or purpose	
distinguish	find differences that set one thing apart from another	Unit 16
select	choose from among alternatives	
arrange	organize information	Unit 17
organize	arrange in a systematic pattern	
outline	arrange information into a systematic pattern of main ideas and supporting details	
Review all levels		Unit 18

Category	Meaning	Location
Evaluate Units 19–21	Require judgments based on criteria and standards	
assess	determine value or significance	Unit 19
justify	prove or give reasons that something is right or valid	
critique	examine positive and negative features to form a judgment	Unit 20
judge	form an opinion or estimation after careful consideration	
Review **Evaluate** level		Unit 21
Create Units 22–24	Assemble elements to form a whole or product; reorganize elements into a new pattern or structure	
compose **design** **plan**	make or create by putting parts or elements together devise a procedure to do a task devise a solution to solve a problem	Unit 22
hypothesize **revise**	formulate a possible explanation; speculate modify or change a plan or product	Unit 23
Review all levels		Unit 24

Noun Form and Function (Units 1, 2, 3, 4, 7, 8, 9, and 11)

Form	Function
Adding the suffix **-s** to most singular nouns	makes a **plural noun**.
• map + s = maps • cab + s = cabs • mast + s = masts	• I had the **maps** at camp. • The **cabs** are fast. • The bats sat on the **masts**.
Adding the suffix **-es** to nouns ending in **s**, **z**, **x**, **ch**, **sh**, or **tch**	makes a **plural noun**.
• dress + es = dresses • fizz + es = fizzes • box + es = boxes • rich + es = riches • dish + es = dishes • match + es = matches	• Rose bought three new **dresses**. • They drank cherry **fizzes**. • The **boxes** were full of books. • The safe contains many **riches**. • The **dishes** fell to the floor. • The wet **matches** did not light.
Adding the suffix **-'s** to nouns	makes a **possessive singular noun**.
• Stan + 's = Stan's • van + 's = van's • man + 's = man's	• **Stan's** stamps are at camp. • The **van's** mat is flat. • The **man's** plan is to get clams.
Adding the suffix **-'s** to nouns	makes a **possessive plural noun**.
• boy + s' = boys' • girl + s' = girls' • dog+ s' = dogs'	• The **boys'** cards were missing. • The **girls'** snacks are on the table. • The **dogs'** bowls are empty.
Adding the **'** to a plural noun ending in **-es**	makes a **possessive plural noun**.
• foxes + ' = foxes' • fishes + ' = fishes'	• The **foxes'** den is snug. • The **fishes'** fins make waves.

Noun Form and Function (*continued*)

Count Nouns—Nouns that can be specifically counted		
Rules	**Form**	**Examples**
• Can be preceded by the indefinite articles in the **singular** form	a an	a **bicycle**, a **cat**, a **table** an **insect**
• Can be made **plural**	-s -es	**bicycles, cats, tables, insects** **dresses, riches, suffixes**
• Can be preceded by the definite article in the **singular** form • Can be preceded by the definite article in the **plural** form when referring to specific objects, groups, or ideas	the	the **pencil**, the **pencils** the **insect**, the **insects** the **truck**, the **trucks**
• Can be preceded by the zero article (Ø) in the **plural** form	zero article (Ø)	(Ø) **Bicycles** are fun to ride. I see (Ø) **stars** in the sky. (Ø) **Insects** are not fun.
• Can be preceded by determiners in the **singular** form	this	This **bicycle** is red. This **lunch** is good. This **table** is round
	that	That **insect** is big. Do not light that **match**! That **truck** is running.
• Can be preceded by determiners in the **plural** form	these those	These **trucks** are red. Those **workers** are strong.
• Can be preceded by quantity adjectives **a lot of**, **any**, **many**, **some**, and **a few**	a lot of any many some a few	He has a lot of **friends**. I don't have any red **pencils**. She has many **cats**. I saw some **stars** in the sky. I need a few **paper clips**.
• Cannot be preceded by the quantity adjectives **much** or **a little**		NOT: She has much apples. There are a little stars in the sky.

Noncount Nouns		
Cannot be specifically counted, but can be measured		
Rules	**Form**	**Examples**
• Can only be used in the singular form	singular	That was **fun**. The plant needs **water**. The pen is out of **ink**.
• Never take indefinite articles **a** and **an**		The room is filled with **smoke**. You need **cash** for the movie. I want **mustard** on my sandwich.
• Sometimes take the definite article **the**, if it refers to a specific object, group or idea.	**the**	Please pass me the **pasta**. The **soup** is on the table. Wash the **dirt** from your hands.
• Can be preceded by determiners **this** and **that**.	**this** **that**	This **corn** tastes great! That **water** looks dirty.
• Can be preceded by quantity adjectives **a lot of**, **any**, **much**, **some**, and **a little**.	**a lot of**	There is a lot of **mud** on the truck. I have a lot of **stuff**.
	any	This isn't any **fun**. I don't smell any **smoke**. Do you want any **rice**?
	much	This isn't much **fun**. That man has so much **hair**! Don't give me too much **jelly**.
	some	I want some **water**. Please pass me some **mustard**.
	a little	This popcorn needs a little **salt**. Please give me a little **pasta**.
• Cannot be preceded by the quantity adjectives **many**, and **a few**.		NOT: I have many stuff. She has a few cash.

Verb Form and Function (Units 4, 5, 7, 8, 10, 11,15, and 16)

Form	Function
Adding the suffix -**s** to most verbs . . .	makes the verbs **third person singular**, **present tense**.
• sit + s = sits • skid + s = skids • pack + s = packs	• The rabbit **sits** in the grass. • The cab **skids** on the ramp. • She **packs** her bags for the trip.
Adding the suffix -**es** to verbs ending in **s**, **z**, **x**, **ch**, **sh**, or **tch**	makes the verbs **third person singular**, **present tense**.
• press + es = presses • buzz + es = buzzes • wax + es = waxes • switch + es = switches • wish + es = wishes • pitch + es = pitches	• He **presses** the button to open the door. • The bee **buzzes** around the room. • John **waxes** his car once a month. • She **switches** on the radio. • Jamal **wishes** he had a wagon. • Monica **pitches** her trash into the can.
Adding the suffix -**ed** to regular verbs	makes the **past tense**.
• jump + ed = jumped • smell + ed = smelled • end + ed = ended	• She **jumped**. • Stuart **smelled** the roses. • The class **ended** well.
Adding **will** before main verbs	makes the **future tense**.
• will + nap = will nap • will + send = will send • will + use = will use	• The baby **will nap** after lunch. • They **will send** it later. • Ron **will use** blue paint.

Form	Function
Adding the suffix **-ing** to main verbs with the helping verb **am**, **is**, or **are**	makes the **present progressive**.
<ul><li>go + ing = going</li><li>come + ing = coming</li><li>drop + ing = dropping</li></ul>	<ul><li>I **am going** to the circus.</li><li>She **is coming** over to visit.</li><li>Leaves **are dropping** from the tree.</li></ul>
Adding the suffix **-ing** to main verbs with helping verbs **was** or **were**	makes the **past progressive**.
<ul><li>push + ing = pushing</li><li>dump + ing = dumping</li><li>run + ing = running</li></ul>	<ul><li>He **was pushing** the cart.</li><li>They **were dumping** sand into the water.</li><li>She **was running** down the street.</li></ul>
Adding the suffix **-ing** to main verbs with helping verbs **will be**	makes the **future progressive**.
<ul><li>act + ing = acting</li><li>bring + ing = bringing</li><li>swim + ing = swimming</li></ul>	<ul><li>I **will be acting** in the play.</li><li>She **will be bringing** her list.</li><li>They **will be swimming** at 6:00.</li></ul>

Verb Form and Function (*continued*)

Form	Function
Adding the suffix **-ing** to verbs	forms a **present participle**, which can also act as an **adjective**.
• skid + ing = skidding • cry + ing = crying • migrate + ing = migrating	• The **skidding** car crashed into the tree. • I picked up the **crying** baby. • The **migrating** birds were high in the sky.
Adding the suffix **-ed** or **-en** to a verb	forms a **past participle**, which can also act as an **adjective**.
• hurry + ed = hurried • drive + en = driven	• The **hurried** effort did not help. • The **driven** athlete set new records.

Subject and Object Pronouns (Units 4, 6)

Person	Singular		Plural	
	Subject	Object	Subject	Object
First Person	I	me	we	us
Second Person	you	you	you	you
Third Person	he, she, it	him, her, it	they	them

Verb Forms (Units 4, 5, 7, 9, 10, and 11)

The Present Tense (Unit 4)

Person	Singular	Plural
First Person	I pass.	We pass.
Second Person	You pass.	You pass.
Third Person	He, she, it passes.	They pass.

The Past Tense (Unit 7)

Person	Singular	Plural
First Person	I passed.	We passed.
Second Person	You passed.	You passed.
Third Person	He, she, it passed.	They passed.

The Future Tense (Unit 10)

Person	Singular	Plural
First Person	I will pass.	We will pass.
Second Person	You will pass.	You will pass.
Third Person	He, she, it will pass.	They will pass.

Verb Forms (*continued*)

The Present Progressive (Unit 5)

Person	Singular	Plural
First Person	I am sitting.	We are sitting.
Second Person	You are sitting.	You are sitting.
Third Person	He, she, it is sitting.	They sit.

The Past Progressive (Unit 9)

Person	Singular	Plural
First Person	I was passing.	We were passing.
Second Person	You were passing.	You were passing.
Third Person	He, she, it was passing.	They were passing.

The Future Progressive (Unit 11)

Person	Singular	Plural
First Person	I will be passing.	We will be passing.
Second Person	You will be passing.	You will be passing.
Third Person	He, she, it will be passing.	They will be passing.

Forms of *Be*, *Have*, and *Do* (Units 13, 15, and 16)

Be	Present		Past		Future	
Person	Singular	Plural	Singular	Plural	Singular	Plural
First Person	I **am**	we **are**	I **was**	we **were**	I **will be**	we **will be**
Second Person	you **are**	you **are**	you **were**	you **were**	you **will be**	you **will be**
Third Person	he, she, it **is**	they **are**	he, she, it **was**	they **were**	he, she, it **will be**	they **will be**

Have	Present		Past		Future	
Person	Singular	Plural	Singular	Plural	Singular	Plural
First Person	I **have**	we **have**	I **had**	we **had**	I **will have**	we **will have**
Second Person	you **have**	you **have**	you **had**	you **had**	you **will have**	you **will have**
Third Person	he, she, it **has**	they **have**	he, she, it **had**	they **had**	he, she, it **will have**	they **will have**

Do	Present		Past		Future	
Person	Singular	Plural	Singular	Plural	Singular	Plural
First Person	I **do**	we **do**	I **did**	we **did**	I **will do**	we **will do**
Second Person	you **do**	you **do**	you **did**	you **did**	you **will do**	you **will do**
Third Person	he, she, it **does**	they **do**	he, she, it **did**	they **did**	he, she, it **will do**	they **will do**

Irregular Verbs (Units 1–24)

Base Verb	Past Tense	Past Participle
be (am, is, are)	was/were	been
beat	beat	beaten
become	became	become
begin	began	begun
bend	bent	bent
bleed	bled	bled
blow	blew	blown
break	broke	broken
breed	bred	bred
bring	brought	brought
buy	bought	bought
catch	caught	caught
come	came	come
cost	cost	cost
creep	crept	crept
cut	cut	cut
deal	dealt	dealt
dive	dove	dived
do	did	done
drink	drank	drunk
drive	drove	driven
eat	ate	eaten
feed	fed	fed
feel	felt	felt
fit	fit	fit
flee	fled	fled
fly	flew	flown
forget	forgot	forgotten
forgive	forgave	forgiven
freeze	froze	frozen

Base Verb	Past Tense	Past Participle
get	got	gotten
give	gave	given
go	went	gone
grow	grew	grown
have	had	had
hit	hit	hit
keep	kept	kept
know	knew	known
lay (= put)	laid	laid
lead	led	led
leave	left	left
lend	lent	lent
let	let	let
lie (= recline)	lay	lain
make	made	made
meet	met	met
mistake	mistook	mistaken
overcome	overcame	overcome
overtake	overtook	overtaken
pay	paid	paid
put	put	put
read	read	read
ride	rode	ridden
ring	rang	rung
rise	rose	risen
run	ran	run
say	said	said
see	saw	seen
seek	sought	sought
sell	sold	sold

Irregular Verbs (*continued*)

Base Verb	Past Tense	Past Participle
send	sent	sent
shake	shook	shaken
shine	shone	shone
show	showed	shown
sing	sang	sung
sit	sat	sat
sleep	slept	slept
speak	spoke	spoken
speed	sped	sped
spend	spent	spent
spread	spread	spread
spring	sprang	sprung
stand	stood	stood
steal	stole	stolen
stick	stuck	stuck
string	strung	strung
sweep	swept	swept
swim	swam	swum
swing	swung	swung
take	took	taken
teach	taught	taught
think	thought	thought
throw	threw	thrown
thrust	thrust	thrust
wake	woke	woken
weave	wove/weaved	woven/weaved
weep	wept	wept
win	won	won
withstand	withstood	withstood
write	wrote	written

Spelling Rules (Units 5, 6, 10, 15, and 17)

Rule	Examples
Words Ending With Double Letters	
At the end of one-syllable words, after a short vowel, / s /, / f /, / l /, and / z / are usually represented by double letters -**ss**, -**ff**, -**ll**, -**zz**.	• pa**ss** • blu**ff** • wi**ll** • ja**zz**
Doubling Rule	
Double the final consonant in a word before adding a suffix beginning with a vowel when: • The word is one syllable. • The word has one vowel. • The word ends in one consonant.	• sip + ing = si**pp**ing • skid + ed = ski**dd**ed
Drop e̲ Rule	
When adding a suffix that begins with a **vowel** to a **final silent e̲** word, drop the e̲ from the base word.	• hope + ing = **hoping**
When adding a suffix that begins with a **consonant** to a **final silent e̲** word, do not drop the e̲ from the base word.	• hope + ful = **hopeful**

Spelling Rules (*continued*)

Rule	Examples
Words Ending in <u>o</u>	
When a word ends in a consonant followed by <u>**o**</u>, form plural nouns and third person singular, present tense verbs by adding -**es**. Adding -**es** keeps the sound for <u>**o**</u> long.	• hero**es** • zero**es** • go**es**
When a word ends in a vowel followed by <u>**o**</u>, form the plural noun by adding -**s**.	• video**s**
Change <u>y</u> Rule	
When a base word ends in **y** preceded by a consonant, change **y** to **i** before adding a suffix, except for -**ing**.	• try + ed = tr**i**ed • try + ing = tr**y**ing • happy + est = happ**i**est • happy + ness = happ**i**ness

Adjectives (Units 14, 15, and 17)

Adjective	Comparative
Adding the suffix **-er** to an adjective	compares one person, thing, or group to another person, thing, or group. The suffix **-er** means "more."
• fast + er = faster • small + er = smaller • big + er = bigger	• She is a **faster** runner than Sam. • Her backpack is **smaller** than my backpack. • That group of boys is **bigger** than this group of boys.

Adjective	Superlative
Adding the suffix **-est** to an adjective	compares one person, thing, or group to two or more persons, things, or groups. The suffix **-est** means "most."
• fast + est = fastest • small + est = smallest • big + est = biggest	• She is the **fastest** runner in school. • I got the **smallest** slice of pizza. • That gym has the **biggest** swimming pool of all.

Prepositions (Units 4–24)

about	before	during	on	unlike
above	behind	except	onto	until
across	below	for	outside	up
after	beneath	from	over	upon
against	beside	in	past	with
along	besides	inside	since	within
amid	between	into	than	without
among	beyond	like	through	
around	by	near	to	
as	despite	of	toward	
at	down	off	under	

Phrasal Verbs (Units 22 and 23)

Phrasal Verb	Meanings
blow up	destroy by using an explosive
catch on	learn, understand
do over	repeat, redo
dream up	devise, invent
dust off	brush
eat out	dine in a restaurant
fill out	complete
fill up	fill to capacity
find out	discover
get by	survive
give away	give something to someone else for free
give back	return
go on	continue
hand in	submit
leave out	omit
look into	investigate
look up	search for
make up	invent
pass down	teach or give something to someone who will be alive after you have died
pick out	choose
point out	show, indicate
put off	postpone
put on	put clothing on
put out	extinguish
puzzle out	identify
puzzle over	ponder
run across	find by chance
run into	meet someone unexpectedly

Phrasal Verbs (*continued*)

Phrasal Verb	Meanings
set up	arrange
show up	arrive
switch off	turn off
take after	resemble
take down	write, lower
throw away	discard
try on	test the fit
turn down	lower, reject
wake up	arise from sleep

Idioms

Idioms (Units 1–24)

Idiom	Meaning
at the drop of a hat	immediately and without urging
be a fly in the ointment	be a detrimental detail; a drawback
be a horse of a different color	be another matter entirely; something else
be a live wire	be a vivacious, alert, or energetic person
be a thorn in your side	be a constant annoyance or pain to you
be all wet	be entirely mistaken
be at sixes and sevens	be in a state of confusion or disorder
be at the end of your rope	be at the limit of one's patience, endurance, or resources
be beside yourself	be very concerned or worried
be down to the wire	be the very end, as in a race or contest
be fishy	cause doubt or suspicion
be fit as a fiddle	be in good health
be in a pickle	be in trouble or out of luck; be in a difficult situation with little hope of getting out of it
be in full swing	be at the highest level of activity
be in hot water	be in serious trouble or in an embarrassing situation with someone in authority
be in on the act	be included in an activity
be in the cards	be likely or certain to happen
be in the doghouse	be in great disfavor or trouble
be in the public eye	be frequently seen in public or in the media; be well-known
be in the red	be operating at a loss; in debt
be in the swim	active in the general current of affairs
be in the wind	likely to occur; in the offing
be like a fish out of water	appear completely out of place
be on pins and needles	be in a state of tense anticipation

Idiom	Meaning
be on the blink	be out of working order
be on the button	be exactly; precisely accurate
be on the rack	be under great stress
be on to	be aware of or have information about
be on your last leg	be unable to continue
be out at the elbows	be poorly dressed; lacking money
be out of line	be uncalled for; improper; out of control
be out of your hands	be no longer within your responsibility or in your care
be out to lunch	not be in touch with the real world
be over the hill	be past the prime of life; be slowing down
be over the hump	be past the worst or most difficult part or stage
be the bottom line	be the final result or most crucial factor
be under the wire	be at the finish line; just in the nick of time; at the last moment
be up a creek	be in a difficult situation
be up to speed	perform at an acceptable level
be water over the dam	be something that is past and cannot be changed
be within an inch of	be almost to the point of
be your own worst enemy	believe things that prevent you from becoming successful
bite the bullet	face a painful situation bravely and stoically
bite the dust	fall dead, especially in combat; be defeated; come to an end
bite the hand that feeds you	repay generosity or kindness with ingratitude and injury
blow a gasket	explode with anger
blow the whistle on someone or something	expose a wrongdoing in the hope of bringing it to a halt
break a leg	used to wish someone success in a performance
bring down the house	get overwhelming audience applause
bring home the bacon	support a family by working; earn a living
burn the candle at both ends	work from early in the morning until late at night and so get very little rest

Idiom	Meaning
call it quits	stop working or trying
call the shots	exercise authority; be in charge
call your bluff	challenge another with a display of strength or confidence
catch red-handed	catch someone in the act of doing something wrong
catch you in the act	catch you doing something illegal or private
catch you later	see or speak to you at a later time
come apart at the seams	become so upset that you lose all self-control
come over to our side	join our group; take another position on the issue
come to life	become excited
come up smelling like a rose	result favorably or successfully
cost an arm and a leg	be high priced, though possibly not worth the cost
cover your tracks	hide evidence in order to dodge pursuers
cry uncle	show a willingness to give up a fight
cry your eyes out	weep inconsolably for a long time
cut the mustard	perform up to expectations or to a standard
do the trick	bring about the desired result
don't bug me	leave me alone
drive you crazy	make you angry, confused, or frustrated
drop you like a hot potato	get rid of someone or something as quickly as possible
eat your words	retract something you have said
feed you a line	deceive you
fill the bill	serve a particular purpose
get down to brass tacks	begin talking about important things; get down to business
get it off your chest	let go of your pent-up feelings
get off your back	have someone stop bothering you
get on the stick	begin to work
get on your nerves	irritate or exasperate you

Idiom	Meaning
get ripped off	be taken advantage of
get the ax	get fired
get the short end of the stick	get the worst of an unequal deal
get this show on the road	get started with an act or project
get up on the wrong side of bed	be in a really bad mood
give it your best shot	try as hard as you can to accomplish something
give me a ring	phone me
give someone the shirt off your back	be extremely generous
go along for the ride	join an activity for no particular reason
go bananas	go crazy
go down the tubes	fall into a state of failure or ruin
go fly a kite	go away or stop annoying someone (usually said in anger)
go to bat for	give help to; defend
go to the dogs	decline, come to a bad end
go up in flames	be utterly destroyed
go up in smoke	be totally destroyed
have a bone to pick	have grounds for a complaint or dispute
have a domino effect	have a cumulative effect produced when one event sets off a chain of related events
have a leg to stand on	have a good defense for your opinions or actions
have a skeleton in your closet	have a source of shame or disgrace that is kept secret
have an iron in the fire	have an undertaking or project in progress
have cabin fever	feel uneasiness or distress because of being in an enclosed space
have you in stitches	have you laughing uncontrollably
have your fingers crossed	hope for a successful or advantageous outcome

Idiom	Meaning
have your head in the clouds	be unaware of the facts of a situation
hit close to home	affect your feelings or interests
hit the deck	get out of bed; fall or drop to a prone position; prepare for action
hit the jackpot	win; have success
hit the sack	go to bed
hit the spot	be exactly right; be refreshing
hold your horses	slow down; wait a minute; be patient
keep it under your hat	keep something a secret
keep your ear to the ground	pay attention to everything that is happening around you and to what people are saying
keep your fingers crossed	hope for a successful or advantageous outcome
keep your shirt on	don't get angry; be patient
kick the habit	free oneself from an addiction, such as cigarettes
lay your cards on the table	discuss the issue honestly
lend a hand	help someone
let sleeping dogs lie	don't make someone angry by stirring up trouble or talking about something that has caused problems in the past
let the cat out of the bag	let a secret be known
live in a dream world	have unrealistic goals or expectations
look down your nose at	regard with contempt or condescension
look up to	admire
make a beeline	go straight toward something
make a dent in	get started with a series of chores
make a drop in the bucket	make an insufficient or inconsequential amount in comparison to what is required
make a mountain out of a molehill	exaggerate a minor problem

Idiom	Meaning
make no bones about	be forthright and candid about; acknowledge freely
make the grade	measure up to a given standard
make tracks	move or leave in a hurry
make waves	cause a disturbance or controversy
make your toes curl	make you feel very embarrassed for someone; frighten or shock someone
miss the boat	arrive too late and miss out on something
open your eyes	become aware of the truth of a situation
paint the town red	go on a spree; go out and have a good time
pass the buck	shift responsibility or blame to another person
pass the hat	take up a collection of money
pat on the back	congratulate; encourage someone
play into the hands of	act or behave so as to give an advantage to (an opponent)
play possum	pretend to be sleeping or dead
play the game	behave according to the accepted customs
play with fire	take part in a dangerous or risky activity
pound the pavement	travel the streets on foot, especially in search of work
pull a fast one	play a trick or carry out a fraud
pull the rug out from under you	remove all support and help from you; ruin your plans, hopes, or dreams
pull your leg	kid, fool, or trick you
push your luck	expect continued good fortune
put all your eggs in one basket	risk everything all at once
put the cart before the horse	do things out of order; not do things logically
put to bed	make final preparations for completing a project
put two and two together	draw the proper conclusions from existing evidence or indications
put your finger on something	point out or describe exactly; find something

Idiom	Meaning
put your house in order	organize your affairs in a sensible, logical way
ring a bell	arouse an indistinct memory
rock the boat	make trouble; risk spoiling a plan
rub your nose in it	remind you of something unfortunate that has happened
run in the family	be characterized by something common to many members of the same family
run like clockwork	operate with machinelike regularity and precision; perfectly
run out of gas	exhaust your energy or enthusiasm
saved by the bell	rescued from a difficult situation just in time
see eye-to-eye	be in agreement
send someone packing	dismiss someone abruptly
shake a leg	hurry
sink or swim	fail or succeed on your own
snap out of it	go back to your normal condition from depression, grief, or self-pity
stack the deck	order things against someone
step on your toes	offend or hurt someone's feelings
stick to your ribs	be substantial or filling (used with food)
stick your neck out	take a risk
stretch the rules	do something or allow someone to do something which is not usually allowed
stretch your legs	walk
strike it rich	gain sudden financial success
stuck in a rut	staying in a way of living that never changes
take a hike	leave because your presence is unwanted
take a rain check	ask to do something at a later date
take a shot in the dark	take a wild guess; an attempt that has little chance of succeeding
take a stand	take an active role in demonstrating your belief in something

Idiom	Meaning
take an eye for an eye	permit an offender to suffer what a victim has suffered
take at your word	be convinced of your sincerity and act in accord with what you say
take five	take a short rest or break, as of five or ten minutes
take it from the top	start from the beginning
take the bull by the horns	deal with a problem directly and resolutely
take the cake	be the most outrageous or disappointing; win the prize; be outstanding
the sky is the limit	have no limit to what you can spend, how far you can go, or what you can achieve
throw a curve ball	surprise someone with something that is difficult or unpleasant to deal with
tilt at windmills	confront and engage in conflict with an imagined opponent or threat
turn your back on	deny; reject; abandon; foresake
waste your breath	accomplish nothing after talking to someone
weave a tangled web	be involved in a complicated decision
(when) push comes to shove	(when) the situation becomes more difficult or matters escalate
whistle in the dark	attempt to keep up your courage
win by a landslide	get the most of the votes in an election
wing it	go through a situation or process without any plan
work like a dog	work very hard
work like a dream	work very well
work your fingers to the bone	labor extremely hard; toil
wouldn't dream of doing something	never do something because you think it is wrong or silly

Books A, B, C, and D include these terms. Unit numbers following each definition indicate where these terms first appear.

Adjective. A word used to describe a noun. An adjective tells which one, how many, or what kind. A prepositional phrase may also be used as an adjective. Example: *The **quick** team **from the school** won the game.* (Unit 6)

Adjective, possessive. A word that comes before a noun and is used to describe the noun in terms of possession. Examples: *my, your, his, her, its, our, their.* ***My** desk is messy.* (Unit 7)

Adverb. A word used to describe a verb, an adjective, or another adverb. An adverb answers the questions *when, where,* or *how.* A prepositional phrase may also be used as an adverb. Examples: *He ran **yesterday**. She hopped **in the grass**. He batted **quickly**.* (Unit 4)

Antonym. A word that means the opposite of another word. Examples: *good/bad; fast/slow; happy/sad.* (Unit 2)

Apostrophe. A punctuation mark used in possessive singular and plural nouns. Examples: *Fran's hat, the boys' cards.* It is also used in contractions. Examples: isn't, can't. (Units 2, 7)

Assimilation. The change in the last letter of a prefix to sound the same as or more similar to the first letter of the base word or root to which it is attached. This change makes pronunciation easier. Examples: *in + legal = illegal; con + bine = combine.* (Unit 21)

Attribute. A characteristic or quality, such as size, part, color, or function. Examples: *She lost the **big** stamp. Fish have **gills**. He has a **green** truck. A clock **tells time**.* (Unit 5)

Base verb. The form of a verb without any suffixes; the infinitive form without *to.* Examples: *be, help, spell.* (Unit 7)

Biography. A type of literature that tells the story of someone's life. Example: *"Leonardo da Vinci: The Inventor."* (Unit 13)

Comma. A punctuation mark used to signal a pause when reading or writing to clarify meaning. Example: *Due to snow**,** school was cancelled.* (Unit 5)

Command. A sentence that makes a request. Example: *Show the parts of the invention.* (Unit 13)

Compound word. A word made up of two or more smaller words. Examples: *backdrop, hilltop.* (Unit 3)

Conjunction. A function word that joins words, phrases, or clauses in a sentence or across two sentences. Examples: *and, but, or.* (Unit 7)

Consonant. A closed speech sound in which the airflow is restricted or closed by the lips, teeth, or tongue. Letters represent consonant sounds. Examples: **m**, **r**, **g**, **w**, **q**. (Unit 1)

Consonant blend. Consonant sound pair in the same syllable. The consonants are not separated by vowels. Initial blends are letter combinations that represent two different consonant sounds at the beginning of a word. Examples: **bl**ack, **br**im, **sk**ill, **tw**in. Final blends are letter pairs that represent two different consonant sounds at the end of a word. Examples: bu**mp**, se**nd**, la**st**. (Unit 11)

Consonant cluster. Three or more consecutive consonants in the same syllable. Examples: **scr**, **spl**. (Unit 11)

Contraction. Two words combined into one word. Some letters are left out and are replaced by an apostrophe. Examples: *isn't, can't, I'd*. (Unit 7)

Digraph, consonant. Two-letter grapheme that represents one consonant sound. Examples: **ch** (chop), **sh** (dish), **th** (thin). (Unit 8)

Digraph, vowel. Two-letter grapheme that represents one vowel sound. Examples: **ai** (rain), **ee** (see), **oa** (boat). (Unit 19)

Direct object. A noun or pronoun that receives the action of the main verb in the predicate. It answers the question: Who or what received the action? Examples: *Casey hit the **ball**. She dropped the **mitt**.* (Unit 3)

Direct object, compound. Two direct objects joined by a conjunction in a sentence. Example: *The bugs infest **crops and animals**.* (Unit 9)

Doubling rule. A spelling rule in English that doubles a final consonant before adding a suffix beginning with a vowel when 1) a one-syllable word 2) with one vowel 3) ends in one consonant. Examples: *hopping, robbed*. (Unit 6)

Drama. A story, such as a play, musical, or opera, written for characters to act out. Example: *"These Shoes of Mine."* (Unit 15)

Expository text. Text that provides information and includes a topic. Facts and examples support the topic. Example: *"What Is Jazz?"* (Unit 5)

Expression. A common way of saying something. An expression is similar to an **idiom**. Example: *all wet* means "mistaken; on the wrong track." (Unit 7)

Fable. A literary genre whose main characters are usually animals. A fable teaches a moral lesson. Example: *"The Tortoise and the Hare"* is an example of a fable. (Unit 19)

Fiction. A literary genre that includes stories that are not true. Fiction is sometimes based on real people, places, or events. *"Raymond's Run"* is an example of fiction. (Unit 19)

First-person account. A type of writing, either fiction or nonfiction, in which the narrator recalls personal experiences. Example: *"A. H. Gardiner's Account"* in *"King Tut: Egyptian Pharaoh."* (Unit 17)

Folktale. A literary genre consisting of an old story, told over many generations, about a hero or nature. Early folktales were told orally and often changed as they were retold. Example: *"A Collection of Puzzling Tales."* (Unit 22)

Future perfect. A verb form that refers to a past situation in a future time. The future perfect is formed with **will have** plus the past participle. Example: *By next Friday,* **I will have finished** *Anne Frank's diary.* (Unit 21)

Genre. A literary category. Examples of genres include: biography, fiction, folktale, nonfiction, science fiction, and short story. (Unit 13)

Homophones. Words that sound the same but have different meanings. Examples: *son/sun; some/sum; one/won.* (Unit 7)

Idiom. A common phrase that cannot be understood by the meanings of its separate words—only by the entire phrase. Example: *be in the wind* means "likely to occur." (Unit 4)

Indirect object. A noun or pronoun often placed between the main verb and the direct object. It tells to whom or for whom the action was done. Example: *The king offered his* **son** *a gift.* (Unit 17)

Metaphor. A figure of speech that compares people, places, things, or feelings without using the words *like* or *as*. Examples: *He is a* **prince**. *Her* **sunny** *smile.* (Unit 14)

Mood. A literary device that conveys a general emotion of a work or an author. Example: *"The First Transcontinental Railroad"* uses mood as a literary device. (Unit 18)

Mystery. A literary genre in which the author creates suspense around an unknown and provides clues for the reader, who tries to predict the unknown. Example: *"The Disappearing Man."* (Unit 22)

Myth. An anonymous tale based on the traditional beliefs of a culture that often includes supernatural beings and heroes. Example: *"Legendary Superheroes."* (Unit 15)

Narrative text. Text that tells a story. A story has characters, settings, events, conflict, and a resolution. Example: *"Atlas: The Book of Maps."* (Unit 2)

Noun. A word that names a person, place, thing, or idea. Examples: *teacher, city, bat, peace.* (Unit 1)

Noun, abstract. A word that names an idea or a thought that we cannot see or touch. Examples: *love, Saturday, sports, democracy.* (Unit 3)

Noun, common. A word that names a general person, place, or thing. Examples: *man, city, statue.* (Unit 3)

Noun, concrete. A word that names a person, place, or thing that we can see or touch. Examples: *teacher, city, pencil.* (Unit 3)

Noun, proper. A word that names a specific person, place, or thing. Examples: *Mr. West, Boston, Statue of Liberty.* (Unit 3)

Onomatopoeia. A literary device created when a word's sound suggests its meaning. Examples: *crash, bang, zip.* (Unit 16)

Open syllable. A syllable ending with a vowel sound. Examples: *go, be, pay.* (Unit 15)

Past participle. The **-ed** or **-en** form of a verb after the helping verbs **have**, **has**, or **had**. It can also act as an adjective to describe a noun. Examples: *Traffic clogged the **divided** highway. The **driven** athlete set new records.* (Unit 16)

Past perfect. A verb form that shows that one action in the past happened before another action in the past. The past perfect is formed with **had** and the past participle of the main verb. Example: *Anne Frank **had received** a diary before she went into hiding.* (Unit 21)

Perfect. A verb form used to place the time of one action relative to the time of another action. (Unit 21)

Personification. Figurative language that assigns human characteristics to an animal, idea, or a thing. Example: *"Roberto Clemente: The Heart of the Diamond."* (Unit 16)

Phrasal verb. A verb that usually consists of two parts. The first part is the verb and the second part is a word that looks like a preposition but does not function like a preposition. Instead, it is part of the meaning of the phrasal verb. The meaning of a phrasal verb is usually different from the meanings of its individual words. Example: *She **tried on** her new dress.* (Unit 22)

Phrase. A group of words that does the same job as a single word. Examples: *at lunch, in the park, to stay in shape.* (Unit 4)

Plot. A literary term referring to the pattern of events in a narrative or drama. Example: *"The Marble Champ."* (Unit 20)

Plural. A term that means "more than one." In English, nouns are made plural by adding **-s** or **-es**. Examples: *figs, backpacks, dresses.* (Unit 1)

Predicate. One of two main parts of an English sentence. It includes the main verb of the sentence. Examples: *He **digs**. She **lost the big stamp**.* (Unit 2)

Predicate adjective. An adjective that follows a linking verb and describes the subject. Example: *Kokopelli's music is **beautiful**.* (Unit 20)

Predicate, complete. The verb and all of its modifiers in a sentence. Example: *The class **clapped during the song**.* (Unit 8)

Predicate, compound. Two or more verbs joined by a conjunction. Example: *The class **sang and clapped**.* (Unit 8)

Predicate nominative. A noun that follows a linking verb and renames, or tells more about, the subject. Example: *The girl is a **runner**.* (Unit 19)

Predicate, simple. The verb in a sentence. Example: *The class **clapped** during the song.* (Unit 8)

Prefix. A morpheme added to the beginning of a word to modify its meaning. Examples: **mis**interpret, **non**stop, **un**plug. (Unit 13)

Preposition. A function word that begins a prepositional phrase. Examples: *at, from, in.* (Unit 4)

Prepositional phrase. A phrase that begins with a preposition and ends with a noun or a pronoun. A prepositional phrase is used either as an adjective or as an adverb. Examples: *at the track, from the old map, in traffic.* (Unit 4)

Present participle. The **-ing** verb form that expresses present action. It follows a helping verb, such as *am, is, are*. The **-ing** forms of verbs can also act as adjectives to describe nouns Examples: *She **is coming** to the picnic. The **running** water spilled on the floor.* (Units 5, 15)

Present perfect. A verb form that shows a connection between the past and the present. The present perfect is formed with **have** or **has** and the past participle of the main verb. Examples: *I **have been** here for two years. She **has been** here for four years.* (Unit 21)

Progressive. A verb form that indicates ongoing action in time. Examples: *I **am going** (present); I **was going** (past); I **will be going** (future).* (Units 5, 9, 11)

Pronoun. A function word used in place of a noun. Pronouns can be subject, object, or possessive. (Units 4, 6, 7)

Pronoun, indefinite. A pronoun that refers to an unspecified or unknown person or thing. Examples: *anyone, nobody, something.* (Unit 23)

Pronoun, object. A pronoun that takes the place of the object in a sentence. Example: *Jason threw **it**.* (Unit 7)

Pronoun, possessive. A pronoun that shows possession. Examples: *mine, yours, his, hers, ours, theirs. Mary's desk is neat. **Mine** is messy.* (Unit 7)

Pronoun, subject. A pronoun that takes the place of the subject in a sentence. Also called a nominative pronoun. Example: ***He** ran down the street.* (Unit 7)

R-controlled syllable. A syllable that contains a vowel followed by **r**. Examples: *her, far, sport.* (Unit 14)

Root. The basic meaning part of a word. It carries the most important part of the word's meaning. A root usually needs a prefix or suffix to make it into a word. Roots of English words often come from other languages, especially Latin. Example: *ex + **tract** = extract.* (Unit 20)

Schwa. A vowel phoneme in an unstressed syllable that has reduced value or emphasis. The symbol for schwa is ə. Example: *lesson (lĕsʹən).* (Unit 13)

Science fiction. A type of literature that features a setting and people that are futuristic or fantastic. Example: *"Podway Bound: A Science Fiction Story."* (Unit 13)

Sentence. A group of words that has at least one subject and one predicate and conveys a complete thought. Examples: *She ran. The map is in the cab.* (Unit 1)

Sentence, simple. A group of words that has one subject and one predicate and conveys a complete thought. Example: *The man ran fast.* (Unit 2)

Simile. A figure of speech that makes a comparison. A simile always uses the words "like" or "as." Examples: *He runs **like the wind**. Her dreams are **as big as the ocean**.* (Unit 14)

Statement. A sentence that presents a fact or opinion. Examples: *The map is flat. The twins are remarkable.* (Unit 2)

Story. An account of events. A story has characters, setting, events, a conflict, and a resolution. Example: *"Floki, Sailor Without a Map."* (Unit 2)

Stress. The emphasis that a syllable has in a word. Examples: *atlas (atʹləs), lesson (lĕsʹən).* (Unit 13)

Subject. One of two main parts of an English sentence. The subject names the person, place, thing, or idea that the sentence is about. Examples: ***She** raps. **Boston** digs.* (Unit 2)

Subject, complete. A subject (noun or pronoun) and all of its modifiers. Example: ***The blue egg** fell from the nest.* (Unit 7)

Subject, compound. A subject that consists of two or more nouns or pronouns joined by a conjunction. Example: ***Ellen and her class** passed.* (Unit 7)

Subject, simple. The noun or pronoun that is the subject of a sentence. Example: *The **bird** sings. The blue **egg** fell from the nest.* (Unit 7)

Suffix. A word ending that modifies a word's meaning. Examples: *-ing, -ed, -ly, -ment*. (Unit 17)

Syllable. A word or word part that has one vowel sound. Examples: *bat, dig, tox-ic, pic-nic.* (Unit 3)

Symbol. An image, figure, or object that represents a different thing or idea. Example: *In ancient Egypt, a pyramid is a **symbol** of the creation mound.* (Unit 17)

Synonym. A word that has the same or a similar meaning to another word. Examples: *big/huge, quick/fast, fix/repair.* (Unit 3)

Tense. Changes in the form of a verb that show changes in time: present, past, or future. Examples: *act, acted, will act.* (Units 4, 7, 10)

Trigraph. A three-letter grapheme that represents one sound. Example: *-**tch*** (wa**tch**). (Unit 8)

Verb. A word that describes an action (*run, make*) or a state of being (*is, were*) and shows time. Examples: *acts* (present tense, happening now); *is dropping* (present progressive, ongoing action); *acted* (past tense, happened in the past); *will act* (future tense, will happen in the future). (Units 4, 5, 7, 10)

Verb, helping. An auxiliary verb that precedes the main verb in a sentence. Helping verbs include forms of *be, do,* and *have.* (Unit 11)

Verb, linking. A verb that connects, or links, the subject of the sentence to a word in the predicate. Forms of **be** can act as linking verbs. Example: *The girl **is** a runner.* (Unit 19)

Verb phrase. A group of words that does the job of a verb, conveys tense, and has two parts, which are the helping verb and the main verb. Example: *The bus **is stopping**.* (Unit 9)

Vowel. A speech sound in which the airflow is open. Letters represent vowel sounds. Examples: <u>**a**</u>, <u>**e**</u>, <u>**i**</u>, <u>**o**</u>, <u>**u**</u>, and sometimes <u>**y**</u>. (Unit 1)

Vowel diphthong. A speech sound that moves from one vowel position to another, producing a gliding sound. The two vowel diphthongs each have two letter combinations: <u>**oi**</u>/<u>**oy**</u> and <u>**ou**</u>/<u>**ow**</u>. Examples: *oil, boy, out, cow.* (Unit 23)

Sources

Unit 19

Early Olympic Speeders

Hickok, Ralph. 2000. "Biography: Ethelda Bleibtry," from the website http://www.hickoksports.com/biograph/bleibtry.shtml (accessed October 13, 2004).

International Olympic Committee. 2004. "Elizabeth Robinson: The Runner Who Returned from the Dead," from the website http://www.olympic.org/uk/athletes/heroes/bio_uk.asp?PAR_I_ID=47512. (accessed October 13, 2004).

Elliott, Sheila. 1984. "Riverdale Girl 1st With Gold," from The Times (July 30), from the website http://www2.sls.lib.il.us/RDS/Community/BettyRobinson/riverdalegirl.html (accessed October 13, 2004).

International Swimming Hall of Fame. 1967. "Ethelda Bleibtrey," from the website http://www.ishof.org/67ebleibtrey.html (accessed October 13, 2004).

Encyclopædia Britannica Online. 2004. "Thunberg, Clas," from Encyclopædia Britannica Premium Service. http://www.britannica.com/eb/article?tocId=9125273 (accessed October 13, 2004).

Wikipedia, the Free Encyclopedia. 2004. "Betty Robinson." http://en.wikipedia.org/wiki/Betty_Robinson (accessed October 13, 2004).

Chart Sources

BBC Sport. 2002. "Statistics: Speed Skating: Women's 5000m." http://news.bbc.co.uk/winterolympics2002/hi/english/static/winter_olympics/statistics/events/speed_skating_results.stm (accessed October 13, 2004).

Official Website of the Athens 2004 Olympic Games. 2004. "Swimming: Women 100m freestyle results." http://www.athens2004.com/en/SwimmingWomen/results?rsc=SWW011101&frag=SWW011101_C73A1 (accessed October 13, 2004).

Official Website of the Athens 2004 Olympic Games. 2004. "Athletics: Women 100m final results." http://www.athens2004.com/en/AthleticsWomen/results?rsc=ATW001101&frag=ATW001101_C73A (accessed October 13, 2004).

Fiber Optics: High-Speed Highways for Light

Day, Nancy. 1996. "High-Speed Highways for Light: Optical Fibers," from Odyssey (February), vol. 5, no. 2. Carus Publishing, 315 Fifth St., Peru, IL 61354. All rights reserved. Adapted with permission.

Grise, William, and Charles Patrick. 2002. "Passive Solar Lighting Using Fiber Optics," from the Journal of Industrial Technology, vol. 19, no.1. www.nait.org.

Korenic, Eileen. 1994. "Zooming In on Light Speed," from Odyssey, vol. 3, no. 4. Carus Publishing, 315 Fifth St., Peru, IL 61354. All rights reserved. Adapted with permission.

O'Meara, Stephen James. 1996. "Space-Time and the 'Ether' Bunny," from Odyssey. Carus Publishing, 315 Fifth St., Peru, IL 61354. All rights reserved. Adapted with permission.

Raymond's Run

Bambara, Toni Cade. 1971. "Raymond's Run," from Gorilla, My Love. New York: Random House. Copyright 1971 by Toni Cade Bambara. Used with permission.

A Slow Take on Fast Food

International Slow Food Movement. 2004. "All About Slow Food," from the website http://www.slowfood.com/eng/sf_cose/sf_cose.lasso (accessed May 17, 2004).

Chadwick, Benjamin. 2002. "The Slow Food Movement Takes on Fast Food Culture," from *E/The Environmental Magazine Online*. http://www.enn.com/news/enn-stories/2002/11/11152002/s_48688.asp (accessed May 17, 2004).

Dorfman, Marjorie. 2002. "Fast Food Versus Slow Food: Are You Dancing as Fast as You Can," from the website http://www.ingestandimbibe.com/Articles/fastfood.html (accessed May 18, 2004).

Manhattan User's Guide. 2004. "Fast Food/Slow Food," from Charlie Suisman's Manhattan User's Guide website. http://www.manhattanusersguide.com/archives_content.php?contentID=020204&category=food (accessed May 18, 2004).

American Dietetic Association. 2004. "Fast Food and Slow Food," from the American Dietetic Association website. http://www.eatright.org/Public/NutritionInformation/index_17822.cfm (accessed May 18, 2004).

Hodgman, Ann. 2004. "What's for Dinner?" from *The Atlantic Online* (June). http://www.theatlantic.com/doc/prem/200406/hodgman (accessed June 18, 2004).

Johnson, Jennifer. 2003. "In Our Hectic Lives, Can We Make Room for the SlowFood Movement?" from *NYC24*, vol. III, issue 1. http://nyc24.jrn.columbia.edu/2003/issue1/story3/page3.html (accessed May 18, 2004).

Britannica Concise Encyclopedia. 2004. "Kroc, Ray," from Encyclopædia Britannica Premium Service. http://www.britannica.com/ebc/article?tocId=9369449 (accessed May 18, 2004).

Voyatzis, Diane. 2002. "Not So Fast...," from *The Tufts Daily* (October 7). http://nutrition.tufts.edu/news/matters/2002-10-07.html (accessed May 18, 2004).

The Tortoise and the Hare: A Fable

____. 2004. "The Tortoise and the Hare: One of Aesop's Fables," from the website http://childhoodreading.com/Arthur_Rackham/Tortoise_and_the_Hare.html.

Word History

American Heritage Dictionary (Fourth ed.). 2000. Boston: Houghton Mifflin. http://www.yourdictionary.com/ahd/s/s0620700.html (accessed November 29, 2004).

Unit 20

Nash's Bashes: Word Play

Nash, Ogden. 1995. *The Selected Poetry of Ogden Nash: 650 Rhymes, Verses, Lyrics, and Poems*. New York: Black Dog & Leventhal. Copyright 1931, 1935, 1941, 1942, and 1956 by Ogden Nash. Reprinted by permission of Curtis Brown.

The Marble Champ

"The Marble Champ" from *Baseball in April and Other Stories*, copyright 1990 by Gary Soto, reprinted by permission of Harcourt. This material may not be reproduced in any form or by any means without prior written permission of the publisher.

A Game of Catch

Wilbur, Richard. 1953. "A Game of Catch," from *The Sea-Green Horse: A Collection of Short Stories*. New York: Macmillan. Copyright 1953 by Richard Wilbur. Reprinted by permission of Harcourt. Originally appeared in *The New Yorker*, 1953.

Yo-Yo Ma Plays the World

CultureConnect. 2004. "Cultural Ambassadors: Yo-Yo Ma," from the CultureConnect website. http://cultureconnect.state.gov/?p=YMBiography (accessed November 18, 2004).

Green, Aaron. 2004. "Yo-Yo Ma: World Class Cellist," from the Classical Music section of the About.com website. http://classicalmusic.about.com/od/performerbiographies/p/yoyoma.htm (accessed November 18, 2004).

Jong, Mabel. 2003. "Yo-Yo Ma: Family Is the Best Investment," from the Bankrate.com website. http://www.bankrate.com/brm/news/investing/20030821a1.asp (accessed November 18, 2004).

Tassel, Janet. 2000. "Yo-Yo Ma's Journeys: Making Music with Humanity, from Sanders to the Silk Road," from *Harvard Magazine* (March–April), vol. 102, no. 4. http://www.harvardmagazine.com/issues/ma00/yoyoma.html. By permission of the author.

Young Playwright on Broadway: Lorraine Hansberry's *A Raisin in the Sun*

Atkinson, Brooks. 1959. "A Raisin in the Sun," from *The New York Times* (March 12). http://theater2.nytimes.com/gst/theater/trevlist.html?author=Brooks%20Atkinson. Copyright 1959 by *The New York Times*. Reprinted with permission.

Hambleton, Vicki. 2001. "A Raisin in the Sun," from *Footsteps* (May/June), vol. 3, no. 3. Carus Publishing, 315 Fifth St., Peru, IL 61354. All rights reserved. Adapted with permission.

eNotes. 2004. "Profile of Lorraine Hansberry," from the website http://www.enotes.com/raisin-sun/4870 (accessed November 18, 2004).

Hughes, Langston. 1994. "Harlem," from *The Collected Poems of Langston Hughes*. Copyright 1994 by The Estate of Langston Hughes. Used by permission of Alfred A. Knopf, a division of Random House, Inc.

Unit 21

Plant Families

Watson, L., and M. J. Dallwitz. 2000. "The Families of Flowering Plants: Descriptions, Illustrations, Identification, and Information Retrieval," from the DELTA database. http://biodiversity.uno.edu/delta (accessed November 22, 2004).

Flora of North America Association. 2004. "Flora of North America," from the eFloras website. www.efloras.org (accessed November 22, 2004).

Calgary Allergy Network. 2004. "Botanical List of Food Families," from the Calgary Allergy Network website. http://www.calgaryallergy.ca/Articles/botanical.htm (accessed November 22, 2004).

A Family in Hiding: Anne Frank's Diary

Frank, Anne. 1995. *The Definitive Edition: Anne Frank: The Diary of a Young Girl*. Edited by Otto H. Frank and Mirjam Pressler. Translated by Susan Massotty. New York: Bantam Books. Copyright 1995 by Doubleday, a division of Random House. Used by permission of the publisher.

The Anne Frank Center USA. 2003. "Anne Frank: Life and Times," from the Anne Frank Center USA website. http://www.annefrank.com/0_home.htm (accessed November 19, 2004).

My Side of the Story

Bagdasarian, Adam. 2002. "My Side of the Story," from *First French Kiss and Other Traumas*. New York: Melanie Kroupa, Farrar, Strauss, and Giroux. Copyright 2002 by Adam Bagdasarian. Reprinted by permission of Farrar, Straus, and Giroux.

Bringing Up Baby: Family Life in the Animal World

Johnson, Genevieve. 2003. "Sperm Whales and Elephants," from the PBS.org website. http://www.pbs.org/odyssey/odyssey/20030425_log_transcript.html (accessed November 19, 2004).

Brewer, Duncan. 2003. "Parental Care in Mammals," from *1000 Things You Should Know About Mammals*, from the MasterFILE Premier database (accessed November 19, 2004).

Ehrlich, Paul R., D. S Dobkin, and D. Wheye. 1988. "Precocial and Altricial Young," from the website http://www.stanfordalumni.org/birdsite/text/essays/Precocial_and_Altricial.html. (accessed November 19, 2004).

Wikipedia, the Free Encyclopedia. 2004. "Bird." http://en.wikipedia.org/wiki/Bird (accessed November 20, 2004).

Cheater, Mark. 2001. "Granny Knows Best," from *National Wildlife* (August/September), vol. 39, no. 5, from the MasterFILE Premier database (accessed November 17, 2004).

Woodland Park Zoo. 2004. "Animal Fact Sheets: African Elephant.," from the Woodland Park Zoo website. http://www.zoo.org/educate/fact_sheets/elephants/africel.htm (accessed November 19, 2004).

Wikipedia, the Free Encyclopedia. 2004. "Three-spined stickleback." http://en.wikipedia.org/wiki/Three-spined_stickleback (accessed November 21, 2004).

Goodman, Susan. 1996. "A Father's Day Top Ten," from *National Wildlife* (June/July), vol. 34, no. 4, from the MasterFILE Premier database (accessed November 17, 2004).

Kranking, Kathy Walsh. 1994. "Ranger Rick: Let's Hear it for Dad!—Animal Fathers," from the website http://www.findarticles.com/p/articles/mi_m0EPG/is_n6_v28/ai_16829042 (accessed November 21, 2004).

Wikipedia, the Free Encyclopedia. 2004. "Cichlid." http://en.wikipedia.org/wiki/Cichlid (accessed November 21, 2004).

____. 2004. "Threespine Stickleback—Gasterosteus aculeatus (Linnaeus)," from the website http://elib.cs.berkeley.edu/kopec/tr9/html/sp-threespine-stickleback.html (accessed November 19, 2004).

Mason, Jeffrey Moussaieff. 1999. *The Emperor's Embrace: Reflections on Animal Families and Fatherhood*. New York: Pocket Books.

Grace-Pedrotty, Barbara, and Alan MacBain. 1995. "Fabulous Fathers," from *Jack & Jill* (June), vol. 57, no. 4, from the MasterFILE Premier database (accessed November 17, 2004).

Churchman, Deborah. 2000. "All in a Mother's Day," from *Ranger Rick* (May), vol. 34, no. 5, from the MasterFILE Premier database (accessed November 17, 2004).

MSN Encarta. 2004. "Maximum Life Span of Some Plants and Animals," from the Microsoft Encarta Online Encyclopedia website. http://encarta.msn.com/media_461516708/Maximum_Life_Span_of_Some_Plants_and_Animals.html (accessed November 22, 2004).

MSN Encarta. 2004. "Animal," from the Microsoft Encarta Online Encyclopedia website. http://encarta.msn.com/encyclopedia_761558664_2_67/Animal.html (accessed November 22, 2004).

Morales, Manuel. 2004. "Ant-Pubilia Mutualism," from the website http://mutualism.williams.edu/Research/ (accessed November 22, 2004).

Taflinger, Richard F. 1996. "Taking Advantage: Endnotes for Human Cultural Evolution," from the website http://www.wsu.edu:8080/~taflinge/notes.html (accessed November 19, 2004).

Milius, Susan. 2004. "The Social Lives of Snakes," from *Science News* (March 27), vol. 165, no. 13, from the MasterFILE Premier database (accessed November 17, 2004).

____. 2002. "Lion Adopts Antelope," from *Current Science* (April 12), vol. 87, no. 15, from the MasterFILE Premier database (accessed November 17, 2004).

Wikipedia, the Free Encyclopedia. 2004. "Insects." http://en.wikipedia.org/wiki/Insects (accessed November 22, 2004).

____. 2004. "How Fish Spawn," from the Petfish.net website. http://www.petfish.net/how.htm (accessed November 20, 2004).

____. 2002. "Fish," from *World Book* Copyright 2002 by World Book, Inc., 233 N. Michigan, Chicago, IL 60601. All rights reserved.

Who Cares About Great-Uncle Edgar?
Excerpt from "Who Cares About Great-Uncle Edgar?" from *The Great Ancestor Hunt: The Fun of Finding Out Who You Are*, by Lila Perl. Text copyright 1989 by Lila Perl. Adapted and reprinted by permission of Houghton Mifflin. All rights reserved.

Unit 22

How To Make a Crossword Puzzle
Eliot, George. 2004. "Introducing Crossword Puzzles: This is a Puzzling World," from the American Crossworld Puzzle Tournament website. http://www.crosswordtournament.com/more/wynne.html (accessed November 22, 2004).

Frantz, Christine. 2004. "The History of the Crossword Puzzle," from the Information Please Database, Pearson Education, Inc. http://www.infoplease.com/spot/crossword1.html (accessed November 22, 2004).

____. 2004. "History of the Crossword Puzzle," from the Information Please Database, Pearson Education, Inc. http://www.infoplease.com/ipa/A0856331.html (accessed November 22, 2004).

A Collection of Puzzling Tales
Shannon, George. 1985. Stories to Solve: Folktales From Around the World. New York: Harper Collins. Text copyright 1985 by George Shannon. Used by permission of HarperCollins Publishers.

The Disappearing Man
Asimov, Isaac. 1985. "The Disappearing Man," from *The Disappearing Man and Other Mysteries*. New York: Walker. Reprinted by permission of the Estate of Isaac Asimov c/o Ralph M. Vicinanza, Ltd.

Puzzle People
Bellis, Mary. 2004. "Rubik's Cube—Rubik and the Cube: The History of Rubik's Cube and Inventor Erno Rubik," from the About website. http://inventors.about.com/library/weekly/aa040497.htm (accessed November 19, 2004).

Frost, Caroline. 2004. "Tetris: A Chip Off the Old Bloc," from the BBC Online website. http://news.bbc.co.uk/1/hi/magazine/3479989.stm (accessed November 19, 2004).

Rosinsky, Natalie. 2002. "The Puzzling Business of Sam Loyd & Enro Rubik," from *Odyssey* (October), vol. 11, no. 7. Carus Publishing, 315 Fifth St., Peru, IL 61354. All rights reserved.

____. 1998. "A Puzzling Occupation: Will Shortz—Enigmatologist," from the American Crossword Puzzle Tournament website. http://www.crosswordtourn ament.com/1998/art01.htm (accessed November 19, 2004).

____. 1959. "Puzzling Question: Margaret Farrar Anecdotes," from the Anecdotage.com website, originally published in *The New Yorker*. http://www.anecdotage.com/ index.php?aid=1328 (accessed November 19, 2004).

____. 2004. "A Maze: The World's Latest Craze," from the CBS Broadcasting website. http://cbsnews.com/stories/ 2004/09/08/earlyshow/living/travel/ main641936.shtml (accessed November 19, 2004).

Encyclopædia Britannica. 1999. "Farrar, Margaret Petherbridge," from the Encyclopædia Britannica's Women in American History website. http: //search.eb.com/women/articles/Farrar_ Margaret_Petherbridge.html (accessed November 19, 2004).

Encyclopædia Britannica. 2004. "Farrar, Margaret," from Encyclopædia Britannica Premium Service. http:// www.britannica.com/eb/article?tocId=912 5716&query=%22margaret%farrar%22&c t=eb (accessed November 19, 2004).

Encyclopædia Britannica. 2004. "Rubik, Enro," from Encyclopædia Britannica Premium Service. http:// www.britannica.com/eb/article?tocId=9 001210&query=rubik&ct=eb (accessed November 19, 2004).

The Rosetta Stone: A Linguistic Puzzle

Wikipedia, the Free Encyclopedia. 2004. "Rosetta Stone." http://en.wikipedia.org/ wiki/Rosetta_Stone (accessed January 17, 2005).

____. 2005. "Rosetta Stone," from the Astra Corporation website. http: //www.egyptologyonline.com/rosetta_ stone.htm (accessed January 17, 2005).

____. 2005. "The Rosetta Stone," from the website http: //www.ancientegypt.co.uk/writing/ rosetta.html (accessed January 17, 2005).

____. 2005. "Rosetta Stone," from the website http://www.kingtutshop.com/ freeinfo/rosetta-stone.htm (accessed January 17, 2005).

Encyclopædia Britannica. 2005. "Hieroglyphic Writing," from Encyclopædia Britannica Premium Service. http://www.britannica.com/eb/ article?tocId=53614 (accessed January 17, 2005).

Dyke, Daniel J. 2005. "Chapter IV: Language and Writing," from the website http://www.dabar.org/Rawlinson/Raw- Ch4/RAE-p57.html (accessed January 17, 2005).

____. 2005. "Napoleon in Egypt: A Short Account," from the website http: //www.geocities.com/athens/styx/3776/ Nap.html (accessed January 17, 2005).

Millmore, Mark. 2005. "Hieroglyphs," from the website http://www.eyelid.co. uk/hiero1.htm (accessed January 17, 2005).

The British Museum. 2005. "Cracking Codes: The Rosetta Stone and Decipherment," from the website of the British Museum, London. http:// web.archive.org/web/20030608203320/ http://www.thebritishmuseum.ac.u k/egyptian/ea/ccodes/decipher.html (accessed January 17, 2005).

Brier, Bob. 1999. "Napoleon in Egypt," from *Archaeology* (May/June), vol. 52, no. 3, from the EBSCOhost database (accessed January 17, 2005).

Sproat, Richard. 2005. "Decipherment," from the website http://catarina.ai.uiuc. edu/L403C/decipherment.html (accessed January 17, 2005).

____. 1996. "Giants of Egyptology: Jean Francois Champollion," from *KMT: A Modern Journal of Ancient Egypt* (Winter 1995–1996), vol. 6, no. 4, from the website http://www.egyptology.com/kmt/winter95_96/giants.html (accessed January 17, 2005).

Strachan, Richard A., & Kathleen A. Roetzel. 1997. "Ancient Egyptian Culture," from *Ancient Peoples: A Hypertext View*, from the website http://www.mnsu.edu/emuseum/prehistory/egypt/hieroglyphics/rosettastone.html (accessed January 17, 2005).

The Dust Bowl

The Dust Bowl (*Interactive Text*, p.180). Adapted from, Roop, Peter. 1983. "Living in the Dust Bowl," from *Cobblestone* (December), vol. 4, no. 12. Carus Publishing, 315 Fifth St., Peru, IL 61354. All rights reserved. Used with permission.

Unit 23

Horsepower

Casey-Meyer, Brigid. 1982. "Horsepower Helped," from *Cobblestone*. Carus Publishing, 315 Fifth St., Peru, IL 61354. All rights reserved.

____. 2005. "What Is Horsepower?" from the website http://www.web-cars.com/math/horsepower.html (accessed January 24, 2005).

Wikipedia, the Free Encyclopedia. 2005. "James Watt." http://en.wikipedia.org/wiki/James_Watt (accessed January 18, 2005).

The International Museum of the Horse. 2005. "The Domestication of the Horse," from the International Museum of the Horse website. http://www.imh.org/imh/kyhpl1b.html (accessed January 24, 2005).

Zaaaaaaap!

Ratliff, Jennifer A. 2004. "Zaaaaaaaap!" from *Odyssey* (April), vol. 13, no. 4. Carus Publishing, 315 Fifth St., Peru, IL 61354. All rights reserved. Adapted with permission.

Satyagraha: Power for Change

Carter, Alden R. 2001. "Satyagraha," from *On the Fringe*, edited by Donald R. Gallo. Copyright 2001 by Alden R. Carter. Used by permission of Dial Books for Young Readers, A Division of Penguin Young Readers Group, a Member of Penguin Group (USA) Inc., 245 Hudson St., New York, NY 10014. All rights reserved.

Mohandas Gandhi: Soul Force

Oldenburg, Veena Talwar. 1993. "Mahatma Gandhi and the Untouchables of India," from *Faces* (February), no. 2. Carus Publishing, 315 Fifth St., Peru, IL 61354. All rights reserved. Adapted with permission.

Beck, Sanderson. 2003. "Gandhi's Nonviolent Revolution," from the website http://www.san.beck.org/GPJ20-Gandhi.html (accessed January 14, 2005).

Falk, Richard. 2004. "Gandhi, Nonviolence and the Struggle Against War," from the Transnational Foundation for Peace and Future Research website. http://www.transnational.org/forum/Nonviolence/2004/Falk_GandhiNonviolence.html (accessed January 14, 2005).

Blackout!

Kowalski, Kathiann M. 2004. "Blackout!" from *Odyssey* (April), vol. 13, no. 4. Carus Publishing, 315 Fifth St., Peru, IL 61354. All rights reserved. Adapted with permission.

Word History

Roget's II: The New Thesaurus (Third ed.). 1995. Boston: Houghton Mifflin. http://www.yourdictionary.com/ahd/thes/p/p1158300.html (accessed February 8, 2005).

Unit 24

Dream While You Sleep

Brynie, Faith Hickman. 2002. "The Brain Never Sleeps," from *Odyssey* (January), vol. 11, no. 1. Copyright 2002 by Faith Hickman Brynie. Reprinted with permission of the author.

____. 2005. "Dream Research: The Sleep Cycle," from the Dream Moods website. http://www.dreammoods.com/dreaminformation/dreamresearch.htm (accessed January 14, 2005).

Saleeby, J. P. 2003. "Sleep: The Often Ignored Guardian of Wellness," from the *JIVE Magazine* website. http://www.jivemagazine.com/column.php?pid=945 (accessed January 14, 2005).

Dreaming the Night Away

Herbst, Judith. 1985. "The Great Shut-Eye Mystery," from *Bio Amazing: A Casebook of Unsolved Human Mysteries*. New York: Antheum Publishers. Reprinted with the permission of Atheneum Books for Young Readers, an imprint of Simon & Schuster's Children's Publishing Division. Copyright 1985 by Judith Herbst.

Dream Team

Jones, Ron. 1976. "Winning," from *The Co-Evolution Quarterly* (Summer). By permission of the author. Copyright 1976 by Ron Jones.

Pursuit of a Dream

Eaglesham, Barbara. 2002. "Out of Her Hands: The Woman Who Didn't Win the Nobel Prize," from *Odyssey* (February), vol. 11, no. 2. Carus Publishing, 315 Fifth St., Peru, IL 61354. All rights reserved. Adapted with permission.

Maddox, Brenda. 2002. Rosalind Franklin: The Dark Lady of DNA. New York: Perennial.

Piper, Anne. 1998. "Rosalind Franklin: Light on a Dark Lady," from the Contributions of 20th Century Women to Physics website.http://cwp.library.ucla.edu/articles/franklin/piper.htm (accessed January 14, 2005).

The San Diego Supercomputer Center. 2005. "Rosalind Elsie Franklin," from the San Diego Supercomputer Center's "Women in Science" website. http://www.sdsc.edu/ScienceWomen/franklin.html (accessed January 14, 2005).

Martin Luther King, Jr.: The Freedom Dreamer

King, Martin Luther, Jr. 1963. "I Have a Dream." Reprinted by arrangement with the estate of Martin Luther King, Jr., c/o Writers House, as agent for the proprietor, New York. Copyright 1963 by Martin Luther King, Jr. Copyright renewed 1991 by Coretta Scott King.

Haskins, Jim. 1994. "Timely Leader," from *Cobblestone* (February), vol. 15, no. 2. Carus Publishing, 315 Fifth St., Peru, IL 61354. All rights reserved. Adapted with permission.

Whitman, Sylvia. 1994. "To the Promised Land: The Civil Rights Years," from *Cobblestone* (February), vol. 15, no. 2. Carus Publishing, 315 Fifth St., Peru, IL 61354. All rights reserved. Adapted with permission.

Roop, Peter. 1983. "Five Leaders for Freedom," from *Cobblestone* (February), vol. 4, no. 2. Carus Publishing, 315 Fifth St., Peru, IL 61354. All rights reserved. Adapted with permission.

Word History

American Heritage Dictionary (Fourth ed.). 2000. Boston: Houghton Mifflin. http://www.yourdictionary.com/ahd/n/n0104100.html (accessed January 14, 2005).

Photo and Illustration Credits

Cover

Illustration

©Martin French/Morgan Gaynin Inc.

Unit 19

Photographs

16: by Photo©IOC. 17: Sports Museum Of Finland. 19: ©Brandxpictures. 19: ©PhotoDisc. 35: ©Kai's Power Photos.

Illustrations

1: ©Martin French/Morgan Gaynin Inc. 18: Steve Clark. 21–31: Lea Lyon. 32–33: Steve Clark. 37–40: Karen Lee.

Unit 20

Photographs

41: ©1999–2004 Getty Images, Inc. 56: ©Bettmann/Corbis. 71: 1999–2004 Getty Images, Inc. 71: ©2001 Cylla von Tiedmann 75: The Minneapolis Institute of Arts. 77: *t.* ©Underwood & Underwood/Corbis 77: ©Bettmann/ Corbis. 79: ©Bettmann/Corbis.

Illustrations

58–63: Alan Flinn. 65–70: Dennis Balogh.

Unit 21

Photographs

83: ©Bob Torrez/Getty Images. 99: ©2004 Jupiter Images. 100: ©2003 Getty Images. 100: ©2003 Getty Images. 107: ©1999–2005 Getty Images, Inc. 114: ©Comstock, ©Kai's Power Photos, ©Digital Vision, and ©Photo Disc. 116: ©1999–2005 Getty Images, Inc. 117: ©1999–2005 Getty Images, Inc. 120, 126: ©Comstock IMAGES. 123: ©Bettmann/CORBIS. 124: ©Royalty-Free/Corbis.

Illustrations

98–99, 118: Steve Clark. 109, 112: Jing Tsong.

Unit 22

Photographs

127: ©Digital Vision. 157: ©Jason Hawkes/CORBIS. 162: ©2005 Jupiter Images. 163: ©2004 Jupiter Images. 159–161, 164: ©Artville.

Illustrations

142–144, 150–154: Steve Clark. 156: David Danz. Use of Rubik's Cube® is by permission of Seven Towers Ltd. 158: David Danz.

Unit 23

Photographs

165: ©PhotoDisc.
188: ©Royalty-Free/image100.
191: ©2005 Jupiter Images.
192: ©2005 Jupiter Images.
195: © Bettmann/Corbis.
196: ©Comstock IMAGES.
199: ©Bettmann/Corbis.
201: ©Bettmann/Corbis.
207: ©Andrew Lichtenstein/Corbis.

Illustrations

180: ©2005 Jupiter Images.
181–187, 204–205: Steve Clark.

Unit 24

Photographs

224: ©Royalty-Free/Corbis.
232: ©D. Madison/Masterfile.
237: ©Photex/W. Smith/Masterfile.
243: ©1999–2004 Getty Images, Inc.
245: detail ©National Portrait Gallery,
London. 247: Norman Collection on the
History of Molecular Biology.
248: A Barrington Brown/©2005 Photo
Researchers, Inc. 250: ©Hulton-Deutsch
Collection/CORBIS.
251–256: ©2003 Getty Images.

Illustrations

209: Steve Clark. 225: Becky Malone.
227: ©1999–2004 Getty Images.
231: ©1999–2004 Getty Images.
245: ©Royalty-Free/Corbis.
247: Steve Clark.